Image and Cognition

Michel Denis

Directeur de Recherche au C.N.R.S.
Centre d'Etudes de Psychologie Cognitive
Université de Paris-Sud, Orsay

Translated by Michel Denis and Constance Greenbaum

HARVESTER
WHEATSHEAF

New York London Toronto Sydney Tokyo Singapore

First published 1991 by
Harvester Wheatsheaf,
66 Wood Lane End, Hemel Hempstead,
Hertfordshire, HP2 4RG

A division of
Simon & Schuster International Group

Printed and bound in Great Britain by BPCC Wheatons Ltd, Exeter
Typeset by VAP Publishing Services, Kidlington, Oxford

British Library Cataloguing in Publication Data

Denis, Michel
Image and cognition.
I. Title
153.3

ISBN 0-7450-0863-1
ISBN 0-7450-0864-X (pbk)

1 2 3 4 5   95 94 93 92 91

Contents

Preface

The themes explored in this volume are linked to the issue of representation. Representation can be defined as a human activity which consists in generating *symbols*, i.e., entities which *stand for* other entities. Human beings are symbol-makers. Individuals can create material objects which stand for other objects. But the human mind itself is also a medium for the creation of representations, cognitive end-products of what individuals derive from their interactions with the environment. One of the aims of psychology is to account for the processes underlying the construction of these cognitive representations, and the forms under which these representations are expressed in individuals' cognitive systems.

Image and Cognition is devoted to imagery, that specific form of representation which enables the human mind to store and process information from the perceptual environment. What makes imagery a specific modality for the representation of information is that it can maintain perceptual information in a form having high structural similarity with perception. In the passage from percept to image, information is obviously transformed, but the encoding processes in imagery have the specific property of preserving the spatial extension of perceived objects. Imagery is a form of representation which involves a certain amount of abstraction, but this degree of abstraction does not prevent representation from keeping its structural isomorphism with perception. This major feature of imagery provides it with most of its functional value in activities such as language comprehension, problem-solving and action planning.

As groundwork to a better understanding of imagery as one facet of the broader area of representation, the first chapter of this volume analyzes the properties and functions of representational systems in general. What emerges from this analysis is that there is a plurality of representational formats which can be adapted to individuals' needs. But the issue is also to specify what makes imagery different from other forms of representation. The second chapter is devoted to an historical review of theoretical debate on the status of imagery in human cognition. This chapter is followed by a detailed analysis of the properties of images and their relationships to perception – a necessary preliminary to an examination of the role of imagery in other psychological activities.

The bulk of this volume deals with the role of images in language processing. Language comprehension is generally viewed as a representation-generating activity. The psychology of language aims at accounting for the processes underlying semantic representations (or meanings) elaborated by individuals when they process verbal utterances. The construction of these representations, which are transient psychological events, involves the activation and combination of permanent conceptual representations associated with the lexical entries making up these utterances. Combined efforts in both psychology and linguistics have been made to specify the nature and structure of meaning, and the processes underlying its construction. A considerable number of studies nevertheless disregard the fact that imagery processes are frequently elicited during language comprehension. The functional value of imagery in comprehension thus needs to be addressed directly. What are the relationships of images to the meaning of an utterance? Can images and meaning be equated? Or are images mere epiphenomena with no functional value as regards meaning?

These questions are examined in depth in this book, with emphasis on responses provided by empirical approaches. Space is also devoted to an exploration of assumptions and experimental data motivated by the general hypothesis that imagery plays a specific (although optional) role in representation as a complement to the necessary role played by the processes which elaborate meaning.

The basic argument is that imagery is not the *locus* of meaning, but rather a medium for the *figuration* of meaning. When imagery acts as a supplement to comprehension processes, there is elaboration of optional cognitive products whose nature and structure are basically distinct from the outcomes of representations which encode the *meaning* of utterances. The semantic representation of an utterance is an abstract entity which is rendered appropriately by propositional notation. Images essentially express the *figural* part of the semantic representation. The representational format of images is modal in that it has an internal structure that mirrors sensory modalities. Images are not predicative in nature. They do not *describe* situations reported in utterances, but rather *figure* them. Because images preserve the structural relationships (in particular, spatial relationships) between the elements that make up a representation, they can act as 'models' having structural properties and access rules similar to those for perceptual events. In particular, given the structural properties images derive from perception, they are cognitive representations which enable individuals to perform computations, simulations, inferences, comparisons, etc., without recourse to formal logic.

This conception of imagery in its relations to language is illustrated by data from an extensive research programme involving materials at varying levels of complexity. First, imagery as a medium for mental representation is analyzed in terms of its relationships to lexical meaning. The assumption that lexical meaning can be broken down into semantic features is the basis for a series of experiments dealing with features denoting the figural aspects of concepts. Mental images of an object are seen as the cognitive end-products of the activation of figural features making up the conceptual representation of this object in a specialized processing system.

These analyses lead to the further assumption that there is selective activation of figural features during the processing of utterances describing concrete scenes. The data here show that the implementation of a conceptual representation may only tap a fraction of this representation. In addition, the linguistic context differentially affects the cognitive orientation of a subject to one part of the representation rather than another.

The progressive shift in this research program to more complex linguistic materials (texts) makes it possible to focus on imagery as an activity which provides the reader with a non-linguistic model of the events or situations described in the text, in addition to the semantic text-base. The findings here demonstrate that this representation greatly enhances memory storage of the text content.

Lastly, in a book devoted primarily to the relationships of imagery to language processing, it seems crucial to extend the issue of mental imagery to other situations calling for the processing of verbal information. For this reason, the contribution of imagery to reasoning, problem-solving and, more generally, human thinking are explored. Finally, while imagery is dealt with in this book as a psychological event involved in other psychological events, a presentation is made of the role of imagery in action and creation, in situations where individuals interact with the outside world.

Advances in cognitive research reveal the value of examining mental imagery in terms of human engineering. Future avenues of exploration are put forward in the final section of this book to serve as perspectives for cognitive research on mental imagery.

M.D.

1 Cognitive Psychology and the Concept of Representation

One of the major features of the term 'representation' is its polysemy. Psychologists involved in the study of representations must invariably grapple with the diversity of meanings associated with 'representation' and the range of interpretations connected to the concepts underlying these meanings. Effort, however, reaps benefits, since it can either lead to theoretical advances in circumscribing a federating concept of cognitive psychology, or eliminating a concept that is too fuzzy to be really useful.

As a prologue to the examination of the problems associated with the exploration of mental imagery – a specific form of representation – this chapter overviews some broad notions on representation. Representation is one of the cornerstones of cognitive psychology, but clearly has importance in other branches of psychology and in other fields of science and human activities.

1.1 Meanings of 'representation'

1. In psychology, as in other fields, *'representation'* can refer to both a process and the outcome of this process. When representation is defined as a process, it refers to an *activity* (generally human) whose goal is to generate objects, or (on a more abstract level) entities possessing certain properties. (These properties are discussed below.) When representation is seen as the outcome of a process, it refers to these *entities* themselves rather than to the activity which produced them. The semantic flowchart for 'representation' in Figure 1.1 shows that misinterpretation can arise as of the first branching node, since the same term is used for a process and for its outcome.

1

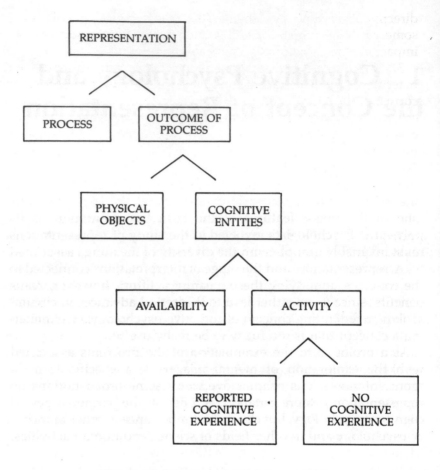

Figure 1.1 Meanings for 'representation'

2.   Moving down the flowchart to the outputs of representation (i.e., entities defined as 'representations of . . .') shows that these entities also require further subdivision. The outcomes of representational processes can either be physical objects or cognitive entities. A *drawing* of the Eiffel Tower and a *mental image* of this edifice both evoke a physical entity which in the two cases is absent. However, these two outcomes differ considerably as to the type of activity which generated them. In the first case, the process of representation results in the creation of a physical object, a new object which can continue to exist in the physical world and be potentially available even when not in actual use. In the second case, the process of representation results in a specific psychological event, a transient cognitive reality which is not

directly observable by others. This psychological event can in some cases be reinstantiated at later times, but as such has no impact on the individual's physical environment.

3. Cognitive representations themselves can be differentiated in terms of *state*. The state of *availability* of a cognitive representation corresponds to the encoding of knowledge in memory. The state of *activity* of a cognitive representation is the result of activating processes which cause available representations to become active in the working memory of the individual's cognitive 'here and now'. To return to the Eiffel Tower example, this distinction captures the difference between evocation of the Eiffel Tower in the form of a mental image (or an alternative form), and the cognitive entity standing for the Eiffel Tower which is stored permanently in the individual's mental structures even when the Eiffel Tower is totally extraneous to his or her current mental activities.

A similar distinction has been proposed by Le Ny (1985) between 'type' and 'token' representations. A type representation corresponds to the information a person has about a given object. Token representations correspond to specific occurrences of activation of this information. Occurrences can vary in form. For instance, the picture-postcard version of the Eiffel Tower can be evoked either mentally or graphically, but it is equally possible to generate an 'improved' version: an Eiffel Tower bedecked with flags and banners, Christmas tree lights or – why not? – painted lemon yellow. These variants (some of which could be real or virtual physical states) probably result from the addition of specific details to the activation of the same base representation. Whether these modifications can actually be made in real life is, of course, another issue entirely.

4. As indicated in Figure 1.1, availability for report is an additional criterion which splits current psychological events as a function of the way individuals experience them. A representation can be activated transiently in a form which allows the subject to report some conscious cognitive content: the subject either 'hears' the words '*Eiffel Tower*', or visualizes its figural features. In other words, the activation of the representation which was available in memory turns into a *transient cognitive experience* the subject can report by some explicit reponse, either verbal or graphic. Alternatively, transient activation may take place and be detected by an empirical procedure without the subject being aware of consciously experiencing the representation. This implies that a distinction should be made between the activation of representations where

no cognitive content is consciously experienced by the subject, and activation of representations accompanied or prolonged by a cognitive experience the subject can report.

This exploration of the semantic tree for *'representation'* in no way exhausts its full range of meanings. The tree presented here covers the concerns of cognitive psychology and corresponds to a need to tackle the issue of the structure and functions of representations in the human cognitive system. Researchers in semiotics or aesthetics would probably trace different routes in the semantic field of representation.

This being said, it is obvious that further pinpointing can be made with respect to representation in cognitive psychology. For instance, the distinction between declarative vs. procedural knowledge has a bearing on the concept of representation in that it extends the notion of computational modelling to psychological processes (see Mandler, 1983; Rumelhart, 1979; Winograd, 1975). In other words, a representation is more than a collection of 'facts'. Procedures (such as how to knot a necktie, find one's way on a subway map, compute the square root of a number, etc.) also have to be stored. They need to be 'represented' in the cognitive system in some form, i.e., remain available to the system in order for them to be put into use.

The declarative/procedural distinction raises the issue of the purpose or goals of representations. In other words, a 'representation-*of*' something is also a 'representation-*for*' some purpose. Naturally, all representations are the representations *of* something, and this *referential* function of representations should not be overlooked. However, beyond the nominal content of physical and cognitive representations, all have a *purpose*, i.e., an objective for which they have been elaborated, activated and stored. This perspective on representation emphasizes the goal-oriented nature of human activities, and the fact that goals can in turn affect the processes underlying the elaboration of representations.

1.2 Properties of representational systems

Before reviewing the major properties of representational systems, two preliminary comments are in order. The first concerns the use of the term *'system'* with respect to representation. 'System' here refers to the fact that in a set of representations there is a need to view the units making up the set in terms of their organization, mutual relations and dependencies; in short, in terms of the general properties of all 'systematic collections'. Psychology, in particular, focuses on cognitive representations. Thus, it is useful to define cognitive representations in terms of the basic features they have in common with other types of representation.

1. One definition most psychologists would probably agree upon is that a process of representation can be said to have occurred when an object or a set of objects are re-expressed or 'figured' in the form of a new set of objects in systematic correspondence with the original set. Proof of correspondence can be found in the *preservation* (or a certain degree of preservation) of the relationships between the elements in the represented set. This type of correspondence is the main feature of pictorial systems of representation. It is also true of imaginal mental representations. An entire chapter is devoted to the empirical data confirming the structural isomorphism between mental images and the perceptual events they are elaborated from (see Chapter 3).

2. The counterpart to the notion of preservation is that of *transformation*. Information undergoes transformation during the representation process. There is a qualitative change in the *nature* of the information provided by the initial objects in that information appears in a new and different form. Note that various encoding formats which serve to construct representations vary in their degree of structural similarity with the objects they represent. Analogical representational systems (which preserve the structural, mainly spatial properties of the represented objects) contrast with systems based on arbitrary signs. Analogical systems themselves can be further differentiated as a function of the number of parameters retained for the construction of the representation. A map, for example, generally preserves the relative positions and relative distances between points. Some maps, however, only preserve relative positions or do not use the same scale to represent different lengths (such as stylized maps of railway systems, or three-dimensional map representations). The creator of a representation can sometimes deliberately introduce distortions to highlight a dimension which serves a specific purpose of the representation.

3. Even when coding results in a representation having high analogy with the represented objects, representation always involves *information loss* in the form of reduction of the original informational content, a feature common to all systems of abstraction. Calculating the degree of information loss is a critical problem, and is dependent upon assessment of the amount of

information which must be incorporated in the representation, the way in which the representation will be used, and the cognitive capacities of the individual the representation is elaborated for. Some uses will call for a greater amount of preserved information, others less.

Abstraction is part of virtually all representational activities. Even the most detailed drawings or the most fine-grained photographs cannot preserve all the features of the object they represent. Photocopying is a borderline case. A photocopy of a page of a book reproduces all the original information (both semantic and graphic) with virtually no distortion or deformation. But is a photocopy a *representation*? When a system of representation is designed to preserve the perfect or near-perfect identity of the original and resultant objects, what is involved is something other than representation. Even the most picture-like cognitive representation is the end-product of a system of *transformation*.

Another case in point is computer systems, which can reproduce alphanumerical information with no distortion, and thus with no information loss between original and copy. This again is a borderline issue since the upper limits of representational accuracy have been attained.

4.   The notion of transformation is related to another property of systems of representations, their *directionality*. When a representational process applies to a set of objects A to generate a set of objects B, the latter represents the former, and not the reverse. In other words, although an individual equipped with adequate representational processes can construct representation B of the set of objects A, this does not entail that a correct reconstruction of A can be always derived from B alone.

5.   These are very general properties of representational systems, which psychologists must take into account in research. Note that in many instances psychologists, in fact, are dealing with *representations of representations*. This, for instance, takes place when a concrete event is represented in a photograph, which in turn is represented in a drawing (which itself can be copied and reproduced in a variety of different forms).

More complex situations, however, are common in the domain of cognition, when representations in different modalities occur in series. For instance, a person may have noticed a building when on a trip, and stored a mental image of this building. This person can construct cognitive entities, such as visual images of the building, and may also be asked to provide information on this building to another person. Starting from the mental representation activated for this purpose, the person will implement another representational system designed to evoke a representation in the addressee's mind via language. Additional representational systems can also be involved. The addressee may use the linguistic information to draw a picture. This picture may be seen by a third person, and so on. The information loss in this case is likely to be considerable, owing to the approximation inherent to switch-overs between representational systems.

This example points to the fact that the study of representations goes far beyond examination of representing–represented world pairs. In the vast majority of cases, psychologists are called upon to deal with series of interlocking binary worlds.

1.3 Functions of representational systems

Representational systems are goal-oriented. Representations are never elaborated in a vacuum. Representational systems have functions, and representations, whether physical or cognitive, are to be used ultimately.

1.   The first function of representational systems is to *preserve* information which would otherwise be lost or deteriorate, or information people know they will no longer access directly. This is typically the prime function of family or holiday snapshots. Photos such as these are representations which can serve as partial substitutes for the original objects. The notion of *partial* substitutes is a crucial one since these representations will stand for the original objects essentially for cognitive purposes. For instance, a snapshot of a person or a place enables viewers to retrieve certain pieces of information when the object itself is no longer there or no longer accessible in memory. Did the building have two or three rows of windows? Was Alexandra's hair short or long last year on her birthday? Photographs can also trigger memories of emotional experiences. But this approaches the limits of human activities drawing on representation. Actions performed by humans on physical representations have no effect on the original objects (except in magical beliefs that pins in wax models can hurt the person whose effigy is being stabbed). Having a representation is not the equivalent of possessing the object itself.

2.   Beyond preservation of previously perceived information, representations provide individuals with explicit displays of

information that is either not explicit or not readily accessible. This is the case for maps, diagrams, blueprints (e.g., wiring or electronic circuitry), where information concerning functional relationships between elements is expressed in a symbolic, short-ened and abstract form whose explicitness, however, depends on the accessibility of this coding system to the individual who is consulting it.

3. The idea behind these forms of representation is that information abstracted and stored in a map or diagram can be used as a basis for further behaviour such as planning a route for a trip or understanding how a complex apparatus operates. This coincides with the well-known function of representations to serve as tools for *guiding, orienting* and *regulating* individuals' behaviours.

4. Another important function is *systematization*. For instance, taxonomies, such as the taxonomy of animal species or plants, represent sets of elements and their relations. Such representations provide systematization of complex corpora. The same goes with genealogical trees, which express the system of dependencies among a set of people spatially. Similar functions are found in charts or flow diagrams which express the steps of complex processes.

5. Representations also serve other functions. A particularly important one is that of *signalling*, which itself is closely related to that of communication in systems of representation such as road signs, shop signs, pictograms conveying instructions, etc. Certain more specific functions can be found in emblematic or metaphorical representations (such as the cornucopia, the fleur-de-lis or Uncle Sam).

Note that the functional characteristics of physical, concrete representations described above also apply to cognitive representations. Cognitive representations preserve information, including information not easily accessible to perception (relations or structures). They can be used as tools for action planning, information hierarchization, and can be integrated into more complex systems involving communication.

Cognitive representations are more than concatenations of past experiences, or purely a storehouse of information maintained for future inspection. Cognitive representations are crucial to problem-solving, coping with novel situations and creating new behavioural algorithms – i.e., elaboration of new plans and goals in contrast to merely recollecting previous events. Representation is probably the core concept in that branch of psychology dealing with the relationships between permanent knowledge and incoming information, since this relationship is the basis for new behaviours.

Cognitive representations cannot be reduced to mere *substitutes* for objects. In particular, images do more than stand for absent objects. Rather, images act as *internal models* of objects in individuals' cognitive systems, and can be used for purposes of simulation in the absence of objects or when it is impossible to act upon these objects physically (cf. Rumelhart and Norman, 1988).

1.4 Forms and uses of representations

Issues connected to representation are not new to psychology. The history of psychology has been marked by debate on representation, and perhaps the real question is why representation remains controversial to this day (see Fodor, 1975; Johnson-Laird, 1983, 1989; Kosslyn, 1984; Le Ny, 1989; Mehler, Walker and Garrett, 1982; Paivio, 1986).

Representation has gradually emerged as one of the basic motivators for modern cognitive psychology. This topic locates cognitive psychology as a field firmly within the framework of the cognitive sciences. The aim of cognitive psychology is to study the activities individuals engage in when collecting, processing and storing information, and later retrieving and using this information in new contexts. As amply illustrated above, processing and storing information are clearly representational activities. They are used to construct cognitive products which can either be used in the short term or stored for future use. The basic issues in cognitive psychology are the nature of these products, how, when and why they are stored, and defining the processes involved in their activation and long-term use. Exploration of these issues prompted major efforts in the late 1960s to rehabilitate imagery as a vital part of psychological activity. These same issues were the basis for the queries underlying research in the 1970s on the nature of images and the potential existence of alternative forms of representation. Chapter 2 traces this historical debate. The next section centres on one of the major advances in cognitive psychology to have emerged from this debate, and from recent epistemological convergence in cognitive sciences on the notion of representation.

One of the most important preliminaries to any understanding of representation is the distinction between *content* and *form*. In linguistics, it is fairly trivial to stress the fact that a variety of forms can express the same conceptual content. Glass and Holyoak (1986) provide a useful illustration of this distinction as regards object representation (see Figure 1.2). One adequate linguistic rendering of this picture is the sentence: *'This is a picture of a cup without a handle on a flat saucer.'* The same picture could be represented by a series of equations. The 'saucer' could be represented by $(x - a)^2 + (y - b)^2 = R^2$ (the equation for a circle) and the 'cup' by $x^2/a^2 + y^2/b^2 - 2z = 0$ (the equation for an elliptic paraboloid). The linguistic description will probably appear to be more 'intuitive' or less 'complex' than the equations, which nevertheless describe the same content. The most spontaneous form of coding subjects tend to produce for this picture is linguistic, even if they are advanced mathematics students. However, if subjects are asked to calculate the volume of the 'cup', the linguistic description is of much less help than the equation.

This points to another major feature of representations, which will receive a great deal of attention in this book. The same information can be represented in a variety of forms, but the utility of these forms (or codes) depends on the use the individuals intend to make of them. Kosslyn and Pomerantz (1977) show that the structural characteristics of different systems of representation can result in differences in the nature, rapidity and efficiency of the processes operating within these systems. Suppose you have to represent the

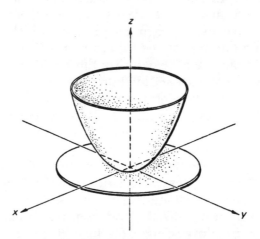

Figure 1.2 An illustration of the plurality of forms of representation
Source: Glass & Holyoak (1986). Reproduced with permission from
Random House, Inc.

same pieces of geographical information (all the cities with more than 100,000 inhabitants in a country, for example) on a map and in the form of a table of intercity distances. The two representations are isomorphic in the sense that they contain the same information and that map information can be derived from table information, and vice versa. However, each representation has distinct *properties*, which are related to the specific use they are put to.

For example, a map provides information in an analogical format which enables people to solve problems such as: 'Are Nantes, Orléans and Metz on a straight line?' On the other hand, the table of intercity distances, which contains numerical information, can be used easily to find the answer to such questions as: 'What is the overall distance from Nantes to Metz via Orléans?' Thus the efficiency of a representation is closely linked to the use individuals make of it. This is equally true for mental representations, and shows to what extent the issue of *purpose* is critical to a grasp of the concept of representation.

In models where several forms of mental representation are thought to coexist in the human cognitive system, it is argued that a given piece of information can be stored in memory in several different forms. This hypothesis runs counter to more parsimonious models which postulate that an individual piece of information is only represented once and in a single form in human memory. It is conceivable that a given piece of information may be stored in memory in different forms as a function of optimal utility – i.e., in terms of cognitive constraints and type of goal, but also in terms of individual differences (partially covered by the notion of 'cognitive style').

This overview of issues in representation shows that psychologists who deal with the concept of representation must inevitably come to terms with problems related to *forms* of representation, and by extension to the way in which these forms are actually *used*.

1.5 Cognitive psychology and the issue of representation: a question of theoretical and empirical appropriateness

Is psychology the right field for a systematic account of representation? Like researchers in other domains, psychologists need to find cogent responses to two questions: (*a*) Why has representation emerged as an integral part of psychology and what can account for its growth as a fundamental concept? (*b*) How can representation best be defined within psychology, and what are the optimal methods for studying it?

The growing importance of the concept of representation in psychology reflects researchers' need for a concept having a relatively high level of generality, which would enable them to account for behaviour. The notion of representation emerged in psychology at the same time that the field was reacting against exclusively behaviouristic theories. In other words, introducing representation was a way of placing psychology in a position to conceptualize and develop a scientific approach to the cognitive entities which were seen as the bases for behaviour. Representation developed from the notion of *strategy*, i.e., a theoretical construct linking behaviour and the hypothetical mental structures governing it.

In social psychology, the notion of representation was introduced as a more general term than the more restricted notions of *stereotype* or *ideology* which failed to account for characteristics of cognitive representations. The social sciences, in general, contributed to drawing attention to one of the major features of representations, namely, that the *values* attached to representations are important determinants of behaviour.

Educational psychology was quick to integrate the notion of representation to account for difficulties experienced by teachers in the transfer of scientific knowledge. Teachers must take learners' preconceptions and prior knowledge into account when introducing new knowledge. In other words, the goal of teaching is to substitute scientific models for pre-scientific representations while bearing in mind that pre-scientific models in fact do not fade from memory. A significant trend in educational psychology has developed to adopt the notion of representation, which works on the assumption that 'representation' is more useful as an operational term than 'knowledge' because it does not necessarily entail the notion of truth.

The study of representations which began in the field of social psychology and then expanded to cognitive psychology has gradually penetrated fields with little previous history of theoretical recourse to representation as a concept, such as the field of human motor skills. Similarly, the notion of representation is becoming more common in accounts of animal behaviour. It is worth recalling that one of the watershed publications of the North American cognitivist movement dealt with 'cognitive maps' purportedly used by both rats and men (Tolman, 1948).

The notion of representation is now widely used in areas of psychology other than cognitive research. As elsewhere its meaning varies. However, the core concept linking the semantics of 'representation' in all the sub-branches of psychology is that relatively permanent entities exist which can be transiently activated and restructured, and form the functional bases for behaviour. Representations are *internal models* of individuals' environments and their actions in these environments. As models, they provide individuals with information on the world and serve as instruments for the regulation and planning of behaviour.

The dangers of so broad a definition are obvious, as are the potential objections to one general concept of representation in psychology. Advances in science are characterized by differentiation of concepts rather than generalization. What would psychology gain from a unified concept of representation when the term is assigned such a variety of meanings? In other words, does the need expressed by many psychologists to tackle the concept of representation warrant the creation of this 'hyperconcept'?

The question is worth consideration. If psychology as a field orients towards a general approach to representation, this approach and its preconditions need to be defined in advance. The first of these preconditions is to avoid drifting to the oversimplified claim that 'psychology is the study of representations'. There is certainly no benefit from making representation an exclusively psychological topic, nor from artificially proclaming one definition of representation to subsume all the activities investigated by psychology. Nevertheless, branches of psychology dealing with the individual as an information processing system would be at a loss without a fairly general concept of representation covering such notions as information extraction and appropriation, and internal (symbolic) expression of this information. For this reason, the issue of representation in cognitive psychology must be closely associated with the issue of *information processing*. Here, representation is an integral part of the manipulation and appropriation of information collected from the environment and from individuals' own behaviour.

Any understanding of mental representation also calls for defining the systems involved in the temporary *activation* of representations (in the absence of objects), and the systems involved in the *construction* of representations during perceptual processing (in the presence of objects). Representational processes operate on both perceptually available objects – during initial information extraction – and on the cognitive reactivation of represented objects from memory. This is why research on representations needs to devote special attention to characterizing these encoding and storage processes (operating on specific inputs), in addition to the processes involved in the activation of representations.

The processes involved in the construction or implementation of representations always operate within a general economy of behaviour. Representations can be seen as functional bases for behaviour, acting as permanent structures that anchor actions which can only be in the here and now. Thus, all theories on mental representations need to account for the *processes* operating on these representations. This notion of representation–process pairs is gaining a wider audience as an epistemological prerequisite for cognitive psychology (cf. Anderson, 1978, 1990; Kosslyn, 1981; ▶ Palmer, 1978).

There are more than epistemological reasons for situating the study of representation within the broader conceptual framework of information processing. Representation deserves to be approached at some level of generality because it is central to most branches of *cognitive science*, in particular those areas focusing on the definition of algorithms for the regulation, acquisition, storage and manipulation of knowledge. In particular, the aim of artificial intelligence is to create systems for the representation of knowledge in a 'rational' way, which maximizes internal consistency. One of the requirements for this type of system is that knowledge can be manipulated easily and that in some cases new knowledge can be deduced from the knowledge base. Knowledge representation is thus a core issue in artificial intelligence research.

In many cases the knowledge stored in artificial intelligence systems is derived from the same areas as knowledge acquired in 'natural' ways by humans. The conceptual and methodological links between human and artificial systems is evident and has given rise to the notion of *cognitive modelling*. In artificial intelligence, representations are generally ascribed meanings, but in contrast to cognitive representations, artificial representations do not need to be meaningful to be manipulated. System engineers work to eliminate ambiguous symbols which cannot be handled by the inference mechanisms of the system. Human systems obviously raise other problems for psychologists dealing with 'natural' representational systems. Nevertheless, advances in artificial intelligence can shed light on human cognitive modelling by making the characteristics of the human system more explicit and pinpointing constraints on human–machine interactions.

1.6 Conclusion

Cognitive psychology aims at accounting for the processes allowing a cognitive entity to *stand for* an absent entity. A fundamental feature of all representations is their ability to make absent entities symbolically *present* to the individual. This function of representation is closely related to the basic inclination of the human mind to differentiate 'what is here' from 'what is no longer here'. This dichotomy reflects a basic psychological act and probably constitutes one of the most elementary distinctions in human understanding.

To explain the fact that individuals behave in a way suggesting that absent objects are present in transient memory, cognitive psychology postulates the existence of two systems: an activation system, and a system that monitored and stored the features of these objects when they were available for perceptual inspection. The existence of these systems forms the basis of debate on cognitive representations and in particular the issue of whether all other psychological processes are subordinated to representational processes. The most fruitful approach appears to be a dual one: placing the issue of cognitive representation within the general framework of the study of representation, and defining it as an activity basic to all organisms which store and reinstate information. At the same time, the scientist must view representation operationally in order to analyze its various forms in human cognition, its outputs and its potential significance in behaviour.

2 Recent Developments in Imagery Research

Imagery is a perennial and controversial theme in psychology. The classic source of information about mental imagery (as far back as Plato and Aristotle) comes from introspection. The upsurge in imagery research in the last twenty years, however, has yielded a treasure chest of new data. This 'golden age' has also been marked by changes in psychology's traditional stance towards imagery. Interested readers will find ample documentation in several historical overviews (see Denis, 1979b; Holt, 1964; Mandler and Mandler, 1964; Richardson, 1980). The major turning points are presented below.

The first era of imagery research dates back to the beginnings of scientific psychology in the nineteenth century. At that time, the dominant trend in psychology was Associationism (cf. Binet, 1886; Titchener, 1898). This 'new psychology' defined itself as the science of mental life, and viewed introspection as the prime means of accessing mental events. In the classic paradigm of the time, subjects were asked to introspect either during or just after execution of tasks, and then report on their mental states and subjective representations during the task. Today we know that certain types of inner experiences are more likely than others to reach consciousness through introspection. Introspection can tap 'ideas', 'affects' or 'feelings', but above all *images*, i.e., mental evocations of previous perceptual experiences. Images are not only easy to access but are also experiences that subjects can put into words, for example, in verbal reports. This explains why imagery was so central to Associationist psychology. Simply, methodology at that time was particularly adapted to the study of images.

The first attack on the Associationist view that imagery was a prime means of analysis of mental experiences came from the

Würzburg group. The Würzburg premises were that there are two types of mental experiences. One type has sensory contents like images; the other is imageless and non-analyzable. The Würzburg group was arguing, in other words, that images are not the locus of thought, but rather are secondary features which, at best, illustrate thought on those occasions when thought can be pictorialized. The original Associationist position emerged substantially weakened from the debate on 'imageless thought'. The death-blow, however, was to come from Watson's (1913) article, 'Psychology as the behaviorist views it'. The science of behaviour, in Watson's view, rejected Associationism as well as the imageless thought approach on the grounds that both had recourse to the same methods of introspection and the same mentalist conceptions. Behaviourism not only excluded images from psychology ('ghosts' devoid of any functional significance, in Watson's opinion), but all mentalist constructs – attention, sensation, mental processes, etc., – whose functional role in behaviour was not (and in any case could not be) proved.

In the thirty or so years following the Behaviourist revolution, imagery was to be relegated to purgatory. Virtually excluded from prevailing research trends until the 1950s, imagery was slowly resurrected in indirect and then gradually more explicit ways in the theories of that time. Neo-behaviourists were first to view non-verbal processes as possible mediators of behaviour (cf. Mowrer, 1960; Skinner, 1953; Staats, 1961). Visual images were then referred to in 'acceptable' terminology such as 'conditioned sensations' (Mowrer), 'operant seeing' (Skinner), 'conditioned sensory responses' (Staats). Regardless of circumlocution, imagery was, however, recognized as making a decisive contribution to the 'representational' part of word meaning.

Imagery once again became a major issue in psychology with the emergence of Cognitivism in the early 1960s (Bruner, 1964; Neisser, 1967; Piaget and Inhelder, 1966). Researchers set themselves clearly apart from the Associationist tradition (which viewed images as residual forms of sensations) by stressing the role of images as end-products of symbolic activity, and the difference in nature (rather than in intensity) between images and percepts. Imagery, like language, was linked to the symbolic function. Placed on the same level, yet differentiated from other symbolic activities, mainly language, imagery was on the brink of being incorporated into more ambitious and more comprehensive models of cognitive activity. The works of Allan Paivio in the mid-1960s constitute the turning-point for the return of imagery, and full acknowledgment of its role in cognition.

2.1 Neomentalism and the dual coding model

The originality and impact of Paivio's approach stemmed from his aim to study mental structures and processes through an objective analysis of behaviour rather than through a subjective approach to mental states. His orientation differed from the Behaviourist position in that his stated purpose was not the study of behaviour, but the use of behaviour to study mental representations and the central processes governing their construction. In contrast to Associationist paradigms, introspective analysis was no longer used as the means of accessing the processes underlying mental experiences. Because Paivio grounded his theoretical constructs on objective methodology and procedures, his work had the immediate effect of placing imagery in the forefront of scientific psychology (see Paivio, 1971, 1975a). Neomentalism, as it stands today, is still considered to be of high heuristic value (see Paivio, 1986, 1991; Paivio *et al.*, 1989).

Using a variety of paradigms, Paivio not only defined a psychological phenomenon but, more importantly perhaps, conferred major status on imagery in his model of cognitive activity. Paivio's studies clearly show that the functional properties of imagery, in particular its ability to generate analogue representations, make it a key component of a wide range of activities. In the area of verbal memory, for instance, where factors such as word frequency and associative meaning were considered to be critical, Paivio showed that word imagery value, i.e., the capacity for words to elicit mental images, was much more powerful than other variables and could in addition account for them. Further, he showed that imagery, either spontaneous or elicited by instructions, was a significant factor in the enhancement of mnemonic coding in most subjects.

Researchers rapidly took interest in imagery effects at this time. This led to a proliferation of theoretical models and accounts of imagery effects in psychological activities. Paivio's work, however, was to have the greatest impact, primarily because it was the most systematic, but also because it was an integral part of his more comprehensive theory, the dual coding model. In this model, psychological activities are regulated by two 'coding systems' or 'modes of symbolic representation', each of which has specific structural and functional properties. The imagery system, whose elaboration is linked to perceptual experience of the physical world, is more likely to be implemented when the situation involves concrete objects or events. The verbal system, linked to language exposure and experience, is assumed to be less dependent on the concreteness of the situation and has greater utility in more abstract tasks. In other words, the imagery system is brought into play when the individual needs to process information with a figural content (interpreting scenes, forming visual images, etc.), whereas the verbal system is reserved for linguistic processing. Paivio collected a considerable body of empirical data to test the validity of these two constructs and measure their differential effects.

2.2 The rise of Propositionalism and the first imagery debate

The publication of Paivio's major book in 1971, *Imagery and Verbal Processes*, was decisive for the return of imagery, although battles were still being waged on several fronts. Neo-behaviourists proferred harsh judgements. In particular, Skinner (1975) challenged the alleged functional role of representations in behaviour and argued that the study of representations hinders the advancement of psychology as a science. The major source of controversy, however, was to arise from the publication in 1973 of a paper by Zenon Pylyshyn, whose impact can be felt to this day. Pylyshyn did not challenge the idea that imagery is a genuine facet of mental life. Rather, his tightly wrought set of arguments criticized the excessive number of functional properties attributed to imagery as a hypothetical construct.

Pylyshyn was the first to point to the need for analysis of the representational structures underlying images rather than their phenomenal properties. His most far-reaching claim was that there are forms of representation that are more abstract, unavailable to introspection, and neither imaginal nor verbal. These 'amodal' representations, which Pylyshyn termed 'propositions', were also considered by Anderson and Bower (1973) to play a critical explanatory role in psychological activity. The core idea was that although imagery can be used to form a representation of a spatial relationship between objects, what is stored in long-term memory is not an image, but a propositional *description* of the objects and their relationships.

The Pylyshyn as well as Anderson and Bower positions can be seen as variants on Conceptualism, whose basic aim (from Rationalist philosophy to the Würzburg group) is to account for human thought processes in a way which excludes that thought can be vehicled by symbolic representations. In Paivio's theory, symbolic representations (images and verbal representations) are the very loci of mental activity. In contrast, the Conceptualist approach defines thought as a type of activity involving specific cognitive entities. Images and verbal representations are not the necessary mediators of thought but rather optional byproducts (see also Chase and Clark, 1972). Perhaps the most extreme version of this position is the postulate of a 'language of thought' to which all other systems of representation, including imagery, are subordinated (cf. Fodor, 1975).

Thus, practically as soon as imagery had regained some credibility as a scientific object of investigation, it was once again threatened with banishment into the murky doom of cognitive chimera.

2.2.1 *The theoretical counter-offensive*

In these suddenly troubled waters, reactions were swift and varied. Paivio (1975a, 1977) was quick to denounce the 'true identity' of his opponents, claiming that what had really penetrated cognitive psychology were artificial intelligence models, and that some researchers working on imagery were in fact primarily interested in exploiting imagery to construct computer models of human cognitive functioning (for examples, see Rumelhart, Lindsay and Norman, 1972; Simon, 1972). Use of the computer metaphor to describe human cognition makes a major concession in Paivio's eyes to Rationalistic approaches and orients researchers towards a reductionist interpretation of mental representations (although the proponents of this approach argue to the contrary). Paivio's main criticism was directed against researchers who were only interested in images to the extent that they could be analyzed in a propositional format, and whose main interest in imagery was that images lend themselves particularly well to formal propositional descriptions.

The rise of propositional theories did not put a halt to the dual coding perspective. A whole series of findings were obtained over the course of the 1970s which were consistent with the model or at least could be interpreted parsimoniously within the framework of the theory. Most of these studies (which made no reference to hypothetical, more abstract forms of mental representation) employed a paradigm designed to investigate memory for pictures vs. memory for verbal material. Some of the data successfully validated an 'elementary' version of the dual coding model, in that they supported the hypothesis of two memory codes with independent and additive effects. The findings in general indicated that better recall of pictorial material is dependent on the possibilities of activating both codes. Operationalizing two codes is simply more efficient than operationalizing only one. Other studies within this framework addressed the issue of whether one of these two codes – namely, the imagery code – was intrinsically more efficient than the other for memory storage (Fraisse, 1974; Paivio, 1974; Paivio and Csapo, 1973; Rowe and Rogers, 1975).

Somewhat later, studies were designed to test dual coding model predictions against predictions from a single coding model. Although a certain amount of evidence was accumulated in favour of the dual coding model (Belmore, 1982; D'Agostino and Small, 1980; Harris, Morris and Bassett, 1977; Santa, 1977), a growing number of researchers turned towards models with a single system of representation, which was tested with semantic decision paradigms essentially.

The working hypothesis was that there is a single 'memory base' and that pictorial and verbal stimuli activate the same semantic code. One of the first convincing pieces of evidence for a single processing system was that the coding of pictures and the coding of words have similar functional properties. Findings suggesting there were similar 'laws' for the memorization of pictorial and verbal material were taken as a positive empirical argument for a single coding system (cf. Anderson and Paulson, 1978). The differences which subsist between the processing of pictures and words are not assumed to reflect the existence of two distinct representational systems, each containing qualitatively different types of information. In other words, the nature of information in the memory store which is activated by the stimulus is the same, regardless of type of stimulus. Differences between pictures and words stem from the differential discriminability of each (Friedman and Bourne, 1976) or from differences in rate of activation in the system (Durso and Johnson, 1979). This more lenient version of the single system model introduces the complementary idea that there are different *access paths* to one single system, some of which are faster than others. More specifically, it is argued that a given semantic representation is more likely to be activated or is activated in a more 'automatic' fashion (i.e., faster) by a pictorial than a verbal stimulus (Carr *et al.*, 1982; Nelson, Reed and McEvoy, 1977; Rosch, 1975). Thus, although all stimuli are ultimately coded in an amodal propositional system, the processing of pictures should be easier than the processing of sentences describing these pictures (Seymour, 1975). The information contained in propositional representations is conceptual in nature and stored in an abstract form which preserves little of the specifically figural or linguistic information of input messages (Guenther, 1980).

In a variant on this perspective, although pictures and words tap the same *sort* of information in the individual's representational system, they are likely to activate different subsets of semantic information. In other words, if activation occurs in the *same* semantic system, it may address specific subparts of this system as a function of whether the input is figural or verbal. This version of a single system model is thus more flexible than the original, in that although all components are identical in nature (i.e., abstract or propositional), the model allows for differentiation between figural components and those unrelated to figuration. Studies conducted in this newer framework were thus illustrative of a more 'analytic' approach to conceptual representations and made an explicit attempt to differentiate components of the system that handle the 'appearance' of objects from other components. This approach was to lay the groundwork for the future notion that constructing an image consists of the activation of some parts of a more general representation, i.e., the implementation of specific activating processes (cf. Denis, 1982a, 1982b).

In this period of theoretical upheavals and reappraisals, Paivio cautiously entertained the possibility of extending the dual coding model to incorporate another representational system in addition to the two existing systems. Data indicating that mental representations of concrete and abstract sentences have some features in common prompted Marschark and Paivio (1977) to put forward a common (amodal) mode of representation to account for these similarities. They, however, preserved the modal representational systems so that the model could handle differences between the memorization of concrete and abstract verbal material. In his later reassessments of this version of the model, Paivio was clear about his preference for a dual coding system, with no recourse to a third system unless the evidence clearly argues for it. Paivio's main contention, however, was that the abundant data confirming the dual coding model make it uneconomical to abandon it since more comprehensive models, i.e. models accounting for data that can be handled by the dual coding model and data which this model fails to account for, are not available (Paivio, 1982, 1986).

2.2.2 Compromise solutions

In the debate opposing dual coders and hard-line propositionalists, a number of researchers took a middle path which basically consisted of associating modal forms of representation (such as visual images) and amodal forms (such as propositions) in the same model. This type of mixed model was thus expected to account for all forms of representation, whether input information was related or unrelated to perceptual experience. In addition, mixed models incorporated the additional premise that figural information could be represented in memory in *both* modal and propositional forms. In a comprehensive approach to imagery processes, there was a need for investigation of the specific properties of the relevant modalities as well as an investigation of the 'deeper' components of representation (cf. Kosslyn, Holyoak and Huffman, 1976; Kosslyn *et al.*, 1977).

Other compromise models attributed more weight to abstract forms of representation and considered that modal forms were tightly subordinated to abstract ones. For example, Mary Potter (1979; Potter, Valian and Faulconer, 1977) developed a model around the premise that mental evocation of an object in an individual's mental system results primarily from the activation of a conceptual representation which itself is neither verbal or sensory. Language inputs, for example, are not shunted to a 'verbal system' where meanings are purportedly located, but rather to a 'conceptual system' where non-modal information is stored. Perceptions of objects or pictures are likewise directed towards this conceptual system. Thus, in this model, the prime elements of thought are conceptual, and the representations processed by modal systems (the lexical system, the visual imagery system) are only 'relays' for the activation of conceptual information. Modal systems are still included in Potter's model, but have an ancillary role. Their role is, for instance, to preserve the surface or literal features of input information.

A comparable search for theoretical compatibility between an abstract level of representation and modal levels can be found at this time in works by Paivio's former associates, who although entirely versed in the dual coding model, were nevertheless responsive to propositionalist arguments. This dual attraction prompted them to raise two fundamental issues concerning the concept of representation: (a) Can the functioning of a representational system be reduced to more abstract, basic principles? (b) In what form is knowledge ultimately stored? One particularly interesting response can be found in Yuille and Catchpole (1977), whose model defines an 'abstract plane' and a 'representational plane' for cognitive operations. Knowledge is stored in a conceptual form in the abstract plane where it can be treated by propositional analysis whereas this same knowledge can be activated as transient mental representations in a modal fashion in the representational plane.

This partitioning, which differs totally from the dichotomy in the dual coding model, can in a sense be seen as a variant or extension of the Piagetian distinction between operative and figurative levels. In the Piagetian theory, the figurative level is subordinated to operational thought and is the level where internal representations (for instance, images) are formed and then acted upon by operations. Although the operative/figurative level distinction can be interpreted as an alternative form of dual coding, it in fact differs considerably from it in that the two representational systems operate in parallel in Paivio's model, whereas they are in a hierarchical relationship here (cf. Marschark et al., 1987). Another striking feature of this model is that an imagery theory no longer revolves around imagery proper. Rather, imagery is one of many modules in the cognitive system the model is constructed to account for. The model thus focuses more heavily on the instrumental role of images as possible (or virtual) tools for thinking rather than making them essential components of thought, and as figural expressions of the meaning of verbal outputs rather than inherent parts of meaning. In other words, images are the products of a processing system (rather than stored entities in long-term memory), and serve as 'models' for operations which cannot be carried out or implemented on other forms of representation.

One of the seminal influences in the field of imagery can be traced back to Stephen Kosslyn's first paper (1973) which reflected his interest in incorporating propositional notions into a theory of imagery. Another key-paper was to follow in 1975. The core of Kosslyn's approach – similar to the conceptualizations motivating Roger Shepard's first works on mental rotation (cf. Shepard, 1975) – was that imagery researchers are amenable to the idea that there may be other forms of mental representation than images but that this in no way detracts from the value of data obtained from studies devoted exclusively to identifying the specific properties of imagery. This position was adopted and reinforced in a major paper by Kosslyn and Pomerantz (1977) which took the stance that images need to be investigated in their own right, as genuine forms of mental representation which cannot be reduced to other, purportedly exclusively functional forms of representation.

Although Kosslyn explicitly focused his attention on the analysis of images, he nevertheless attached enormous importance to propositions which he viewed as modes of representation of information in long-term memory. In a certain way, the Kosslyn position exemplifies a 'third Propositionalist approach' in cognitive research on imagery. The first approach, which was put forward by the earliest anti-imagists, rejected the hypothesis of specific functional properties of images and considered images at best to be epiphenomena with no functional significance for psychological activity. In this view, functional processes, which do not intervene on the level of imagery, are assumed to tap abstract mental entities or entities whose nature is not specified but which in any case are best characterized by propositional analysis (cf. Pylyshyn, 1973). The second approach is reflected by researchers who showed renewed interest in imagery but who opted for propositional notation to describe the structure of images and their transformations (cf. Anderson and Paulson, 1978; Baylor, 1971). In a similar vein, some authors argued that perceptual information could also be coded propositionally (cf. Light and Berger, 1976; Palmer, 1977). What differentiates the third approach is that propositional notation is not used to describe images themselves (as transient psychological events), but rather their infrastructure and type of coding in long-term memory. This feature is what most clearly distinguishes Kosslyn's theory from Paivio's. Paivio sees the imagery system as modal both during activation and in long-term memory. Kosslyn, in contrast, considers that information is stored permanently in propositional form and that imagery experiences are generated from this amodal data base when specific modal processes are implemented.

2.2.3 *The indeterminacy hypothesis*

The theoretical counter-offensive and the ensuing compromise solutions in response to Pylyshyn's (1973) paper were soon to be complemented by John Anderson's (1978) position. Rather than a counter-attack or a compromise position between imagists and propositionalists, Anderson argued for indeterminacy. His position was that both families of models are on an equal footing in terms of their ability to account for imagery phenomena, and that neither do so conclusively. That is, a propositional model can always 'mimic' an imagistic model and thus account for data supporting imagistic theories (for example, data from mental rotation experiments). If, as Anderson shows, a set of assumptions on propositional representations and their associated processes can be derived from a set of assumptions on imagistic forms of representations and the processes acting on them, the raw behavioural data cannot be used as proof of the existence of one form of internal representation or another. In the absence of primary (for instance, physiological) data, ultimate theoretical choices should be based on the parsimony of the models. The best theory in Anderson's opinion is thus the most parsimonious one, in which both figural and verbal inputs are stored in a single representational form, and which assumes a single set of psychological processes to account for the processing of information.

Anderson's (healthy) epistemological scepticism, which is reflected in his position that internal representations indeed exist but that their nature cannot be specified, in fact placed him closer to the propositionalist camp. His ties with Propositionalism are reinforced by his position on 'exactness'; that is, that propositions are especially easy to formalize and model in simulations (cf. Anderson and Bower, 1973; Kintsch, 1974; Norman and Rumelhart, 1975). Anderson's reasoning is illustrative of the pull of propositionalist theories which began at that time to supplant dual models.

Anderson's 'agnostic' position received attention from authors who had incorporated the notion of proposition into their theories of imagery (Keenan and Moore, 1979; Kosslyn *et al.*, 1979). However, Anderson's theory attracted little support, and debate shifted to a new area, the issue of the spatial nature of images and that of 'tacit knowledge' as an account for the effects of visual imagery.

2.3 Kosslyn's theory and the new imagery debate

In the meantime, a number of researchers were beginning to argue for an analytical approach to imagery, which aimed at defining the parameters of images and at the same time specifying their deep structure (cf. Denis, 1979b; Shepard, 1978). One of the immediate outcomes of these works was a finer distinction between images seen as transient psychological events having structural properties which can be described, and the deep meaning of these 'surface' events. This new orientation was to have considerable repercussions since it made it clear that no reference could be made to images without also making assumptions about their underlying structures, and the 'modules' of the cognitive system which generate imagery experiences. Further, images were considered to fulfil representational functions only when an 'interpretive function' is applied to them and extracts their meaning. This was to lead directly to the 'semantics' of imagery, a concept developed by researchers to bridge the gap between the analysis of semantic activities as applied to linguistic material (sentences and texts), and the study of imagery.

This period was also marked by an upsurge in work on mental rotation and analysis of how imagery contributes to the comparison of patterns presented at different angles. Roger Shepard and his associates reinforced the new contention at that time that analogical processes were involved in the mental transformations of physical objects (cf. Shepard and Cooper, 1982). A fuller description of mental rotation research is found in Chapter 3.

It was also at this time that Kosslyn introduced the idea of images as 'analogue representations'. Kosslyn defined images as patterns of activation in a medium or 'visual buffer' having the properties of coordinate space. Images correspond to activated portions of the visual buffer and are in a one-to-one correspondence with parts of the objects they represent. Two types of representations in long-term memory can be activated to generate images: 'literal' representations, which encode the overall structural features of objects ('skeletal encoding'), and propositional (abstract) representations, which encode the list of parts making up the object, their locations, the relationship of the object to superordinate categories, etc. Kosslyn postulates four families of processes which apply to images: (*a*) the processes involved in generating images and maintaining them transiently in the visual buffer; (*b*) the processes involved in image exploration; (*c*) the processes involved in the transformation of images (such as mental rotation); *(d)* the processes enabling subjects to use their images to respond to questions about objects.

In Kosslyn's theory, images (in contrast to verbal symbols) are representations which entertain non-arbitrary, analogical correspondences with the objects they stand for. Each part of an image theoretically corresponds to the matching part of the object it represents, in such a way that the relative distances among object parts are accurately reflected by the distances among the corresponding parts of the imaginal representation. One of Kosslyn's most important experiments in this regard shows that there is a linear relationship between distances scanned by visual imagery and scanning durations. These experiments, which lent weight to the contention that images have true 'metrics', also prompted the further hypothesis that images are generated in a medium which has genuine spatial-like properties (cf. Kosslyn, 1973; Kosslyn, Ball and Reiser, 1978).

Kosslyn's most elaborated version of this theory and synthesis of his work, *Image and Mind*, appeared in 1980 and in a sense made him the most articulate spokesman for a position that was rapidly gaining audience. Briefly, Kosslyn's argument was that cognitive research is doing a disservice to the study of imagery by treating images and the processes involved in their elaboration in a vague or metaphorical way. Rather, the psychological events involved in imagery have specifiable, measurable parameters which should be accurately defined and assessed in conceptualizations and terminologies. In other words, images are cognitive products whose constituent parts and internal structures need to be defined and analyzed in an explicit and detailed fashion. Kosslyn's own response to this challenge was to couch his theory in the form of a model and a computer simulation (cf. Kosslyn and Shwartz, 1977). This simulation, which is in no way a mere (albeit elegant) extension of Kosslyn's approach, is in fact a decisive research tool which forces the scientist to adhere to criteria of accuracy and clarity at each step in the conceptualization process. Kosslyn's approach thus reflects the extent to which a whole generation of researchers with training in computer science put their trust in the heuristic value of modelling in cognitive science.

This position did not, however, spare its defenders from attacks, in particular from Pylyshyn, whose new writings challenged the 'spatial' nature of visual images. Pylyshyn (1981) argued that the temporal regularities observed in experiments on mental scanning do not reflect true spatial properties of mental images. Rather, they reflect what the individuals know about spatial properties of the objects they are requested to image and the scanning durations of these objects in the real world. Thus, imagery studies replicating the equation between time, distance and speed in fact reflect subjects' prior knowledge of this equation rather than properties inherent to the image medium. Since subjects know the equation to be true and can apply it correctly to physical events, they make their mental scanning fit the equation. In other words, these experiments measure subjects' ability to apply prior knowledge to imagery experiments. In Pylyshyn's terms, the cognitive function measured in these experiments is 'penetrated' by subjects' prior 'tacit knowledge'.

Kosslyn's (1981, 1983) responses to Pylyshyn drew on a new series of empirical data. Kosslyn pointed out in particular that individuals are unaware of a number of properties shared by both imagery and perception. Yet they respond in a way that shows that the properties of their mental representations correspond to those of the physical objects, thus invalidating the tacit knowledge explanation. Kosslyn (1983) showed that the temporal parameters of imagery differ as a function of whether an individual is told to image an object and then imagine it is being put into motion, or alternatively to image an object and make the image itself move. Kosslyn acknowledged the fact that prior knowledge can affect some mental operations applied to visual images (cf. also Intons-Peterson and McDaniel, 1991; Intons-Peterson and Roskos-Ewoldsen, 1989), but emphasized that prior knowledge tends to be tapped to a greater extent only when subjects are explicitly told to do so.

A number of studies published in this period indicated that prior knowledge might play a role in imagery. Data reported by Richman, Mitchell and Reznick (1979), then by Mitchell and Richman (1980), suggested that if subjects are led to believe that their responses will be examined for the relationship between distance and duration, they can accurately predict the findings of these experiments. Thus, subjects are likely to respond in a way they believe will satisfy the experimenter. This explanation, however, implies that subjects do not respond until they have checked their responses against their prior knowledge. It is doubtful, in fact, that all mental scanning experiments are flawed by this type of bias.

Evidence from other studies showed that prior knowledge

cannot entirely account for performance. In these studies, (a) subjects' responses could not be attributed to any prior knowledge; (b) there was maximal likelihood that subjects actually scanned mental images in the absence of explicit instructions to do so; (c) subjects had no reason to suspect that the experimenter was interested in time–distance relationships. The findings showed that there is still a positive correlation between scanning durations and distances (Finke and Pinker, 1982, 1983; Pinker, Choate and Finke, 1984). The overall conclusion that can be drawn from this evidence is that if some imagery phenomena are penetrated by prior knowledge, all imagery effects cannot be reduced to knowledge alone.

More recent data provide further evidence against the pervasiveness of prior knowledge. If prior knowledge has an effect on visual imagery, and if it is true that imagery phenomena are mere reflections of available tacit knowledge, naive subjects should be able to accurately predict imagery phenomena on the basis of such knowledge. That is, anyone knowing the relationships among time, distance and speed should be able to predict the temporal regularities of his or her responses before engaging in a mental scanning task. In fact, when experimental tasks such as these are described to subjects, most fail to predict the imagery effects, including those which mimic well-known perceptual phenomena (such as increase of scanning times with distance) (Denis and Carfantan, 1985). Furthermore, ability to predict imagery phenomena is no better in subjects who have the highest imagery capacities (Denis and Carfantan, 1986, 1990).

Before putting an end to the imagery debate (at least for this chapter), it is worth pointing out that most of the criticisms of imagery theories have been based on speculation rather than on empirical facts. Pylyshyn, for instance, does not question the empirical validity of the data obtained in imagery studies, but rather challenges the internal logic of the theories put forward to account for these data. Propositionalists rarely presented new empirical data to support their claims. Pylyshyn's extensive list of writings only contains one article which includes data corroborating his hypotheses, a study which indicates that the time to rotate a pattern mentally is affected by both angle of rotation of the pattern and by some of its structural properties (Pylyshyn, 1979). Paivio (1982) was right to stress that imagery theories have produced new factual information whereas Propositionalists primarily 'reacted' to the data and their imagist interpretations. It is a matter of fact that most of the data fuelling the debate between imagery proponents and Propositionalists have been supplied by the former.

Other, more recent skirmishes have shifted controversy to the area of experimenter effects. This criticism is a variant on the more general issue that experimenters can sometimes influence subjects by providing them with implicit cues to respond in a way that fits with the hypotheses. For instance, if an experimenter expects that mental scanning times will be proportional to scanned distances, he or she may give subtle cues to subjects to produce the expected pattern. Intons-Peterson and White (1981) showed that some imagery effects were cancelled out when the experimenter was blind to the purposes of the experiment (cf. Intons-Peterson, 1983). As a test of experimenter effects, Jolicoeur and Kosslyn (1985) had experiments run by testers who had been briefed on hypotheses which in fact were the exact opposite of classic findings. For instance, the testers were given preliminary data highly suggestive of the fact that scanning times are longer for very short distances. The findings show, however, that even when experimenters were led to expect erroneous outcomes, subjects always responded in a comparable fashion, and hence were apparently not affected by experimenter expectations.

Kosslyn's work also shed light on individual imagery differences, an important facet in imagery research. Clearly, people differ in their ability to construct and use visual images (as they do for other cognitive abilities). What remains problematic is how to *measure* these differences and define the most relevant tasks (cf. Denis, 1990a; Ernest, 1977).

Currently, three techniques are used. The first is imagery questionnaires, which consist of presenting subjects with short descriptions of scenes and asking them to visualize and rate their images for vividness, clarity or richness of detail. A good example is Marks' (1973) Vividness of Visual Imagery Questionnaire. The second is the inventory technique where subjects are asked to indicate the frequency of their use of visual imagery in a variety of everyday situations. A typical example is the Individual Differences Questionnaire (Paivio and Harshman, 1983). Objective tests form the third category. Here, subjects are asked to perform a task which has been designed to call for visual imagery. The number of correct answers given within a specified time limit is considered to be a measure of the use of visual imagery. Most of these tasks consist of predicting the outcome of a transformation of a spatial configuration (cf. Bennett, Seashore and Wesman, 1963; Guilford, 1967; Thurstone and Jeffrey, 1956; Vandenberg and Kuse, 1978).

All these instruments probably tap different aspects of visual imagery. Some require subjects to assess their cognitive experience of their own images, whereas others are oriented towards measuring individual aptitudes in manipulating visual information. There is a tendency to use several of these tests at a time to discriminate better between 'high' and 'low' imagers, but appropriate use of a single test can be valid if it corresponds to that aspect of imagery being investigated in the experiment.

There is a growing consensus that the study of individual imagery differences benefits from defining subcomponents of imagery abilities. Kosslyn has carried out a systematic exploration of imagery components using a battery of tests designed to tap different facets of visual imagery (maintaining an image, mentally scanning an image, mentally rotating an image, etc.) (see Kosslyn *et al.*, 1984). The battery thus sheds light on specific abilities corresponding to the implementation of specific and relatively independent 'processing modules'. Some of these modules handle representations in long-term memory from where images are generated; others deal with images once these have been activated in the visual buffer (see also Poltrock and Brown, 1984).

Kosslyn has adopted this same 'modular' approach to study the neurological infrastructure of mental imagery. He tested subjects with specific pathologies suggesting dysfunctions of the processes governed by different processing modules. Functional dissociations of these modules caused by brain lesions are considered to be neuropsychological proofs of this 'componential' theory of mental imagery (cf. Farah, 1984; Kosslyn *et al.*, 1985).

This new direction in mental imagery research has a number of profound implications. First, it adheres to the 'computational' approach to cognition, which consists of building computer models of human performance as an integral part of theory building (cf. Pinker, 1984). Second, Kosslyn's current position reflects his conviction that the features of human 'natural computation' are better investigated by a neuropsychological than the traditional cognitive approach. A number of researchers on imagery have indeed turned to neuroanatomy, neurophysiology and neuropsychology (cf. Farah, 1988; Kosslyn, 1987, 1988; Kosslyn, Van Kleeck and Kirby, 1990).

2.4 Conclusion

Imagery has been at the centre of epistemological debate since the dawn of scientific psychology. Strikingly, it is still here a century later. Is imagery indeed the touchstone of current psychological research? What can be said is that cognitive research must come to terms with mental representations, the symbolic forms in which these representations are expressed, and the processes applied to them. Regardless of outcome, imagery certainly remains the richest and the most controversial of all these forms of representation.

3 The Properties of Visual Images

One of the major obstacles to an exhaustive inventory of the properties of visual images is their variety. Even when classifications are restricted to conscious forms of imagery (eliminating such specific phenomena as after-images and eidetic imagery), the range of imagery activities and the functions they serve is still enormous. There have been many attempts at classifying forms of imagery. Most tend to be dichotomous. The earliest, which scientific psychology derived from the empiricist tradition, distinguishes 'memory images', evoking specific perceptual experiences, from 'imagination images', evoking combinations of several previous experiences (Perky, 1910; Vinacke, 1952).

Piaget and Inhelder (1966) classified visual images into two broad categories: 'reproductive images' and 'anticipatory images'. Reproductive images evoke known objects or events whereas anticipatory images represent objects or events with which subjects have had no prior perceptual experience. This division also corresponds to a developmental order in that reproductive images can be generated at the pre-operational stage or even as early as the emergence of the symbolic function. Anticipatory images are the end-products of the visualization of yet unaccomplished events and as such are not available prior to concrete operations.

This chapter explores the general characteristics of visual images, regardless of their relative positions in existing classifications. Further, the generation of some images may call for more complex processes than others. For instance, looking for a metaphorical image for the concept of FRATERNITY probably requires more steps than elaborating an image for the concept of TOMATO or BICYCLE. However, once constructed, all visual images have a number of characteristics in common, which will be examined in detail in the sections that follow.

3.1 Imagery and perception

There will be repeated reference to visual perception in this chapter on visual imagery. Perhaps the prime reason is that there is a 'surface' resemblance between the psychological events resulting from imagery activities and those stemming from perceptual activities. These two activities deal with physical features of the environment, although these features are absent in one case and present and directly accessible in the other. Both activities also produce cognitive experiences which individuals intuitively feel to be similar although not identical. This sense of similarity is so strong that imaginal and perceptual experiences are often described in the same terms. For instance, 'at the top left' can describe a portion of a visual image as well as a spatial characteristic of a perceived object. Everyday language uses qualifiers such as 'intensity', 'clarity', 'richness of detail', 'vividness', etc., to describe both images and percepts.

The second reason for repeated reference to perception is that the products of imagery are in fact derived from perception. The contents of imagery activities are shaped by the perceptual processings which preceded them, and the raw material for imagery is ultimately perceptual. Although distinct from perception, visual images nevertheless preserve something of perceptual events. Virtually everything can be preserved (as is the case for eidetic imagery), but in most cases imagery is affected by processes of selection and schematization. Even when an image is entirely the product of imagination, the constituents of the image are still dependent on past perceptual events. In this respect, the relationship between imagery and perception is best described in terms of dependency.

This dependency itself can be viewed from several angles. Visual images draw their contents from the repertory of perceptual experiences built up in each individual's personal history. Negative proof comes from studies showing that a given imagery modality is less easily activated when this modality is not functional. For example, the congenitally blind perform less well than sighted subjects on tasks which can benefit from visual imagery, whereas individuals who have lost their sight perform as well as sighted subjects, suggesting they can draw on their past perceptual experiences (cf. Marmor, 1977; Paivio and Okovita, 1971; for the issue of imagery in the blind, see De Beni and Cornoldi, 1988; Ernest, 1987). Besides, once the system enabling storing of incoming perceptual experience in the form of visual images has been instated, positive proof comes from the very brief, even subliminal perceptions which persist either in daydreaming or indirectly in drawing (cf. Eagle, Wolitzky and Klein, 1966; Singer, 1966).

Once the relationship between imagery and perception has been established, the problem is to determine to what extent the two activities are functionally similar. This has led some researchers to hypothesize that imagery not only 'derives' from perceptual activity but also that it is linked to perception in that both activate the same mechanisms in a neural substrate common (or partially common) to each.

3.2 Functional similarities

This section provides a selective review of empirical data attesting to the functional similarities between imagery and perception. In general, experiments compare (a) a condition where subjects required to execute a task are presented with an object or a physical configuration, and (b) a condition where the subjects have to execute the same task while forming a visual image of the object or configuration. The question is whether performance is similar in both conditions. Are the effects in the same direction? If so, is the magnitude of these effects identical in both?

Studies in the field of memory using the comparison of perceptual and imaginal conditions have produced data that argue convincingly for the functional similarity hypothesis. There is longstanding evidence that memorizing a list of concrete words is enhanced when these words are accompanied (or even replaced) by pictures or photographs of the objects designated by these words. This effect has been observed in a number of free recall experiments (cf. Denis, 1975; Fraisse, 1970; Paivio, Rogers and Smythe, 1968). In a variant on this paradigm, subjects are presented with the list of words alone and are instructed to create visual images mentally of the objects mentioned, as their names are presented. In experiments comparing picture vs. noun-plus-imagery instructions conditions, not only learning with images has effects on free recall in the same direction as learning with pictures (i.e., better recall), but the magnitude of these effects is extremely similar in both learning conditions (cf. Denis, 1975). Thus, in free recall learning, the purely mental evocation of objects apparently has mnemonic encoding effects which are similar to the processing of corresponding pictures.

In another specific area of verbal learning, memory for phrases describing actions is also facilitated by mental imagery to an equal extent as by the perception of actions. Engelkamp and Krumnacker (1980) compared the four following conditions for memory of phrases such as *'throwing a ball'* or *'playing piano'*: (1) the subjects actually performed the movements making up these actions; (2) the subjects formed a visual image of these actions; (3) the subjects watched a film of these actions; (4) the subjects received standard verbal learning instructions. The first condition results in the highest recognition and recall scores and the latter one is the least favourable. Imaginal (2) and perceptual (3) conditions are at intermediate, equivalent levels (see also Engelkamp, 1986).

Peterson (1975) reports another interesting finding. In her experiment, subjects were first presented with a 4×4 matrix, in which 12 cells contained a letter. After this learning phase, subjects were asked to recall positions of the letters on an empty matrix. On average, subjects' recall was the best for the letters which were located at the periphery of the matrix, and in particular in the four corner cells. As a matter of fact, these cells were also memorized best when subjects had to *imagine* the letters contained in these cells (with letters enumerated orally by the experimenter during the learning phase).

Memory research has also shown that the effects of perceptual presentations are comparable to those of visual imagery with respect to hypermnesia, that is, memory enhancement as the interval between learning and recall increases (within certain temporal limits). Experiments have shown that hypermnesia is significantly higher for lists of pictures than for lists of words. Several hypotheses have been advanced to account for this differential effect (cf. Erdelyi, 1982). The point here, however, is that when subjects are presented with a list of words with the instructions to form visual images of corresponding objects, hypermnesia exhibits exactly the same pattern as when subjects have been presented with pictures (Erdelyi et al., 1976).

Thus, the evidence from several types of memory studies shows that imagery effects are highly similar to those resulting from direct perception. Another approach consists in comparing the judgements made by subjects who are presented with physical stimuli (that is, open to perceptual analysis) with judgements when these stimuli are absent from their perceptual field (that is, when stimuli are mentally evoked). A case in point is Shepard and

Chipman's (1970) experiment, where subjects had to evaluate the shape similarity of fifteen American states presented by pairs of outline drawings. All possible pairs were presented. Subjects had completed the same evaluation task previously, but with pairs of the written names of the fifteen states. The results show a high correlation between the order of the pairs (from the most to the least similar) in the two situations. In addition, the two sets of similarity data for the drawing and the name conditions proved to be highly comparable. These findings suggest that assessment of the figural properties of stimuli that are unavailable to perception rely on information available in memory, which provides an adequate representation of these properties (see also Chew and Richardson, 1980; Gordon and Hayward, 1973).

In Shepard and Chipman's study, the nature of this representation was not investigated as such. However, the role of visual imagery in evoking figural properties in similarity judgements was reflected in subjects' post-experimental verbal reports. Furthermore, there were indications that the equivalence of similarity structures in both conditions (judgements on objects or their verbal substitutes) was more pronounced in subjects who stated they had used imagery extensively in the second condition (cf. Shepard, 1975).

On the whole, Shepard's findings attest to the isomorphism of the similarity patterns in a set of physical stimuli and in the set of the internal representations of these stimuli. In addition, they suggest that individuals with a tendency to use these representations in the form of visual images can produce behaviour that is extremely similar to the behaviour elicited by the stimuli themselves. Similar findings have been obtained in mental comparison experiments, where high imagers make faster decisions than low imagers, mainly on tasks where decisions rely on visualization of verbally described information (Paivio, 1978a, 1978b) (see Chapter 4).

Thus, a considerable body of data converges on the idea that imagery provides individuals with cognitive products which can be used in the same way as products of perception, and have behavioural effects that are often very similar to those of perception.

At this juncture, it is worth pointing to a question which tacitly underlies all these experiments. Researchers interested in mental images, their effects on behaviour and the similarity of these effects with those of perception are in fact dealing with the status that should be assigned to imagery. Images are at times interpreted as mental events which are the *causes* of the observed effects. Images, in this case, have the status of *internal stimuli*, having some of the properties and producing effects on the nervous system which can be interpreted and analyzed in the same terms as the effects of external stimuli. This approach, however, has the drawback of forcing researchers to put *objects* and *images of objects* on the same level in order to compare their effects. In fact, the most valid conceptual approach here consists in comparing entities which are both *cognitive* in nature, that is *mental representations* elaborated from objective stimuli and *mental representations* of stimuli generated in the absence of these stimuli. If mental representations are considered to have functional effects on the generation of behaviour, the investigation of functional similarities of imagery and perception must be set in a conceptual framework designed to specify the properties of these representations, and explain why the properties of some representational systems can be found in other systems as well. Then, if representational systems can 'inherit' properties from other systems, the question here is how extensively one system (imagery) inherits from the other (perception) and what are the limits on this inheritance.

3.3 Structural similarities

If imaginal representations have similar effects on behaviour as representations directly derived from perception, this may be a consequence of the fact that beyond their functional properties, the two sorts of representations have some intrinsic (structural) characteristics in common. This leads to the idea that if images and percepts are analyzed in terms of their internal organization, they should exhibit similarities at this level of analysis as well.

Intuitively, people are inclined to interpret imaginal events as possessing structural characteristics similar to those of perceived objects. Images are thought to possess an internal structure, as perceived objects do. However, although people may have some spatial intuition of their visual images, does this entail that the mental events produced during imagery have characteristics which reflect a genuine internal structure? Furthermore, if it is true that visual images have an internal structure which at least partially reflects the structure of perceptual events, the researcher can go one explanatory step further, and test the assumption that the functional similarities of the two modes of representation derive from their structural similarities.

Research on the mental scanning of spatial configurations has been aimed at defining aspects of the internal structure of visual images. These studies tend to confirm that images possess an internal structure, which reflects the structure of the configurations from which they were elaborated. In a classic study, Kosslyn, Ball and Reiser (1978) presented subjects with the map of an imaginary island, on which seven details were located (a beach, a hut, etc.), in such a way that the twenty-one distances between all pairs of details were different (Figure 3.1). The subjects studied the map until they were able to reproduce the locations of the seven details on a blank map perfectly from memory. The subjects were then asked to form a visual image of the map and focus their attention on one of the details which was mentioned by the experimenter (for instance, the beach). When a second object was named (for instance, the hut), subjects were asked to scan mentally across the map to the location of the second detail and to depress a button to indicate that they had checked for its presence

Figure 3.1 Map used in Kosslyn, Ball and Reiser (1978) experiments.

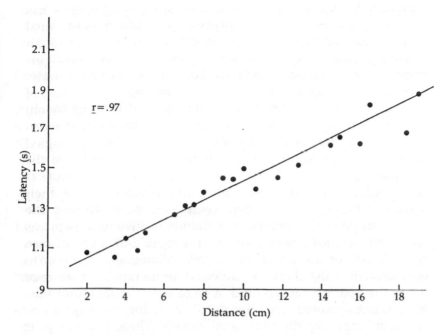

Figure 3.2 Verification latency as a function of distance separating details
Source: Kosslyn, Ball and Reiser, (1978, experiment 2)

in the image. (In some cases, the second detail named did not correspond to any object present on the map.) Figure 3.2 shows the linear relationship between verification latency and the distance separating the two details. This relationship only holds, in fact, in the experimental condition that required subjects to base their decisions on the examination of the visual image of the island. In the absence of explicit instructions to consult the image before stating that a detail was present, decision times were no longer correlated with the distance between details. This finding suggests that information on the presence of details can be stored in other forms than images, but that when this information is expressed in a visual image, it is organized in a way that reflects the spatial structure of the object itself, and in particular the relative distances among its parts.

It should be stressed that experiments designed to evaluate the structural similarity of images and percepts always infer the (hypothetical) *structure* of representations from analysis of the *processes* which operate on these representations (for example, mental scanning). In this respect, it is important to make a distinction between two sets of processes. Visual images are representations constructed in a processing system by specific generating processes. Representations, in addition, can be processed later on, provided other processes are implemented (scanning, rotation, etc.). Thus, images should be conceived of as mental representations which are both *outputs* of processes and *sites* for the implementation of other processes.

Similar to studies on mental scanning of spatial configurations, other studies focus on the properties of the processing system in which visual images are elaborated. Kosslyn (1975, 1976) conducted a series of studies demonstrating that the mental medium for images, or 'visual buffer', has both limits and processing constraints, and that these limits and constraints are highly similar to those which regulate visual perception. In particular, images, as percepts, undergo constraints relative to the apparent size of the imaged objects. Just as it is more difficult to discriminate details of an object on a tiny photograph than on an enlargement, a detail can be 'detected' more rapidly in an image when the object is represented at large size. On the other hand, at constant apparent size, the details covering the largest areas are 'seen' more rapidly than small details. These findings prompted the hypothesis that the processing system in which images are constructed has a maximal capacity, as is the case for the system which processes perceptual information, and that capacity size places limits on the amount of information available simultaneously in a visual image.

Lastly, if visual images are conceived of as 'models' of the objects they stand for, these models not only contain information on the different parts of the imagined objects, but the distance ratio between the different parts of the represented object is preserved in images. Certainly, an image can contain distortions, such as those resulting from the erroneous subjective evaluation of the size of a part of the imagined object. However, the basic idea is that images possess a structure which reflects the structure of the represented objects, that size (or distance) differences can actually be represented in visual images, and that these differences affect the temporal parameters of image processing. Thus, there is some justification in speculation on the 'metrics' underlying mental images. This does not mean that genuine spatial properties are attributed to visual images (which are cognitive, and not physical entities), but rather that this particular representational medium has functional characteristics which are extremely similar to those of the visual processing system.

3.4 Images as analogue representations

For many researchers, the notion of *analogy* is especially appropriate for characterizing a form of representation which has a high degree of structural similarity with visual percepts. It is a matter of fact that the development of research on visual imagery is contemporaneous with the development of the concept of analogy, as applied to the issue of representation. It has become commonplace to refer to the mode of representation which consists in elaborating visual images as *analogical*, by contrast with other modes of representation, qualified either as *propositional*, or *digital* or *conceptual*. What can be said of this property of analogy when it characterizes a form of representation? Does it only apply to representations, or shouldn't the analogy between processes be taken into account as well?

The first property of visual images which warrants their being termed analogical is that they are representations which appear to preserve the values of *continuous* variables. Continuity is a property of analogue representations in general, and not only a property of images. For instance, an individual's memory can encode and store the values of a set of entities on continuous dimensions, such as size, age, pleasantness, and so on. Analogue representations may be abstract in nature and devoid of any spatial qualities.

Another characteristic of analogue representations is that they entertain non-arbitrary relationships with the objects they represent. The corollaries of this characteristic are the notions of *resemblance*, and that of as direct as possible *correspondence* between the elements constitutive of the representation and those composing the represented object.

On the whole, the prime feature which characterizes images as analogue representations is their *structural isomorphism* (that is, their point-to-point correspondence) with representations elicited by perception of objects. Isomorphism is perfect if the different parts of an object, their respective positions, their topological relations, are identical in the perceptual and imaginal representations of the object.

In other words, two basic assumptions are made: (a) image-like representations have an internal structure; (b) there is a systematic relationship between this structure and the structure of perceptual representations. These assumptions are at times extended by the claim that this structural isomorphism not only pertains to images and *percepts*, but is actually present between images and imagined *objects* as well (cf. Cooper and Shepard, 1973).

Thus far, the analogy between perception and images has been examined on the *structural* level. Analogy has also been placed on the level of *processes* with the assumption that the structural isomorphism between images and percepts entails that images are processed by mechanisms similar to those implemented in perception. For instance, judging an imaginal representation (such as comparing the sizes of two objects) taps processes which are functionally similar to those brought into play when judging objects in perception. This hypothesis is confirmed by findings on mental scanning of imagined configurations, showing that there is a linear relationship between scanning times and distances. Thus, the cognitive processes involved in scanning imagined distances can be said to 'mimic' perceptual processes.

Data on another family of processes further reinforce the analogical nature of mental imagery. The processes described above operate on representations of static objects. Processes have no effect on the state of the representations and after process execution, the representation remains unchanged. However, other types of processes *transform* representations such that the final state of the representation differs from the original state.

In mental imagery research, the dynamic transformation which has yielded the greatest amount of data is mental rotation. The first experiment in this field was conducted by Shepard and Metzler (1971). Subjects were presented with pairs of perspective drawings of three-dimensional objects similar to those shown in Figure 3.3, and were asked to decide whether two drawings of a pair represented objects which were identical or different in shape. In some cases, the two shapes were identical, except that one of the objects was rotated, either on the same plane (Figure 3.3a) or in depth (Figure 3.3b); in other cases, the two shapes were different (Figure 3.3c). The main finding of this experiment was that when the two objects had the same shape, subjects' decision times were proportional to the angular difference between the two objects. Furthermore, most subjects stated that in order to check whether the two objects had the same shape, they mentally rotated one of the objects to judge its physical congruence with the other. The Shepard and Metzler (1971) findings on mental rotation have been shown to apply to many other types of stimuli: random polygons (Cooper, 1975; Farrell and Shepard, 1981), alphanumeric characters (Cooper and Shepard, 1973), line drawings of hands

(Cooper and Shepard, 1975) or faces (Cochran, Pick and Pick, 1983), photographs of faces (Valentine and Bruce, 1988).

The results obtained by Shepard and his associates (cf. Shepard, 1975; Shepard and Cooper, 1982) suggest that subjects make use of a procedure that allows them to mentally perform a rotation similar to the rotation which could be physically applied to the real object. Just as a 60° physical rotation requires twice the resources as a 30° rotation from the system which executes it, the psychological activity which mimics this rotation requires an execution time which is proportional to the amount of transformation it is called upon to execute. Mental simulation of the physical process thus undergoes constraints which reflect those that apply to the physical process itself.

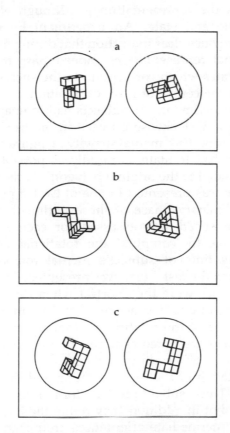

Figure 3.3 Examples of stimuli used in Shepard and Metzler's (1971) experiment.

This notion has led imagery researchers to extend the notion of analogy to the *processes* which operate on images, and not only to the internal structural organization of images in relationship to percepts. In the case of mental rotation, the processes taking place during this sort of mental operation are thought to be comparable to those which take place when subjects observe the physical rotation of objects (Shepard and Podgorny, 1978).

The analogy between perceptual and imaginal processes has been extended further by showing that if the time necessary to perform mental rotation is proportional to the rotation angle, in addition the internal representation goes through intermediary steps which actually correspond to the successive states of the object during physical rotation. Clearly, the linear increment of mental rotation time does not necessarily imply that mental rotation makes the representation go through all the possible positions to the end state. An experiment by Cooper (1976) nevertheless provides clear indication that during mental rotation, subjects' internal representations indeed pass through all the intermediary states which correspond to the successive positions of the object in the course of physical rotation.

In Cooper's experiment, the subjects had to imagine an irregular polygon turning clockwise on itself in the frontal plane. At a specific time during this mental activity, a figure was presented and the subject had to state as rapidly as possible whether the figure corresponded to the original polygon or was a mirror-image of it. The figure was presented in one of twelve possible orientations. In a preliminary phase of the experiment, the individual mental rotation speed was assessed for each subject. It was therefore possible to 'compute' the rotational position of the polygon at any time of subject's mental rotation, and more specifically, when the test figure was presented. The data showed that response times were the shortest when the test figure was presented in the orientation assumed to be congruent with the current orientation of the rotating internal representation. When the test figure was presented at some other orientation, response times increased linearly with the angular difference between the expected orientation of the representation and the orientation of the test figure. Thus, subjects indeed form a visual image of the rotating object, but in addition they rotate the internal representation through intermediate orientations from start to end states.

To sum up, current findings argue convincingly for structural similarity between the psychological events generated by the perception of objects and those resulting from the imaging of these same objects. The image of an object structurally reflects the internal organization of the perceptual experience of this object. This analogy as regards 'appearance' extends to at least some of the processes brought into play in perception and in imagery. Images may undergo types of processing which are similar to those applying to physical stimuli in the perceptual field. When transformational processes, such as rotation, are applied to a visual image, the image goes through the steps corresponding to those of the physical transformation of the object. The data thus consolidate the claim that mental images are truly analogue representations.

Considering that there is an analogy between images and percepts in terms of 'appearance' should not, however, distract from the ultimate issue of the *use* of representations. What use do people make of their images? Do analogical representations serve specific functions, i.e., that other types of representations cannot serve? In this respect, the structural approach to mental imagery is valid only in as much as it helps to shed light on the *functional* properties of this form of representation.

3.5 Similarity of mechanisms involved in the processing of perceptual and imaginal information

The studies described above strengthen the contention that there are functional and structural analogies between image and perception. However, in order to account for the structural similarity between images and percepts, is it sufficient to refer to the fact that images, as derived from previous perceptual experiences, preserve the 'surface' properties of the original perceptual representations? Would it not be more relevant to assume that this similarity in form also reflects a similarity between the *mechanisms* operating on perceptual information and those generating imaginal information?

Furthermore, is it sufficient to claim that the processes brought into play in imagery and those which operate on perceptual information simply 'resemble' each other? Rather, would it not be more relevant to assume that the *same* processes apply to both kinds of information? There are good reasons for hypothesizing that at least some of the mechanisms which process visual images are also those which govern visual perception. From a neurophysiological standpoint, imagery may be assumed to trigger neural mechanisms similar to those involved in visual perception. This idea, originally introduced by Neisser (1967, 1972), is widely acknowledged today (cf. Farah, 1985; Finke, 1980, 1985, 1989; Kosslyn, 1980; Kosslyn and Shwartz, 1977; Shepard, 1975; Shepard and Podgorny, 1978).

The issue of the functional equivalence between imagery and perception has been dealt with in the most detailed fashion in Ronald Finke's works (Finke, 1980, 1985; Finke and Shepard, 1986). Finke starts from the premise that perceiving an object, visually imagining that object or merely 'thinking' about that object (without visualizing it), can in certain circumstances produce equivalent behavioural effects. This equivalence is found at relatively 'high' levels of information processing (for instance, in tasks consisting in classifying objects in conceptual categories). There are, on the other hand, levels of functioning where the perception of an object produces specific effects, which are not found when subjects mentally evoke the object (with or without visualization). For instance, colours after-effects (in complementary colours) consecutive to the fixation of a coloured object for a sufficiently long period of time are generally not reported by subjects who evoked this object mentally, even in the form of a visual image. Lastly, there are cases where the construction of a visual image produces similar effects to those of object perception, and where these effects are directly attributable to visual imagery and not simply to mental evocation of the object. Categorizing these classes of effects is a major enterprise in as much as it can serve to identify the characteristics of processes brought into play in both imaginal and perceptual activities. However, if it can be shown that these processes operate in both activities, it must also be shown that they operate at a level of cognitive functioning that is not influenced by subjects' knowledge, beliefs or expectations. For instance, paradigms need to be designed in such a way that in imaginal situations, subjects will not produce behavioural effects that they *deduce* from their memories of previous perceptual experiences, or produce what they suppose to be the effect expected by the experimenter. In short, it is crucial for experiments to show that the processes thought to be involved are not likely to be 'cognitively penetrated' (cf. Pylyshyn, 1981).

A finding reported by Podgorny and Shepard (1978) strongly suggests there is a similarity of pattern-analyzing mechanisms when an object is imagined and when the same object is actually perceived. Subjects were presented with an empty grid of 5 × 5 cells. In the perceptual condition, a capital letter resulting from the darkening of several cells of the grid was displayed for a short period of time (Figure 3.4). In the imaginal condition, subjects were instructed to mentally 'darken' the appropriate cells, in response to the oral presentation of a given letter. In both conditions, a coloured dot then appeared on one of the cells of the empty grid. Subjects were then asked to state whether the dot occupied one of the cells where the letter had appeared (or had been visualized).

The results show that response latencies in the perceptual condition vary as a function of several parameters (figural complexity of the letter; part of the letter where the dot is located; distance from the letter, when the dot appears in a cell which had not been darkened). The relevant point here is that subjects in the imaginal condition exhibit the very same chronometric regularities, depending on the same parameters (although the absolute reaction times are on the average longer overall than in the perceptual condition). Furthermore, in the part of the experiment where two dots appear on the grid, the respective locations of these two dots (on the same bar of the letter, on two bars, at the intersection of two bars) affect reaction times in the same way regardless of whether the subjects have been in the perceptual or in the imaginal condition (Figure 3.5). The absence of any interaction between conditions (perceptual or imaginal) and the location of points reflects that the mechanisms responsible for the chronometric regularities in the perceptual condition hold true for the imaginal condition as well. Similarly, in tasks requiring the comparison of imagined or perceived block letters, there is evidence that visual images and visual perceptual representations are

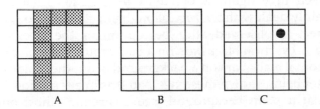

A   B   C

Figure 3.4 Materials used in Podgorny and Shepard's (1978) experiments.

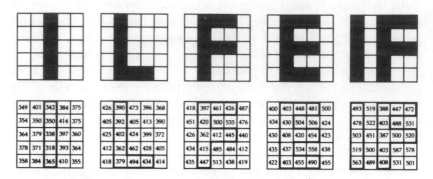

Figure 3.5 Response times (ms) to individual cells in the 5 × 5 grid for
each pattern (averaged over perceptual and imaginal conditions)
Source: Podgorny and Shepard (1978, experiment 1).

equivalent for both the structural properties they possess and the
operations they undergo (Bagnara *et al.*, 1988).

Podgorny and Shepard's findings thus strongly suggest that
similar pattern-analyzing mechanisms are implemented in the
visual system when individuals observe an object and when they
imagine the same object (even though the degree of activation of
these mechanisms is higher in the perceptual condition). In this
particular area, the arguments that tacit knowledge enters into the
imaginal condition fail to be convincing since subjects would need
to have knowledge of the very complex pattern of response times
(in the perceptual condition) for each stimulus and adjust their
responses in the imaginal condition as a function of this
knowledge.

If perceptual and imaginal situations exhibit similarities of this
type at the levels of cognitive functioning required for pattern
processing, there is reason to believe that some effects occurring
consecutive to perception of an object may also occur after imaging
this object. Investigations of after-effects in imaginal situations
have mainly dealt with the McCollough effect (McCollough, 1965).
This effect is observed after perception of the two following
patterns: *(a)* vertical black bars on a background of a given colour;
(b) horizontal black bars on a background of another colour (Figure
3.6). After being shown these two patterns in alternation, subjects
looking at a plain background 'see' achromatic horizontal and
vertical bar gratings faintly tinged with hues of colour complementary to those observed previously.

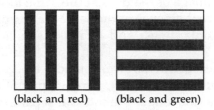

(black and red)   (black and green)

Figure 3.6 Examples of patterns used in experiments on the McCollough effect.

Experiments by Finke and Schmidt (1977, 1978) show that this effect can also be found in subjects who have only been presented with coloured backgrounds, and are instructed to *imagine* horizontal black bars on one of the backgrounds, and vertical ones on the other. (The effect, however, is not found in the condition where subjects see the bars and imagine the background colours.) An even more striking finding is the following: when the group of subjects is split into vivid and non-vivid imagers as a function of their responses to a questionnaire of imagery vividness, only the vivid imagers make a significant number of colour judgements in the direction predicted by the McCollough effect.

Several studies have compared field of resolution in visual perception and in imagery. Kosslyn's (1975) early experiments suggested that visual images present limitations comparable to perception as concerns resolution. For instance, it is more difficult to identify details of an object when this object is placed at a distance in imagination and hence appears smaller. The idea that imagery and perception undergo similar constraints as concerns visual resolution was later extended to works comparing the 'acuity' of visual perception and imagery (Finke and Kosslyn, 1980). In the perceptual condition, the experimenter presented the subjects with a pair of black dots measuring 6 millimetres in diameter. The dots were separated by a 6-, 12- or 18-millimetre interval, and were displayed in the centre of a screen facing the subjects. Subjects were required to track a moving guide-point along vertical or horizontal lines from the centre of the screen outwards. They were asked to make judgements of resolution, i.e., to indicate the point at which they could no longer discriminate the two dots in the periphery of their visual field. In the imaginal condition, the subjects were initially presented with a pair of dots, and then were told to project an accurate and vivid mental image of the dots at the centre of the screen. Then, while maintaining the image of the dots at the same location, they were requested to move their eyes in the same way as previously, along vertical or horizontal lines, and to make similar judgements of resolution.

Resolution measurements were made on each of the four directions (up, down, left, right), for each pair of circles. The first main result is that the longer the interval separating the two dots, the larger the resolution fields in both the perceptual and imaginal conditions. In particular, the size of the field of resolution does not increase linearly with the distance separating the dots in both the perceptual and imaginal conditions. Figure 3.7 shows fields of resolution in degrees (averaged over the four directions). Finke and Kosslyn also classified subjects as a function of the vividness of their visual imagery, as measured on an imagery questionnaire. As shown in Figure 3.7, the fields of resolution in the imaginal condition were larger for vivid than for non-vivid imagers, but the two groups of subjects did not significantly differ in the perceptual condition. Lastly, although vivid imagers had fields of resolution of comparable size in the imaginal and the perceptual conditions, the fields of resolution for non-vivid imagers were smaller in the imaginal than in the perceptual condition.

A closer look at the *shape* of the fields of resolution, covering responses for each of the four directions, shows that the fields are more elongated along the horizontal than along the vertical axis in both the perceptual and imaginal conditions. Furthermore, both perceptual and imaginal fields present the same vertical asymmetry (the lower half is larger than the upper half). Using a similar psychophysical technique, with more complex figures, and measuring in eight rather than four directions, Finke and Kurtzman (1981) replicated the results for the shape similarity of fields of resolution in perception and imagery (Figure 3.8). In addition, they observed that when the imaginal condition is made more difficult (by increasing the complexity of the figures), vivid imagers had larger fields of resolution than non-vivid imagers. For the entire sample of subjects, scores reflecting imagery vividness were significantly correlated with the size of the field measured in the imaginal condition, but did not correlate with the size of the field measured in the perceptual condition. The extremely good match of the shapes of the fields of resolution in both conditions in any case strongly supports the contention that the same mechanisms regulate imagery and visual perception at this level of functioning of the visual system.

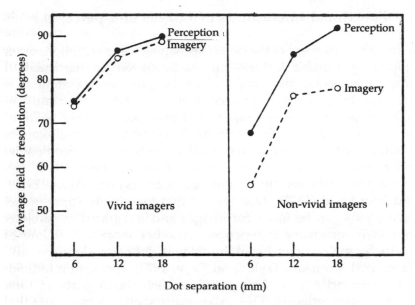

Figure 3.7 Average fields of resolution as a function of the distance
separating the dots, in perceptual and in imaginal conditions, for vivid and
non-vivid imagers
Source: Finke and Kosslyn (1980, experiment 1).

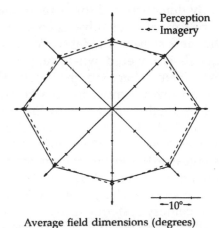

Figure 3.8 Shapes of visual fields in the perceptual and imaginal
conditions
Source: Finke and Kurtzman (1981, experiment 1).

3.6 Functional interactions of images and percepts

If imagery taps some of the same mechanisms as perception, other empirically testable features can be predicted. In particular, if imagery 'occupies' the same part of the processing system as is used for the processing of perceptual information, the simultaneous implementation of imagery and perception should be detrimental to one or the other, or both. The first type of well-known phenomenon is confusion in normal subjects (that is, people who can normally distinguish real events from imagined ones), between genuinely perceptual and imaginary events. Perky (1910), and later Segal (1972), have shown that marginally supraliminal perceptions can be taken for images and integrated by subjects into their imaginary experiences. Another more recent line of research, mainly developed by Marcia Johnson (Johnson and Raye, 1981; Johnson, Taylor and Raye, 1977), focuses on individuals' tendencies to include imaginary events as parts of their perceptual experiences. One experiment shows in particular that subjects with high imagery capacities tend to incorporate imaginary events as actually perceived more than subjects with lesser imaginal capacities (Johnson *et al.*, 1979). Finke, Johnson and Shyi (1988) also provided evidence for memory confusions for real and imagined completions of visual patterns.

Perhaps the most striking experiments deal with functional interactions between the perceptual and imaginal modes. Classic observations have clearly demonstrated that use of imagery in a given modality affects the capacities of subjects engaged in a perceptual task involving the same sensory modality. For instance, the detection of visual signals is lowered when subjects are required to develop concurrent imaginal activity in the visual modality. This drop in sensitivity, however, is much less marked when the concurrent activity involves another modality, for instance, audition (cf. Segal and Fusella, 1970). This kind of result, as well as the phenomena collectively known as 'selective interference' (cf. Baddeley, 1986; Brooks, 1970), suggest that the generation of visual images can affect the functioning of the visual perceptual system. Note that Baddeley's (1986) model of working memory incorporates a visuo-spatial, short-term memory system which is independent of verbal temporary storage, and is involved in both the generation of visual images and visual perception (cf. Baddeley, 1986; Logie and Baddeley, 1990; Logie, 1991). The notion of a 'visuospatial scratchpad' bears much resemblance to Kosslyn's conception of 'visual buffer'.

The most common examples of the effects of concurrent visual imagery on perception are those where this influence produces an interference effect, i.e., where imagery to some extent hinders the deployment of mechanisms involved in perceptual processing. A more comprehensive approach to image-perception interactions, however, also leads to hypotheses on situations where imagery facilitates simultaneous or immediately subsequent perceptual activity (provided the contents of both activities are compatible). Effects of this type have been reported for the detection of visual signals (Peterson and Graham, 1974). Similarly, studies on perceptual masking show that an image which is congruent with the upcoming target facilitates detection (Reeves, 1980), and experiments by Farah (1985) demonstrate that imaging a letter of the alphabet facilitates the visual detection of the same faintly presented letter.

There is also experimental evidence that forming a visual image can, in difficult processing conditions, facilitate subtle perceptual discriminations. For instance, in an experiment by Freyd and Finke (1984), subjects were presented with a stimulus composed of a horizontal line and a vertical line forming a cross (Figure 3.9). Their task consisted in detecting small differences in length between the two lines. When an appropriate context frame (a square positioned on the cross) was presented simultaneously with the cross, length discrimination was facilitated. However, this facilitation also occurred when the subjects were trained to form an *image* of the square positioned on the cross. In contrast, a context frame like an X, which does not facilitate the discrimination of lengths in perceptual condition, is not a facilitator when subjects project an image of this frame on the stimulus. Here,

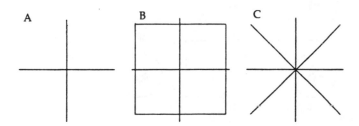

Figure 3.9 Materials used in Freyd and Finke's (1984) experiments.

perceptual and imaginal processes apparently interact very efficiently at this level of functioning of the visual system (see also Cave and Kosslyn, 1989).

The most subtle type of interaction between perception and imagery emerges from studies on mental rotation. Corballis and McLaren (1982) adapted the task originally designed by Cooper and Shepard (1973), where subjects had to decide whether capital letters presented in different orientations were standard or backward letters (Figure 3.10). The authors replicated the classic finding that response times increase proportionally with the tilt of the letter relative to its standard vertical presentation (0°). The longest response times were for the stimulus at 180°. Variations in response times thus were related to the angle assumed to be covered during mental rotation of the letter.

Corballis and McLaren designed a new situation where the subjects, before being presented with the letter, watched a rotating disc. This perceptual activity is known to induce an after-effect of rotary movement on the subsequent stimulus (here, the letter) (the rotary after-effect is in the opposite direction to that of the disc). The findings show that the after-effect systematically affects the time required to respond to the letter. Response times are longer when the direction of the after-effect is the opposite of the expected direction of mental rotation, and are shorter (although to

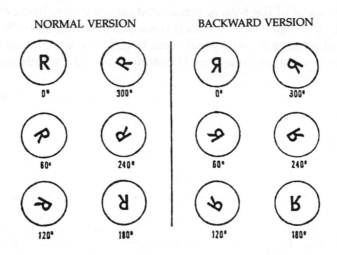

Figure 3.10 Examples of stimuli used in Cooper and Shepard's (1973) experiments.

a lesser extent) when it is in the same direction as mental rotation. More detailed analyses reveal other interesting features. In the absence of any after-effect, that is, in the standard situation devised by Cooper and Shepard, the response times for a letter oriented at 120° are compatible with the hypothesis that mental rotation is counter clockwise, that is, covering a 120° angle. Corballis and McLaren found that subjects tended to perform a 240° clockwise mental rotation for letters tilted to 120° when the induced after-effect was clockwise. In short, this study supports the claim that perceived motion is likely to interact with imagined motion.

The implication from the set of data reported above is that there are intimate functional relationships between perceptual and imaginal processes. Furthermore, the findings are compatible with the assumption that perception and imagery, at least at certain levels of cognitive functioning, bring similar mechanisms into play and tap the same parts of the cognitive apparatus. The neuropsychological and neurophysiological research analyzed in the next section proceeds from the similarity between the mechanisms of imagery and perception and moves towards the hypothesis that the same neural structures are involved in both.

3.7 Neuropsychological and neurophysiological approaches

Neuropsychological and neurophysiological research focuses on identifying the brain mechanisms that produce visual imagery. These studies are designed to identify those parts of the nervous system involved in imagery activities; some in addition raise the issue of whether the same cortical regions are involved in the processing of both images and percepts. Detailed critical reviews can be found in Bruyer (1982), Paivio and te Linde (1982), Sergent (1990) and Richardson (1991).

An early significant contribution to this domain appears in Hebb's (1968) model of hierarchized cell assemblies. Hebb's model was aimed at accounting for differences in levels of mental activity. His major assumption concerning imagery was that evoking a past experience involves at least partial activation of the neuronal structures (or cell assemblies) which were activated during the original experience. Hebb posits that first-order assemblies, directly excited by sensory inputs, are responsible for imagery phenomena closest to perception, such as eidetic images.

Generic images, on the other hand, which do not refer to particular past experiences, would result from the activation of second- or higher-order cell assemblies, without the activation of the first-order assemblies.

More recently, hypotheses on the nervous infrastructure of mental imagery have been strongly influenced by the development of research on cerebral hemispheric specialization. While the left hemisphere is generally known to play a major role in the processing of verbal information, a number of non-verbal tasks, involving the processing of visuospatial information, are apparently highly dependent on the right hemisphere. The analysis of performance of subjects with right cerebral lesions, as well as experimental techniques based on lateralized presentation of stimuli, confirm the dominant role of the right hemisphere in tasks involving spatial localization, depth perception, angle discrimination, pattern matching and face recognition (cf. Milner, 1974). These data lent the greatest weight to the hypothesis that visual imagery is mainly governed by the right hemisphere.

This hypothesis is also supported by several experimental findings. Seamon and Gazzaniga (1973) involved subjects in a short-term recognition memory task. In one condition, the subjects received visual imagery instructions; in the other, they received verbal rehearsal instructions. During the recognition test, probes were presented to the left or right cerebral hemisphere. Recognition decisions were faster for the items presented to the right hemisphere when the subjects used the imagery strategy, but were faster for the items presented to the left hemisphere when the subjects used the verbal rehearsal strategy. This result suggests that the right hemisphere may be specialized for cognitive activities involving the processing of visual images for mnemonic coding.

Convergent data also come from neuropsychological research. Jones-Gotman and Milner (1978) compared subjects with a right or left temporal lobectomy and control subjects in a paired-associate learning task for concrete words or for abstract words. The subjects were instructed to use a visual imagery strategy for learning concrete words and to elaborate sentences to link the abstract words. The results show that right temporal patients, as compared to the other subjects, recall fewer words learned with imagery instructions, whereas they do not differ from the control subjects for recall of words learned with verbal instructions. Furthermore, the recall impairment of the lobectomized subjects is more substantial when the size of the hippocampal region which is removed is larger. In a further study, Jones-Gotman (1979) showed that subjects with right temporal lobectomy exhibit a similar deficit when they are involved in an incidental learning task using visual imagery.

These studies suggest that the right temporal lobe, and more specifically the hippocampus, is involved in memory tasks calling for imagery. Nevertheless, they cannot be taken as definitive arguments that imagery is a specific function of the right hemisphere, an idea that many researchers were quick to adopt. In fact, these studies deal with processes which *use* imagery in the context of mnemonic coding or retrieval. Other aspects of imagery were not investigated as such in these studies, such as the *generation* of visual images. On the other hand, there are indications that *mental comparison* (more specifically, comparison of object sizes) is not affected by the localization, either right or left, of a temporal lobectomy (Wilkins and Moscovitch, 1978). This is compatible with the idea that analogue representations are not electively stored in one hemisphere, while there is much less doubt, on the other hand, that verbal processing systems are primarily associated with the functioning of the left hemisphere.

Electroencephalography does not provide any evidence for differential activity of the two hemispheres in tasks involving visual imagery. For instance, the memorization of sentences with different imagery values is not accompanied by differences in alpha activity in the right and left hemispheres (Haynes and Moore, 1981). Further, when subjects answer questions which are assumed to require the inspection of visual images, the suppression of the alpha rhythm, which is generally considered to be an index of imagery activity, exhibits the same characteristics in the right and the left hemisphere (Barrett and Ehrlichman, 1982). Finally, the data are unclear as to a specific role of the right hemisphere in visual imagery; in any case, the notion of a single hemisphere acting as an executive for the whole set of imagery processes does not seem viable today (cf. Ehrlichman and Barrett, 1983).

Hypotheses on the nervous infrastructure of imagery were to undergo major revision with the development of 'componential' models of mental imagery (cf. Farah, 1984; Kosslyn, 1987; Kosslyn *et al.*, 1984). As mentioned in Chapter 2, these models postulate that imagery is not an elementary psychological process. Rather, the analytical approach to imagery is based on the idea that there are relatively independent 'components' or 'processing modules', whose implementation are not necessarily governed by a single region of the brain. The modular character of the componential theories of imagery can thus be tested by finding situations where these modules are dissociated, for example, in the behaviour of subjects with localized brain lesions.

Specific attention has been directed to the process of *generating* visual images. A converging set of arguments suggest that generation is located in the posterior region of the left hemisphere. Cases of 'imagery loss' have been documented in the neuropsychological literature (cf. Basso, Bisiach and Luzzatti, 1980; Brain, 1954; Goldenberg, 1989). A detailed analysis of thirty-seven cases was carried out by Farah (1984), using a componential model of mental imagery, which differentiated *(a)* deficits in *image generation processes*, *(b)* deficits resulting from damage to *long-term memory representations* from which visual images are generated, and *(c)* deficits affecting *image inspection processes*, once images have been formed. With respect to the first type of deficit, subjects with a generation deficit (frequently associated with a dream imagery deficit) tend to have brain lesions localized in the left posterior region of the brain. This lateralization considerably undermines the hypothesis that the right hemisphere plays a primary role in mental imagery. On the other hand, the data are consistent with other neuropsychological evidence based on examination of split-brain patients required to perform tasks with lateral presentation of stimuli. For instance, the two hemispheres of a patient studied by Farah *et al.* (1985) performed very similarly in a perceptual classification task of lower-case letters (discriminate 'medium' letters, like *a, c, e*, and 'not medium' letters, like *b, d, g*). On the other hand, in a task where the subject was presented with upper-case letters and had to classify the corresponding lower-case letters (a task which elicits the generation and inspection of visual images of lower-case letters), left hemisphere performances were maximal, while those of the right hemisphere were not different from chance. Other studies on split-brain patients (Kosslyn *et al.*, 1985) and patients with brain lesions (Farah, Levine and Calvanio, 1988) provide converging evidence in favour of the localization of structures responsible for the generation of visual images in the left hemisphere. In addition, findings suggest that mental imagery has distinct visual and spatial components, and that these distinct types of representations are neurologically dissociable (Farah *et al.*, 1988a; Kosslyn, 1991).

Neuropsychological and neurophysiological approaches also serve to clarify hypotheses concerning the commonality of mechanisms brought into play in perception and imagery. The idea that the image of an object results from the activation of the same representational structures as in perception receives considerable support from studies using classic psychophysical methods. The hypothesis that both perceptual activity and imagery are implemented in the same processing system (Kosslyn's 'visual buffer') is reinforced by works documenting the existence of functional interactions between these two activities (cf. Farah, 1985, 1989; see also Baddeley, 1986). The existence of such interactions suggests that there may be a common neural substrate involved in perceiving and imaging. Recent neurophysiological studies provide a new set of arguments. For instance, it has been demonstrated that when a subject forms a visual image of a letter, the evoked potential which accompanies the perceptual detection of the same letter, presented simultaneously, has a significantly greater amplitude than the potential which accompanies the detection of a different letter. In addition, the occipital topography of this phenomenon suggests that the cortical areas involved in the interaction between images and percepts are truly specific to the visual modality (cf. Farah *et al.*, 1988b; see also Farah *et al.*, 1989; Péronnet and Farah, 1989). Further arguments in this domain come from studies measuring variations of local cerebral blood flow (cf. Goldenberg *et al.*, 1987; Goldenberg *et al.*, 1988; Roland *et al.*, 1987; Roland and Friberg, 1985).

The hypothesis that imagery 'engages' neuronal structures which belong to the visual system – a hypothesis included in Changeux's (1983) theory of 'mental objects' – is usually extended by the additional postulate of *analogy* between the representations activated by imagery on this nervous substrate and the representations activated by perception (cf. Farah, 1988). The current hypothesis is that the same processing modules are brought into play in perception and in imagery (cf. Kosslyn, 1987). Neuropsychological observations often stress the similarity between deficits affecting perception and imagery. The most remarkable phenomenon, in this respect, is the hemineglect syndrome following a lesion of the right parietal lobe. Patients exhibiting this form of hemineglect in perception (they do not 'see' the left half of configurations which are in front of them) often present the same deficit in imagery (they do not 'see' the left half of known configurations that they are invited to visualize). The mechanisms serving the generation of imaginal representations may thus function like 'analogues' of the mechanisms brought into play in perceptual processing (cf. Bisiach and Luzzatti, 1978; Grossi *et al.*, 1989).

3.8 The temporal characteristics of visual imagery

This chapter illustrates both the abundance and the importance of the contribution made by studies designed to identify the characteristics of visual imagery. What emerges from these works as a whole is that images are psychological events which have a structure, and this structure shares many features of perceptual events. In particular, there is considerable evidence that the spatial properties of objects are coded in the imaginal representations that people generate of these objects. Other structural aspects of images have been less extensively studied, but deserve to be mentioned in this chapter, in particular the temporal structure of visual images. Images, as psychological events, develop over time. A basic question is whether the temporal characteristics of images exhibit any regularities.

The assumption that images result from the transient activation, in a specialized processing system (or visual buffer), of representational units stored in long-term memory, raises two related issues as concerns the temporal parameters of visual imagery: one is connected to the time required to generate images in the visual buffer, and the second, the time during which the images, once generated, are maintained in the buffer.

The time required to generate an image is generally estimated from the time which elapses between verbal stimulus presentation and the subject's statement that he or she has formed an image, by a conventional signal, for instance depressing a key which stops a clock. The latency of image generation depends on several characteristics of the verbal items used as stimuli. It is well known that latencies are shorter as the words increase in rated imagery value. In general, concrete words elicit visual images with shorter latencies than abstract words (Cocude and Denis, 1988; Denis, 1983; Morris and Reid, 1973; Paivio, 1966). In addition, the hierarchical position of a concept in its taxonomy is a relevant factor. Words designating basic level concepts (cf. Rosch *et al.*, 1976) elicit images faster than either more general or more specific words (Hoffmann, Denis and Ziessler, 1983; see Chapter 5).

Generation times are affected as well by intrinsic characteristics of images, such as their complexity or richness in detail. In general, more time is required to generate an image as the number of details composing the image increases (Beech and Allport, 1978; Kosslyn *et al.*, 1983; McGlynn and Gordon, 1973; McGlynn, Hofius and Watulak, 1974; Paivio, 1975b). Empirical data suggest that image generation may be sequential. All the segments of the image of a letter do not seem to be generated at once, but rather sequentially, in roughly the order in which most people draw the letter (Kosslyn *et al.*, 1988).

Findings also show that the time required to generate images is affected by subjects' imagery capacities, as measured by relevant tests or questionnaires. Subjects characterized as high imagers form visual images faster than low imagers (Cocude and Denis, 1988; Ernest and Paivio, 1971; Hoffmann, Denis and Ziessler, 1983; Rehm, 1973).

Persistence of imagery, i.e., how long an individual states that an image lasts, has also been explored. All images fade gradually after being generated. The time when the image subjectively 'disappears' corresponds to the time when the representational units activated in the visual buffer no longer receive enough activation. During the activation period, the image can be subjected to various processes, such as exploration or rotation. Thus, it is crucial to identify not only the processes that generate images, but also the processes affording their persistence, once images have been formed. In Kosslyn's (1980) theory, refreshing processes operate on an image as soon as it has been generated. These processes maintain the image in the buffer. The issue, however, is whether these processes are functionally distinct from those governing image generation.

Only a few studies have dealt with the variables likely to affect image duration. The duration of images (defined from verbal reports) is apparently not directly related to the imagery value of the words which elicited them (Cocude and Denis, 1988). Once images are formed, they are available for a lapse of time which is independent of the difficulty of generation.

In terms of image content, difficulties in maintaining an image are related to degree of internal complexity. Active exploration of images has been reported to enhance their persistence (Kosslyn, 1980). This finding is somewhat similar to the fact that images of objects in motion persist longer than images of static objects. Making an image dynamic may increase the likelihood of implementation of refreshing processes (Cocude and Denis, 1990). Lastly, images with high emotional content are maintained longer than neutral images (Cocude, 1988).

Individual imagery differences do not seem to affect the duration of images, at least as measured by current imagery questionnaires (Cocude and Denis, 1988). However, some subjects can significantly increase the duration of their images. Subjects who are regularly involved in mental concentration techniques, such as yoga, and have presumably developed higher capacities to control their mental activities, have image durations which are almost twice as long as those of control subjects (Figure 3.11). Further, subjects who have done yoga for a long time have image durations which are significantly longer than those of beginning yoga students (Figure 3.12). However, image generation latencies in subjects skilled in yoga do not differ from those of control subjects. Only the duration of images is affected by longstanding yoga practice (Cocude and Denis, 1986).

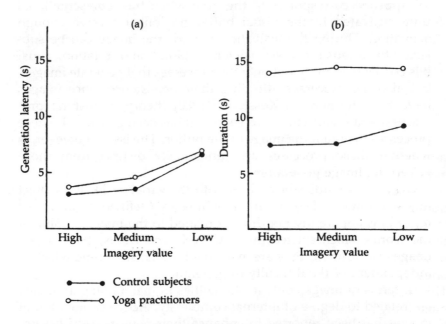

Figure 3.11 Mean generation latencies and mean durations of images as a function of noun imagery value, for control subjects and for yoga practitioners
Source: Cocude and Denis (1986).

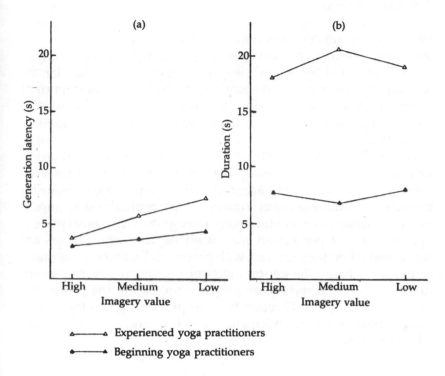

Figure 3.12 Mean generation latencies and mean durations of images as a function of noun imagery, for experienced and for beginning yoga practitioners
Source: Cocude and Denis (1986).

Overall, these data suggest that there is a functional distinction between processes governing the generation of visual images and those governing their persistence, since both types of processes do not respond similarly to the same factors. Generation processes consist in search in memory for the representational units necessary for the formation of images, and then the activation of these units in the visual buffer. Once activation has taken place, another set of processes follow on the previous ones, in order to maintain the level of activation of the image. This refreshing taps cognitive resources which are limited in most individuals. For this reason, image duration is proportional to the amount of available resources. Once these resources have been depleted, the image no longer remains activated, unless other processes are called up, such as those that structurally transform the image.

3.9 Conclusion

Images have functional properties. They also have structural properties which turn them into *figures* which are genuine cognitive reflections of the spatial properties of corresponding objects. It is easy to see why the 'realism' of images is such an important factor of their functional efficiency since they provide subjects with manipulable 'models' of reality when reality is not directly accessible.

The mechanisms which process images are closely related to the mechanisms processing perceptual information. Current research provides some convincing arguments that there is a commonality between the processing mechanisms for perceptual and for imaginal information. This commonality of cognitive 'machinery' serving images and perception may itself explain why images are functional when they interact with perceptual activity. In as much as images activate the neural mechanisms which govern perceptual detection of objects, they prepare subjects for the processing of perceptual inputs. Through this pre-processing of information, images thus serve an anticipatory function and have significant adaptive value.

4 Imagery and Language Comprehension

Chapter 3 defined some of the intrinsic properties of visual images, and deliberately chose to ignore the ways in which imagery is related to other representational systems. This chapter now turns to one of these features: the relationship of imagery to language processing.

The psychology of language describes how individuals construct meaning, i.e., how semantic representations of utterances are elaborated. On a certain level of analysis, constructs and theories of meaning need not account for the processes which enable meaning to be expressed in mental representations derived from sensory modalities. Semantic analysis typically employs abstract symbols, such as those used for propositional notation. In other words, accounting for meaning calls for the coordination of relatively abstract symbols through application of appropriate rules. Another perspective on meaning centres on whether symbolic representations occur as a natural function of comprehension, and are the locus of meaning. This does not imply that these representations account for comprehension, but that if it can be shown that they are actually implemented during comprehension, their relationships to language processing need to be examined as a specific issue. This type of study focuses on (a) how these representations are constructed during the processing of language, and (b) how they contribute, if at all, to the processing of linguistic information, and more specifically to the elaboration of responses required by the task or situation (see Desrochers, 1988).

The questions we will be dealing with in this chapter can be formulated as follows: To what extent does imagery elicited by an utterance play a role in the comprehension of this utterance? Does imagery affect the elaboration of the meaning of utterances and, if so, does imagery always play a mandatory role? For instance, is the image generated by a descriptive sentence (such as *'Frank opens a can of Coke'*) totally identifiable to the *meaning* of this sentence? Or does it merely reflect a part of this meaning? If so, *what* part of meaning is not covered by the image? Are images additional psychological events, grafted to comprehension? And, in this case, do images play a mandatory role or are they purely epiphenomenal?

4.1 A working hypothesis

In the early days of scientific psychology, Associationism illustrated the extremely strong temptation to see images as the basis, or even the very 'locus' of meaning. Binet (1886) argued that, intrinsically, images contain the meaning of descriptive sentences. This assumption is also found in the dual coding theory, except that images are not *the* locus, but *one* of the loci of meaning (Paivio, 1971). In fact, any theory assigning such a preponderant semantic role to imagery needs to account for all cases where images evoked in a listener's mind by a given sentence (a sentence describing a scene, for example) contain pieces of information which were not explicitly transmitted by the sentence. For instance, back from a trip, Sam calls Peter and says: *'During my stay in Paris, I visited the Musée d'Orsay.'* This sentence, devoid of any ambiguity, is understood perfectly by Peter. The image that comes to Peter's mind when hearing this sentence is of himself when he visited the Musée d'Orsay two years previously – and not the image of Sam in the museum. Consider now the following example. A problem statement begins with the sentence: *'A schoolboy has three marbles. . .'* Such a statement may elicit a visual image in which the three marbles are clearly displayed. Will the situation be the same for a statement which starts: *'A schoolboy has 397 marbles. . .'*? The two statements do not differ from each other as concerns either their comprehensibility or the later processing of the problem (*'. . . and he won two more; how many marbles does he have now?'*). Consider also the case of sentences containing a negation (*'Sorry, no orange juice this morning!'*) and which elicit extremely vivid images of the expected yet absent object.

Thus, although images can reflect more, less or an extremely divergent semantic content than what is contained in the literal meaning of a sentence, a real issue is to define whether images are still *identifiable* with the meaning of the sentence. A more workable

approach is to see images as events which accompany the psychological activity of meaning generation and assignment, or events
that illustrate a given part of meaning, or a meaning derived from
the literal meaning (by inferential processes, anticipation of upcoming events or evocation of a past associated event).

Can objections to a narrowly 'imagistic' interpretation of comprehension be reduced by complementing the system of imaginal
representations with a 'verbal' system? This solution was behind
the popularity of the dual coding model. But what tools should the
'verbal' system use to process meaning, and handle more than the
phonemic or graphemic features of language? If a 'verbal' system
of this type can actually process the semantics of utterances, why
assign it a privileged role exclusively in the case of utterances with
low imaginal content? What, in fact, a theory of comprehension
needs is a general interpretive system which is able to elaborate
the semantic content of any sentence, and allows individuals to
compute meanings, regardless of whether the sentence is a
description of a visual scene or not. This is why a 'verbal' system
should not be postulated as operating 'parallel' to the system of
imaginal representations. If imagery has a function as concerns
language comprehension, this function cannot be placed on the
same 'level' as purely semantic processing.

A cohesive approach to these issues can be formulated as
follows: (*a*) There are processes governing the elaboration of
semantic representations of utterances; these representations result from a specific configuration of semantic units activated in
individual's memory by verbal inputs and brought to a transient
state of cognitive activation. This semantic structure becomes the
'meaning' of the utterance and is a mandatory step in processing.
(*b*) This deep semantic representation, which is assumed to be
propositional in nature, can yield other sorts of representations,
which express all or part of the semantic information in non-
linguistic representations structurally similar to perceptual events.
Generation of these representations is optional. Theoretically,
they add nothing to comprehension, but give individuals a
'cognitive supplement' that expresses the relations in the statement in an analogue format. Furthermore, these representations
lend themselves much more easily to certain forms of computation
than propositional representations.

Chapter 4 presents current trends in research on the role of
imagery in comprehension, and examines to what extent the
working hypothesis outlined above receives corroboration from

the data. Chapters 5, 6 and 7 explore these issues further and report data from my own experimental work on three levels of complexity of linguistic material.

4.2 Imagery and language comprehension: how imagery is operationalized

The first question that precedes any examination of the possible role of imagery in comprehension concerns the very existence of this activity during the processing of verbal material. Several studies have aimed at detecting indirect indications of imagery produced while people process linguistic information. Specifically, experiments show that the involvement of the visual system in reading interferes to some extent with the generation of images reflecting the informational content of the verbal message. For instance, Brooks (1970) presented subjects with sentences describing spatial relations, such as: 'The goat is to the right of the fountain and above the rock.' These sentences were presented either in written form (the subjects read them on a screen) or orally (the subjects listened to them). The subjects were then asked to reconstruct the spatial relationships which had been described to them. Performance was better when subjects *heard* the sentences than when they *read* them. One plausible explanation is that when subjects read sentences, there is competition between the activity of reading itself, which taps the visual system directly, and their attempts to visualize the spatial relationships described by these sentences (see also Levin and Divine-Hawkins, 1974).

This indirect evidence, based on the existence of interference between perception and imagery when both involve the same sensory modality, is also reinforced by interpretations of the differential analysis of reading times in high and low imagers (see Chapter 7). All these data suggest that imagery may, and often does, accompany the processing of verbal messages with concrete descriptive content. But what are the *effects* of imagery on the comprehension of the sentences which elicited it?

Experiments in this field are variants on a basic design. A subject is presented with a verbal message. It is expected that processing will be accompanied by some imagery activity. The subject's task is to produce a specific response. The variations of a selected parameter of this response are then related to variations in this imagery activity.

Variations in imagery activity can be operationalized in different ways. First, the importance or amount of imagery developed along with the processing of an utterance is dependent on the nature of the utterance. For instance, some verbal statements, because of the nature of the objects they refer to and the nature of the relationships among these objects, are more likely than others to elicit visual images. Differences in subjects' responses, for instance, in the time necessary to generate these responses, can be related to the intrinsic characteristics of the materials used (for instance, concrete vs. abstract sentences).

Variations in imagery for the same verbal material can also be operationalized in a more direct way, through the use of imagery instructions, for instance, by comparing responses of subjects who have processed verbal material either with or without instructions to visualize. However, even in the absence of such instructions, some subjects may spontaneously produce visual images for this verbal material. Explicit imagery instructions nevertheless tend to maximize the probability that images will be formed while reading.

Lastly, for identical material and in the absence of imagery instructions, an interesting source of variation is the individuals' natural inclination to elaborate visual images. If people classified as high imagers on the basis of appropriate psychometric tests are indeed more likely than others to visualize the content of the verbal material they process, their responses can be related to the amount of imagery actually produced.

4.3 Assessment of comprehension

As stated above, there are a number of ways for the experimenter to manipulate imagery and test its effects on the comprehension of verbal material. The complementary set of operations involves assessing 'comprehension' (of a statement) and selecting valid indices for this process. Although comprehension mechanisms are a complex notion and theories tend to diverge, there is a rather general consensus on a series of assumptions.

First of all, a major notional distinction should be made between the comprehension process, which results in a cognitive product (namely, meaning), and the use the individual will make of this product. Even though meaning can be related to type of anticipated use, and meaning may begin to be used during the elaboration process, there is a need to differentiate between *(a)* the products generated by the comprehension process, and *(b)* what individuals can do with them. At this point, I deliberately avoid the debate on the holistic or componential nature of meaning and its relationship to the lexical units which compose statements. Some of these features will be discussed in later chapters. For the moment, it is sufficient to point out that *(a)* meaning, as the end-product of processing, is a *representation*, and here, a semantic representation of a statement. To be more specific, meaning should not be viewed as a representation of the *statement* as such, but of the *situation* or *state of affairs* described by the statement; *(b)* this representation is a transient entity within the processing system where it has been elaborated; *(c)* this representation is psychological in nature, in that it is the output of an individual's interpretive system.

Clearly, the semantic representation an individual builds from a statement is not accessible to direct observation. On the other hand, what can be observed and will provide indirect measures on this representation is the use individuals make of it, in the context of goal-oriented activities.

These activities can be classified into three categories.

1. In the first type of activities, subjects are presented with a verbal statement, and are then placed in a situation where they have to retrieve the semantic information provided by this statement. What the experimenter can then observe are the outputs of a memory process (late outputs, resulting from further reprocessing of the early semantic representations). The problems with this type of approach are evident. What is tested is in fact a representation resulting from both comprehension and memory processes (either intentional or incidental). A number of experiments, however, have used this memory paradigm appropriately to investigate early encoding processes. A typical example is studies which show differential decrease of memory for the semantic components and the surface aspects of statements (cf. Sachs, 1967).

2. The second set of tasks requires subjects to relate the output of the comprehension process with a piece of information that is already present in memory or has recently been processed.

2.1. Comparison of the semantic representation elaborated from a statement with an available piece of information, for instance, a piece of knowledge in subjects' long-term memory. Typically, subjects have to make truth judgements on sentences describing properties of an object, or the relative positions of several objects along a dimension, as in mental comparison paradigms.

2.2. Comparison of the semantic representation elaborated from a statement with another semantic representation generated by another statement, with, for instance, a judgement on compatibility between the two statements. This paradigm is used extensively in experiments on inference. A special case is when the semantic representation elaborated from the statement must be related to a subsentential unit: a word which appeared in the original statement, or a word linked to one of the words in the original statement, or a candidate word for a title or a summary for the statement.

2.3. Comparison of the semantic representation elaborated from a statement with information provided by a visual configuration. For instance, subjects are asked to judge whether a statement describing the spatial relationships between two objects matches a picture where the two objects are displayed in a certain spatial relationship.

In all these cases, subjects' responses are recorded, and later analyzed in terms, for instance, of the time necessary for their production. The assumption is that these responses reflect, indirectly but in a way that is much closer to the comprehension process than mnemonic task responses, something of the semantic representation of the statement.

3. New approaches have developed as a consequence of new techniques for on-line analysis of reading processes. What characterizes these approaches is that they can capture the comprehension process as it proceeds. In some cases, researchers maintain natural reading situations, which can only yield relatively macroscopic measures, such as reading times for sentences or paragraphs. In other cases, researchers use constraints or display techniques which modify ecological reading conditions considerably but enable them to measure fine-grained components of processing times. This is the case for phrase-by-phrase or word-by-word self-presentation of sentences.

4.4 Imagery, comprehension and memorization of statements

The first research field detailed here is important because it reflects the major thrust in comprehension work in the 1970s and uses sentence memory paradigms.

Begg and Paivio (1969) compared the memorability of concrete sentences (likely to elicit visual images) and that of abstract sentences to approach the issue of the capacity of images to 'picture' the semantic content of sentences. Abundant data as of the classic experiment by Sachs (1967) have shown that memory for sentence meaning and memory for wording decay differently. Sachs's experiment was extended by Begg and Paivio to concrete and abstract sentences (for instance, *'The jagged stone shattered a clear window'*, or *'The national election indicated a secure future'*, respectively). The subjects listened to a series of sentences, some of which appeared twice, either in their original form, or in a modified one. In this case, the modification could either be semantic or simply lexical (by the use of synonyms).

The findings show that in concrete sentences, semantic changes are better detected than lexical changes that do not affect the original meaning. In contrast, lexical changes are detected best in abstract sentences. The interpretation is that the meaning of a concrete sentence is fairly separate from the specific words which compose it. Within the framework of the dual coding model, this suggests that concrete sentences are stored in the form of images constructed on the basis of their semantic analysis. The exact wording of these sentences may be forgotten rapidly, but the images that these sentences elicit tend to resist decay. The meanings of abstract sentences, on the other hand, is more dependent on their constituent words and the memory for their meaning is thus more closely associated to their wording.

In the dual coding framework, the semantic processing of verbal material differs depending on its likelihood to elicit imagery. The more a sentence is likely to elicit imagery, the greater the role of images in the storage of the semantic information extracted from this sentence. Davies and Proctor (1976), for example, showed that the recall of abstract sentences is impaired to a significantly greater extent by verbal than by visual interference, while the reverse is true for the recall of concrete sentences.

However, although Begg and Paivio's (1969) experiment author-izes conjectures as to the form in which meaning is stored in memory, it does not directly address the comprehension process itself. Paivio and Begg (1971) did so in a later experiment designed to examine the contribution of imagery to sentence comprehension by comparing the duration of the two processes. In their study, short sentences were presented to subjects in written form. The subjects were instructed to state when they had understood the meaning of the sentence or when they had formed a visual image of the content of the sentence. The latency of stated comprehension was then compared against the latency of image generation.

Overall, the latencies for stated comprehension were shorter than latencies for imagery, but the magnitude of this effect differed for concrete and abstract sentences. Paivio and Begg hoped to show that comprehension is more closely related to imagery in the case of concrete than abstract sentences. Subjects indeed were faster at comprehending an abstract sentence than at forming an image of it, but this difference was greatly reduced in the case of concrete sentences. Furthermore, imagery latencies were much longer for the abstract than for the concrete sentences, whereas comprehension latencies did not differ considerably for the two materials. An interaction of this type reflects the fact that imagery and comprehension certainly cannot be equated with each other. However, they are probably more closely 'linked' to each other in the case of concrete verbal materials. This conclusion is further corroborated by the fact that the (positive) correlation between comprehension and imagery latencies was significantly higher for the set of concrete than for the set of abstract sentences.

In a study extending the Paivio and Begg paradigm, Klee and Eysenck (1973) compared the comprehension of concrete and abstract sentences. In their study, comprehension was defined as subjects' ability to judge the meaningfulness of auditorily pre-sented sentences. In addition to meaningful sentences like those used in the Paivio and Begg (1971) experiments, subjects were presented with semantically anomalous sentences (for instance, 'The large army beat the wild pearl', 'The mere knowledge brought the true hour'). In this semantic judgement task, comprehension latencies were overall shorter for concrete than for abstract sen-tences (whereas Paivio and Begg did not observe any difference). The assumption that imaginal processes constitute an important component of comprehension is again supported by the fact that comprehension of concrete sentences is particularly long when subjects are given a visual interference task. On the other hand, comprehension of abstract sentences is markedly impaired by auditory interference.

The Begg and Paivio (1969) study on memory for concrete and abstract sentences was criticized on several counts. First, despite Paivio and Begg's (1971) findings on comprehension times for concrete and abstract sentences, these types of sentences are not equivalent in terms of comprehensibility. Differences as concerns memory storage of the meaning of concrete and abstract sentences may thus reflect differences in comprehensibility. More fine-grained examination of the abstract sentences used in the Begg and Paivio (1969) shows that they were in fact more difficult to understand than concrete sentences, even in the absence of a memory task (cf. Johnson *et al.*, 1972). This observation is corroborated by Klee and Eysenck's (1973) findings that comprehension latencies are longer for abstract than for concrete sentences. Obviously, the comprehension of abstract sentences can be facilitated when they appear in context, for instance, if they are placed at the end of a paragraph. This is shown by better recognition of semantic changes in target sentences (Pezdek and Royer, 1974). However, the greater difficulty in understanding abstract sentences is not only due to differential semantic plausibility between concrete and abstract sentences, a feature which can be detected before implementation of memory processes that act on the meaning extracted from these sentences (Holmes and Langford, 1976). Lastly, better recognition of semantic changes in concrete than in abstract sentences was reported by Moeser (1974), even when both types of sentence were equated for comprehensibility (cf. also Kuiper and Paivio, 1977).

However, Green (1977) did not find any evidence that concrete and abstract sentences equated for comprehensibility are processed in fundamentally different ways on a task which consisted in detecting a brief auditory signal while listening to sentences (either for comprehension or for memorization). Green's conclusion is that imagery is not an automatic consequence of the perception of a concrete sentence by the listener and that in addition it is not a prerequisite for sentence comprehension. Images should thus be seen as instantiations of sentence meaning which occur during the construction of meaning, and are highly dependent on individuals' characteristics and cognitive styles.

Other evaluations of the dual coding theory appeared later. In a sentence recognition study, Belmore (1982) reported that the identification of semantic changes does not differ significantly between concrete and abstract sentences – a finding that is discrepant with Begg and Paivio (1969) – but that the identification of syntactic changes is better for abstract than for concrete sentences. Belmore interpreted the poor memorability of the syntactic form of concrete sentences as an indication (albeit indirect) that these sentences are mainly stored in memory in the form of images, that is, memory traces reflecting sentence meaning, and not in their surface form.

In another study (Belmore *et al.*, 1982), subjects were presented with concrete or abstract sentences and were required to state whether each sentence was probably true or probably false on the basis of a previous sentence. The test sentence could either be a paraphrase of the previous sentence or an inference based on it. The data indicate that concrete test sentences are checked significantly faster than abstract test sentences, and that this effect holds true for both paraphrases and inferences. Thus, the regular finding that imagery has a facilitating effect on the processing of the explicit meaning of a sentence is apparently also true for the processing of implicit aspects of meaning.

Other studies on the role of context on the comprehension of concrete and abstract sentences led to new criticisms as regards interpretations based on the dual coding model. One major contention was that the greater difficulty in comprehending abstract sentences may be due primarily to their presentation out of context. Schwanenflugel and Shoben (1983) conducted a series of experiments in which they presented subjects with concrete or abstract sentences either with or without context. Results showed that abstract sentences elicited longer reading times than concrete ones in the no-context condition, but that reading times did not differ when sentences were preceded by a context. Furthermore, more time is required to perform lexical decisions for abstract than for concrete words when these words are presented out of context, but the difference cancels out when these words are preceded by a relevant sentence. This finding highlights factors which can account for the differences in the comprehension of concrete and abstract sentences. These factors are unrelated to the implementation of mnemonic processes, and cannot be interpreted in terms of imagery alone. Further evidence was reported by Wattenmaker and Shoben (1987) in sentence recall experiments (cf. also Schwanenflugel, Harnishfeger and Stowe, 1988).

The studies based on the dual coding model make the assumption that the system of imaginal representations is electively brought into play for the processing of concrete verbal materials. The corollary is that a basic qualitative difference is postulated between memory traces for concrete sentences and traces for abstract sentences. This hypothesis is somewhat problematic. Is the imaginal representation of the imageable part of the semantic meaning of a concrete statement the indispensable functional substrate for understanding this statement? Dual coding theorists have no straightforward – and in any case no explicit negative –

response. The arguments presented at the outset of this chapter cast some suspicion on the idea that images are psychological events that can handle all the semantic information conveyed by a sentence (even of the most concrete type) and to carry out the memory storage of this information alone.

The most questionable feature of dual coding theories as concerns language comprehension is the following. Images are endowed with most of the meaning, but it is not clear whether the notion of verbal coding is restricted to the surface features of the sentences or extends deeper. Furthermore, the dual coding position passes over the form in which the semantic information from an abstract sentence is coded. Abstract sentences clearly have meanings which need to be distinguished from the surface sentence form and, although not expressed in images, are coded and stored in some specifiable format. This conceptual dead end shows why priority must be given to determining which aspects of sentence processing are common to all sorts of sentences, i.e., which processes govern the construction of the *semantic* representation of either concrete or abstract statements. Assumptions need to be made about the processes which elaborate the meaning of all types of sentences, and then additional, distinct assumptions need to be made as to the processes which elaborate modal representations, such as visual images, followed by identification of the effects associated with the implementation of these representations. One outcome of this approach is that reference to a 'verbal' mode of representation is no longer necessary, unless this refers to the system which processes, in a non-modal fashion, the semantics of all types of statements. Another possibility consists of qualifying the system which processes the surface aspects of sentences as 'verbal'; but here again, such a system is theoretically involved in the processing of all sentences. The problems these arguments hint at were not resolved by variants on the dual coding approach which added a super-ordinate system to the two initially postulated systems, while continuing to confer the same functions to imaginal and verbal systems as in the initial model (cf. Marschark and Paivio, 1977).

4.5 Verification paradigms

This section reviews findings from studies on imagery and sentence comprehension, and looks successively at the three paradigms which have proved to be the most successful in recent years.

4.5.1 *Sentence verification*

One of the most popular paradigms in works on comprehension is sentence verification. In this type of task, subjects are presented with statements and required to make judgements about their truth value. Response latencies are recorded and related to experimental factors, including the capacity of these statements to elicit visual images. The first study on this topic was conducted by Jorgensen and Kintsch (1973). They recorded the times required to judge whether sentences presented visually were true or false. They found that subjects' responses were overall faster for sentences that were easy to image (for instance, *'Knife cuts steak'*) than for sentences which were difficult to image (for instance, *'Truck has oil'*).

However, the interpretation of Jorgensen and Kintsch's (1973) data is problematic since the effects which are specific to imagery are hard to disentangle from the effects of the semantic complexity of the sentences. Holyoak (1974) showed that the Jorgensen and Kintsch sentences which were the least likely to elicit images were also judged to be more difficult to understand and contained verbs judged to be more difficult to define. The longer latencies of responses for low imagery sentences could be due to purely semantic factors.

The issue of distinguishing imagery value from the semantic complexity of sentences was also the impetus for a series of experiments by Glass, Eddy and Schwanenflugel (1980). They constructed sentences which only differed for imagery value. In the pre-experimental phase, they required subjects to rate the truth values of a large number of statements, and only retained those sentences which were judged true or false with the highest degree of certainty. Other subjects provided rated estimations of how essential an image was for the verification of each sentence. For instance, a sentence like: *'The stars on the American flag are white'* is highly likely to elicit visual imagery while it is being verified. On the other hand, a sentence like: *'Salt is used more often than pepper'* is less likely to evoke imagery.

In the main experiment, these sentences were presented auditorily to subjects who were required to respond as quickly and accurately as possible whether they were true or false. The first striking finding was that response times were longer for high imagery sentences, which is compatible with the notion that imagery requires the allocation of time-consuming processing resources. Furthermore, in one of the experimental conditions, the subjects had to perform simultaneously a visual pattern identification task intended to 'occupy' their visual system and thus to interfere with imagery activity related with the processing of the sentences. This task, in fact, did not differentially interfere with the verification of high or low imagery sentences. The visual task, however, proved to be more difficult (generating longer response times) when it followed the reading of a sentence which was highly likely to elicit visual imagery. Thus, the development of imagery activity during the processing of high imagery sentences can be shown via its effects on a competing task, but the findings cannot show whether it plays a decisive role in the verification process itself.

In a further study, Eddy and Glass (1981) measured verification times for high or low imagery sentences (for instance, 'A Star of David has six points' or 'Biology is the study of living matter', respectively). Sentences were presented either on a screen (reading was then expected to interfere with the elaboration of visual images) or auditorily (on audiotape). The experimenters selected sentences varying in terms of their imagery value, but equated as to their average verification times in auditory presentation. When sentences were presented on screen, verification times were significantly longer for high imagery than for low imagery sentences. Reading thus interferes more with the verification of high imagery sentences. This effect was stable when subjects were simply requested to make comprehension responses, that is, to judge whether sentences were meaningful (when they were mixed with semantically anomalous sentences). The effect associated with sentence imagery value thus seems to occur prior to verification, that is, on the level of the comprehension process itself. On the other hand, selective interference of reading with the verification of high imagery sentences disappears when subjects are required to make judgements on syntactic aspects of the sentences. These results therefore suggest that although the comprehension of high imagery sentences probably involves mental representations which are more abstract than visual images, genuine visual representations are brought into play as well and seem to play a role in verification. Is, however, this role an obligatory one? Is visual imagery necessarily required when individuals have to judge statements like 'A grapefruit is larger than an orange' or 'Abraham Lincoln had a beard'? Finally, does the imagery activity attested during high imagery sentence verification play a role that it alone can play?

It is worth recalling here that the high imagery sentences used by Glass, Eddy and Schwanenflugel (1980) were sentences that subjects had judged *to require visualization in order to be verified*. This feature, in fact, introduces a further differentiation in the set of high imagery sentences. Some sentences whose referents are physical entities that are easy to evoke in the form of visual images may not necessarily require imagery at all during verification. Eddy and Glass (1981) suggest that of the following two sentences: *'A grapefruit is larger than an orange'*, and *'The sun is larger than an orange'*, both of which refer to easily visualizable objects, the former is more likely to call upon imagery than the latter if they have to be verified. In fact, in the Glass, Eddy and Schwanenflugel (1980) study, where sentences containing high imagery words were compared against sentences containing low imagery words (without the additional restriction mentioned above), sentence type was not sensitive to the effects of selective interference. This observation suggests that if images play a role in sentence verification, they may only do so when the relation or the property to verify is not available in memory in the form of a propositional description, or when it implies subtle distinctions which are not in the subject's knowledge base.

A further set of experiments, including additional methodological refinements and affording better contrast between comprehension and verification, led the authors to conclude that imagery is not crucial to the construction of sentence meaning. It plays a significant role in post-comprehension phases, when the subject is engaged in the *verification* of the statement (Glass *et al.*, 1985). These studies indicate that high imagery sentences which describe physical properties of concrete objects need to be subdivided into: *(a)* sentences likely to lead to automatic access of a description stored in memory: this is the case for statements of overlearned facts (*'A dog has four legs'*); and *(b)* sentences describing an aspect subjects rarely or never paid attention to, at a level of detail that does not allow for automatic access to a representation in memory (*'The Statue of Liberty holds her torch in her right hand'*).

In the first case, speed of verification depends on automatic access to a memory representation. In the second case, verification time is determined by the time necessary to generate and inspect a visual image. This additional response time, however, needs to be differentiated from the additional time observed for abstract sentences or sentences containing general terms.

4.5.2 *Mental comparisons*

Another paradigm is related to sentence verification but is restricted to statements on the relation between two objects for a given dimension. In mental comparison tasks, subjects are required to judge sentences such as *'A horse is bigger than a sheep'* as true or false. Paivio in particular claimed that visual imagery plays a functional role in the evaluation of these sentences.

An effect observed repeatedly in comparative judgement tasks is that, in general, judgements are faster when the actual difference between the two compared objects (in this example, a size difference) is larger. In the case of the above mentioned sentence, designating the horse as the bigger of the two animals is faster than for the sentence *'A horse is bigger than a donkey'*. One interpretation, initially developed by Moyer (1973), is that subjects elaborate analogue representations from the sentence that incorporate information on the size of the two objects and that these analogues are then compared directly, in what Moyer termed an 'internal psychophysical judgement'.

This finding, as such, is not informative on the nature – or more specifically on the imaginal character – of these representations. This hypothesis, however, was defended by Paivio (1975c, 1978b), whose arguments can be summarized as follows. If mental comparisons actually bring representations into play which are analogue to visual representations, decisions should, on the average, be faster when stimuli are pictures than when they are nouns (since pictures are assumed to tap the system of imaginal representations more directly). This is indeed what apparently happens: to decide that a horse is bigger than a sheep takes less time when the animals are presented pictorially than when they are presented as nouns. In addition, for both materials, the pattern of longer decision times for smaller differences between objects on the relevant dimension is confirmed. Lastly, the additional claim in favour of the role of visual imagery in mental comparisons draws on data showing that judgements are faster for high than for low imagers (Paivio, 1978b). Subjects' post-experimental reports also frequently refer to visual imagery (Richardson, 1979).

However, the fact that pictures elicit faster comparison responses than nouns can be interpreted in other ways. This difference may be located at a very early phase of the task. For instance, the difference could simply result from the fact that it is faster to process pictures than nouns. Once the stimulus interpretation has been completed, the comparison processes could be similar in both cases, and the same sorts of cognitive entities would thus form the basis for subjects' computations. This argument was presented by Banks and Flora (1977). These authors showed that when the comparison must be made on an 'abstract', non-imageable dimension (for instance, intelligence, as concerns animals), it is still faster to process pictures than nouns.

Furthermore, the 'analogue-imagistic' interpretation is weakened by the fact that the inverse relationship between comparison times and the distances separating objects on the relevant dimension holds for a number of objects and relations, including highly abstract entities and relations. Friedman (1978), for instance, replicated this in a task where subjects were required to make judgements on the dimension *'better than'* (or *'worse than'*) for entities referred to by words like *hate, peace, suffer*. Thus, images are not the only forms of representation that can preserve information analogically. Holyoak's (1977) experiments showed that when subjects involved in mental comparison tasks are instructed to use visual imagery, fine analysis of chronometric indices suggests that they actually develop the required imagery activity. However, subjects apparently only use imagery when they are explicitly asked to do so. In normal conditions, subjects would not compare visual images before deciding which of two objects is the larger. Rather, they rely on abstract representations of the objects to compare along the relevant dimension.

It is worth pointing out that the two interpretations presented above are to some degree compatible, and that there are advantages in reasoning in terms of 'mixed' models, postulating parallel use of analogical representations, such as images, and propositional representations. Images tend to be used when the comparison involves objects whose differences are minimal on the relevant dimension, or when these objects are unfamiliar (Kosslyn *et al.*, 1977).

4.5.3 *Sentence–picture comparisons*

A third paradigm exploring the relationships between imagery and language comprehension has developed considerably in the last years. In sentence–picture comparison, subjects are first presented with a sentence describing the relation between two objects, for instance: *'The square is above the star'*, then they are presented with a picture, for instance, the picture of a square above a star, and have to check whether the preceding sentence accurately described this picture.

In the early 1970s, two conflicting interpretations of the cognitive processes involved in this task sparked heated debate. The first interpretation, essentially developed by Huttenlocher (1968), stated that judging the compatibility between a sentence and a picture implies that the subjects recode one stimulus in the modality of the other. In particular, the content described by the sentence presented first is likely to be expressed in the form of a visual image, and it is this image that is compared with the picture presented later. This 'imagistic' interpretation was partly supported by Tversky's (1969, 1975) findings. Tversky's experiments indicate that subjects who have processed verbal information and expect that they will have to compare it to a pictorial stimulus build a figural mental representation of the sentence in order to carry out this comparison.

This imagistic interpretation of sentence–picture comparison was attacked by 'propositionalist' interpretations advocated by Chase and Clark (1972) and by Carpenter and Just (1975). The propositionalist position is that representations built up during the encoding of a sentence and a picture lose their specific (linguistic or figural) properties and that the information extracted by the subject from both stimuli is expressed in a common format, namely a propositional format, which corresponds to the 'deep structure' of the two stimuli. Propositional theories do not, in fact, claim that the verbal and the pictorial situations are fundamentally equivalent. Different coding operations are required for their processing and these operations may call for different amounts of cognitive resources. Chase and Clark claimed, however, that there is no difference in the nature of the outputs of these two sets of operations. These outputs are abstract, amodal representations that serve as bases for subsequent comparison processes. This type of representation is assumed to be the actual locus of the meaning extracted by the subject from the sentence, while the proponents of imagistic theories claim that there are distinct systems not only for the processing of pictorial and verbal information, but also for the storage of the representations stemming from this processing.

This being said, propositional theories leave the possibility open that meaning, although located in abstract representational structures, can be translated and expressed in more specific, modal representations, such as those which are constructed by imagery. In this respect, the theory advocated by Chase and Clark does not totally eliminate imagery from cognitive activity. Imagery enables individuals to construct new cognitive representations with a figural content such as, for instance, in paired-associate learning, where the image of two objects shows their specific (spatial or functional) relationships. When prompted by appropriate imagery instructions, subjects can construct a new relationship, abstract this relationship and transfer the (propositional) output of this abstraction rather than the particular image of this relationship in memory. Subjects are able to elaborate other images reflecting either the original figure or new instantiations of the same relationship from these abstract representations. Abstract representations can be used to build up images on which further operations can apply (verification, comparison, inference, etc.). Lastly, if propositional representations are actually the ultimate form of sentence and picture coding, these representations can be constructed in more optimal conditions, for instance, more rapidly, from a picture than from a sentence describing this picture (cf. Seymour, 1975). In any case, there is certainly no fundamental incompatibility between the notion of a propositional format for the semantic representation of a sentence and the acknowledgement of circumstantial utility of imagery in psychological activity, in particular language comprehension (cf. Denis, 1979b).

The sentence–picture comparison paradigm was later applied to a new approach, which focuses on subjects' *strategies* as a source of individual differences. Subjects who have a preference for 'linguistic' strategies (they compare the linguistic description of the picture to the semantic representation of the sentence) can be differentiated from subjects making use of 'visual' strategies (they compare the picture to their visual image of the pattern described by the sentence). This differentiation emerges from a detailed analysis conducted by MacLeod, Hunt and Mathews (1978). This typology is itself related to subjects' verbal and spatial aptitudes. Furthermore, subjects who are inclined to spontaneously use a given strategy are nevertheless capable of adopting an alternate strategy, when this is required by the experimenter (Mathews, Hunt, and MacLeod, 1980).

Other experiments have shown that several characteristics of experimental situations (such as level of uncertainty or temporal constraints) affect the probability that specific strategies will be used. Eley (1981) showed that auditory presentation of a sentence, prior to the presentation of a picture, is an optimal condition for having subjects construct a visual image of the verbal description. Subjects trained to encode the sentence content visually exhibit response patterns very similar to subjects who spontaneously develop this strategy. In any case, it does not seem possible to account for performance in sentence–picture comparison experiments by postulating a single mode of coding. At least two processing modes must be postulated: one based on visual imagery, and the other making use of propositional representations. Arguments have been put forward in favour of the hypothesis of simultaneous implementation of these two strategies in sentence–picture comparison tasks (cf. Beech, 1980).

4.6 Conclusion

The issue basic to all the works reviewed in this chapter is that of the role to be assigned to imagery in comprehension, i.e., the issue of the relationships between the semantic representation of sentences and the images which are constructed from these sentences.

There are several responses to this question of the relationships between imagery and meaning:

1.   These two cognitive entities have identical status: images are equated with semantic representations. This hypothesis, whose shortcomings have been underlined above, has not in fact been expressed in this radical form since Associationist times.

2.   At the other extreme, the claim is that psychologists must analyze semantic representations in terms which do not correspond to the forms of representation likely to be consciously experienced by subjects. The semantic representation of a statement is unrelated to images at all. This position excludes the possibility that images have any functional relationship to meaning and rejects search for potential effects of imagery on the elaboration of meaning (cf. Kintsch, 1974). A large body of experimental data seriously challenge this position as well (in particular, the findings from selective interference experiments).

Two positions midway between these two extremes remain open to the researchers:

1.   Images elicited by sentences cannot be simply identified with meaning; rather, in a multimodal approach to meaning, images

can be seen as components of meaning. Other components likely to contribute to meaning are, for example, implicit muscular responses, autonomic or emotional reactions, etc. (cf. Osgood, 1953). Meaning is a composite entity, of which images are a part. Images play a greater role when sentences refer to physical entities that can be visualized.

2.   Imagery is not the 'locus' of meaning. It is a figuration of meaning or, more precisely, the figuration of the figurable part of meaning. Meaning results from specific processes which do not require the generation of images in order to construct represen-tations likely to be the basis for mental operations. Meaning is the end-product of a computation, and this end-product in turn is subject to . further computations (for instance, inferences). Although imagery may accompany comprehension processes, it is an additional process, which produces its own outputs, whose nature and structure are different from those of semantic rep-resentations. Imaginal representations complement semantic rep-resentations, and are not a prerequisite for completing the comprehension process. However, when imagery is generated, it makes an additional code available, and provides a format for operations which would not be as feasible on more abstract representations.

Interpreted this way, images have properties similar to 'models' (cf. Johnson-Laird, 1983; Rumelhart and Norman, 1988). In par-ticular, they preserve spatial relations among described entities. The advantage of images is that they provide subjects with a representation whose structure, as well as access rules, are similar to those of perceptual events. Images, for instance, enable subjects to derive inferences without mandatory recourse to the rules of formal logic (which, on the other hand, are indispensable when inferences have to be calculated on propositional representations).

Thus images, in their relationships with language comprehen-sion, are better described as cognitive tools subjects use antici-patorily to give themselves the possibility of performing operations in more favourable conditions. If subjects assume that images will be of no help in the situation to be processed, they will refrain from implementing them. The corollary is that subjects have knowledge about the usefulness of images for the processing of the situations they are asked to deal with.

Lastly, this view on imagery facilitates the interpretation of individual differences in spontaneous use of imagery. It also makes it possible to account for the fact that even for poor imagers, comprehension takes place and is operational. Finally, it suggests that some phases of human cognitive development may involve more visual imagery in language comprehension than others (e.g., Kosslyn and Bower, 1974).

5 Imagery and Lexical Meaning

Chapter 4 shows why there are distinct advantages in differentiating the semantic representation of sentences from their imaginal representation. The theoretical and empirical reasons for separating these two cognitive entities serve an overall view which articulates the relationships between them. Thus, an imaginal representation of a statement is the product of complementary and optional activation of all or part of a semantic representation in the form of a modality-specific cognitive event.

The general goal of the studies reported below was to associate imagery and semantics, without however simply merging them. Researchers investigating imagery as a process which can potentially affect language comprehension are clearly aware that the study of imagery needs to be set within a semantic theory and that the minimal requirement is to have appropriate conceptual tools for the analysis of semantic representations. These considerations guided the studies reported in this and the following two chapters on three levels of complexity of linguistic material: isolated words, sentences and texts.

5.1 Images and conceptual representations

Is the distinction between semantic representations and images appropriate at levels of complexity below the sentence level? What are the relationships between word meaning and associated images?

This type of question reflects the perennial interest throughout the history of psychology for topics such as the relationships between images and concepts, or the role of mental images in knowledge (cf. Meyerson, 1932). Classically, the notion of *concept* suggests abstraction, whereas the notion of *image* suggests figuration and concreteness. Concepts are characterized by their generality, whereas images are often defined as singular cognitive instantiations. However, a given object or class of objects can be represented in the mind in both conceptual and imaginal forms. What is the dividing-line between the 'image' of a bird and the 'concept' of bird?

The approach I have taken here is that the relationships between imagery and language comprehension cannot be investigated without a theory of meaning, or at least assumptions regarding the structure of meaning. In fact, researchers are faced with alternative theoretical assumptions and must inevitably make choices as to the appropriate level of analysis to account for the structure and organization of conceptual representations.

One alternative is to see concepts as cognitive entities which provide holistic descriptions of objects or classes of objects. In other words, the object properties reflected in a concept are indissociable (cf. Smith and Medin, 1981, ch. 6). Researchers have no reason to isolate those elements which contribute, in a unitary way, to the definition of the concept. In terms of processing, one implication of this model is that any process which addresses a concept addresses the concept as a whole. Every time a person encounters a given verbal designation, the whole conceptual representation associated with this label is activated, whatever the context in which the word appears.

In contrast to this holistic interpretation of conceptual representations is the notion of 'components' of representations. The basic assumption is that concepts can be broken down into discrete elements, each of which contributes in a non-exhaustive way to the definition of the corresponding class of objects. A concept thus results from the combination of more elementary units, some of which can contribute to other conceptual representations in other configurations. These components are assumed to be relatively autonomous, and thus processes can tap some of the components of a concept rather than the concept as a whole. This approach to concepts has many variants, and theories can be broadly classified as either dimensional or featural (cf. Le Ny, 1979; Smith and Medin, 1981, ch. 4).

Arguments supporting the componential approach, in particular the notion of 'feature' as the minimal semantic unit, have been advanced in recent years. Although initially applied to the analysis of verb meaning, the notion of semantic feature has shown itself to be particularly fruitful for the analysis of comprehension and memory of verbal information (cf. Costermans, 1980; Le Ny, 1979; Miller, 1972; see also Eysenck, 1979; Johnson-Laird, Gibbs and de Mowbray, 1978).

Given the plausibility of theoretical and experimental evidence for a componential analysis of meaning, the working hypothesis here is that the meaning of a word can generally be analyzed into more elementary semantic units than the lexical unit. These semantic units – or features – make up the concept associated with this word. For instance, the concept associated with *eagle* can be decomposed into features, such as: HAS A BEAK, HAS WINGS, HAS CLAWS, IS BROWN, LIVES IN MOUNTAINS, IS WILD, IS DANGEROUS, and so on.

There are two major properties of these sets of features: first, their internal hierarchy, which reflects the fact that some features contribute more to the definition of the concept than others; second, their flexibility, i.e., the fact that the hierarchy can undergo transient restructuring, as a function of linguistic context, subjects' cognitive orientation, and so on. These properties are discussed in Chapter 6. For the moment, the focus is on the main characteristic of verbal meaning in componential analysis, which is that the meaning of a word can be analyzed (and probably in some cases is actually analyzed in this way by individuals) into smaller parts, called 'semantic features'. Meaning can shift to a transient state of availability in working memory when activating processes trigger these features, or some subsets of them.

5.2 The notion of figural semantic features

Of the set of features which define a concept, such as EAGLE in the example above, some correspond to physical properties of eagles which have been experienced perceptually. These features, such as HAS A BEAK, HAS CLAWS, IS BROWN, are termed *figural semantic features*, because they refer to the physical appearance of objects. These features, the psychological counterparts of the perceptual properties of objects, are the basic elements for figuration, whether this process results in physical (for instance, pictorial) end-products or visual images.

In contrast, other features only contribute indirectly to the elaboration of figural representations. In the example above, this is the case for IS WILD or IS DANGEROUS. Probably, although these features are not represented as such in the picture or the

visual image of an eagle, some elaborations of these representations may express the wildness or the dangerousness of eagles.
However, such elaborate representations cannot be accessed as
directly as features like HAS CLAWS or IS BROWN. This leads to
considering that the semantic features which enter into the
definition of a concept are characterized by the probability with
which they can be expressed figurally. Figural features have
maximal probability. Non-figural features are characterized by low
or practically null probabilities.

Figural features play a major role in creating the meanings of
concrete words that denote perceivable physical objects. On the
other hand, the meaning of abstract words is richer in non-figural
features. Finer distinctions can be made among figural features.
For instance, features referring to properties such as size, texture,
colour (IS BROWN), can be set apart from those referring to parts
of objects (HAS WINGS). Similarly, non-figural features can be
classified into features referring to the function of the objects, their
value, and so on.

Arguments in favour of the notion of figural features have been
presented elsewhere (Denis, 1979b, 1982b). Hoffmann (1982) has
also suggested that the relative richness of a concept in figural
features is a relevant criterion for establishing a distinction between what he calls 'categorial' and 'sensory' concepts. The
saliency of figural features in the mental representation of objects
has often been stressed. Katz (1978, 1981) presented data indicating that there is a relationship between the presence of sensory
features in the descriptors of an object and ratings of the saliency
of these features in the visual image of the corresponding objects.
For instance, ROUND is a dominant feature of the concept
BARREL and roundness is found in the visual image of a barrel.
One suggestion that has received attention is to differentiate
'perceptually based' semantic information from 'conceptual' information in word meaning (cf. Flores d'Arcais, Schreuder and
Glazenborg, 1985; Schreuder, Flores d'Arcais and Glazenborg,
1984). Lastly, Tversky and Hemenway (1984) have shown that
figural properties referring to *parts* of objects (WINGS, BEAK, etc.)
have special status. The richness of the description of members of
a class into parts is a criterion for the generality level of that class,
and superordinate concepts in a taxonomy have no features
corresponding to object-parts.

Overall, what emerges from these studies is that it is relevant
when analyzing a concept to define those subsets of features with

a specific cognitive status, which are likely to be activated in figurative activities, in particular mental imagery. Thus, imagery is a constructive process which electively applies to a subset of features, namely figural features, and activates them in a transient way. This activation is accompanied by a psychological experience which is primarily characterized by its structural analogy with perceptual events.

The representational units postulated here have to be considered from two standpoints. I differentiate between two levels:

1. The level where the psychological units are potentially available in permanent cognitive structures; they maintain the individual's world knowledge in long-term memory.
2. The level where these units are activated during psychological activity and are temporarily available. Beyond non-specific activating processes which tap representational units and transfer them to a transient store, imagery can lead to additional, modality-specific activation for a specified subset of features, the figural features.

Imagery is thus a special type of activating process, which has two main characteristics: (a) it electively applies to the features which correspond to figural properties of objects; (b) it is accompanied by a conscious experience whose subjective content has structural properties similar to those of perceptual experience. However, figural features can also be transiently activated without the process being accompanied by a conscious imaginal experience. Figural features may be activated by non-specific activating processes, but can receive additional activation through more specific processes dependent on imagery activity.

What emerges clearly is the need to distinguish a state of *availability* of structures from a state of *activity* of these structures. Further, the tightness of all of the features characterizing a concept is not set once and for all. The activating processes which apply to them are selective to some extent. The specific requirements of situations individuals encounter do not necessarily entail the activation of the entire knowledge base associated with the concept, but rather a search and an appropriate activation of the relevant elements in the processing of the situation.

This type of approach highlights the constructive aspect of imagery. A mental image is the transient activation of a subset of features. This subset corresponds to those physical properties of the evoked object which are useful on the task the individual needs to process.

5.3 Imagery value and semantic structure

This section turns to the ways in which imagery is related to feature-based descriptions of conceptual representations. Several techniques have been developed to measure the amount of imagery elicited by words. One is based on 'imagery value', a notion which has been shown empirically to have psychological relevance and has led to defining 'norms' (cf. Cornoldi and Paivio, 1982; Paivio, Yuille and Madigan, 1968).

The imagery value of a word is defined as its capacity to elicit a mental image in a person's mind. Operationally, it is defined as the mean rating assigned to this word by a group of subjects on a scale whose anchors range from 'no image' to 'very clear and vivid image', for instance. When subjects are required to provide such ratings for a broad set of concrete to abstract nouns, subjects perform readily, indicating that rating the capacity of words to elicit images is meaningful. Subjects tend to distribute their ratings across the whole range of the scale, which is an indication that the concepts of 'no image' and 'clear image' are perceived as applicable. Finally, the ratings show a high degree of intra- and inter-individual consistency. For all these reasons, and given the high correlation between rated imagery value and behavioural measures of imagery, researchers consider word imagery value as a valid reflection of the imagery activity elicited by words.

The hypothesis was advanced above that constructing an image results from processes which apply to the subset of figural features of concepts. To elaborate a visual image, individuals activate figural aspects of concepts in a specialized processing system. This is accomplished by the implementation of specific processes which mimic perceptual experience, and result in cognitive events that are analogous, in terms of their internal structure, to perceptual events. The first step of the research programme reported below consisted in testing one of the major consequences of this hypothesis: that the imagery value of words can be predicted on the basis of the richness of the corresponding concepts in figural semantic features (i.e., the subset of features that are assumed to be the meaning units imagery processes act on) (Denis, 1983).

5.3.1 *Figural features and generality-specificity of concepts*

The first experiment designed to test this hypothesis focused on the imagery value of general and specific words, as related to the semantic composition of these terms. Generality-specificity is a dimension which is closely related to the richness of concepts in figural features. For instance, in a branch of a taxonomy such as LIVING BEING – ANIMAL – BIRD – PARROT, concepts are increasingly richer in figural semantic features as one moves down the branch. Thus, the most specific concepts should be easier to evoke in the form of images, whereas images of the most general concepts would be very difficult to elaborate, or could only be expressed via specifications (retrograding to construction of the image of a lower level concept that is richer in figural features).

General terms, such as *building, furniture* or *clothing,* have been shown to elicit imagery less readily than more specific terms, such as *church, chair* or *trousers.* However, these data have mainly been obtained in experimental settings calling for rapidity of image formation. For instance, image latencies are usually longer in response to general than to specific words (Paivio, 1966). However, the imagery values obtained in self-paced experiments are often not very different for general terms and their subordinates. It is likely that when subjects are invited to rate the imagery value of a word which is poor in figural features, they look for a more specific exemplar in the category and give imagery ratings for the term designating this specific exemplar, and not for the general term itself. This bias probably explains why general words are sometimes assigned equally or in some cases slightly higher, imagery values than more specific words.

The conceptual framework that serves as a basis for the studies presented below is shown in Figure 5.1. The figure represents four theoretical levels of a taxonomy, from the most general (I) to most specific level (IV). Each level lists the features which compose the corresponding concept in the form of a sequence of letters. This type of notation indicates that the concept linked to the term of a given level is composed of the set of features which define the superordinate levels, plus a set of its own features. For instance, the concept BIRD comprises all the features of ANIMAL, plus some additional features: WINGS, FEATHERS, etc. Lower down, the concept PARROT comprises all the features of BIRD, plus new features specific to it: MULTI-COLOURED, TALKS, etc. In this diagram, specification is primarily defined in terms of semantic enrichment.

In Figure 5.1, the figural features, corresponding to object properties that are directly accessible to perceptual experience (here visual) have been italicized. Most taxonomies are so structured

I   {a, b, c}
II   {a, b, c} & {d, e, f}
III   {a, b, c} & {d, e, f} & {g, h, i}
IV   {a, b, c} & {d, e, f} & {g, h, i} & {j, k, l}

Figure 5.1 Schematic representation of four levels of taxonomy.

that the concept at the highest level (level I) is mainly composed of non-figural features which correspond to highly abstract properties (a, b, c). The concept immediately below (level II) is composed of the same set of features (a, b, c), plus a further set (d, e, f), in which d reflects a physical property likely to be represented in imagery. Figural features are hypothesized to be more and more frequent as one moves down the taxonomy, from level to level.

In this componential framework, the diagram accounts for the increasing availability of imagery for more specific terms, not only because of the increase in the number of features which compose the concepts, but primarily because of the increase, in these features, of the relative number of figural features. Note, however, that the sharp distinction between figural and non-figural features was introduced for purposes of clarity. In fact, semantic units are likely to be characterized by their associated probability of being activated imaginally. Some figural features can be represented more easily than others, because of their higher cognitive saliency. This suggests that all the units making up a concept can be activated *to some degree* by imagery processes ('to some degree' implies no degree to a maximum value).

The first step in this imagery value study consisted in demonstrating that (*a*) general concepts are composed of a lower number of features than more specific concepts, and that (*b*) these latter are composed of a relatively higher number of figural features (or, to use the more fine-grained definition above, that the figural value of features composing a specific concept is on the average higher than that of features composing a more general concept).

The experiment assessed two levels of generality-specificity. Pairs of nouns were selected. One designated a relatively general concept, and the other a more specific one. Two types of general concepts were investigated: concepts like VEHICLE, FURNITURE, VEGETABLE (henceforth, general concepts A), and concepts like TREE, BIRD, FISH (henceforth, general concepts B).

These latter concepts subsume a set of specific elements which have a large number of figural characteristics in common. For instance, most fishes are similar to each other as concerns their overall shape, the parts which compose them, and the relations among these parts. Such concepts correspond to what Eleanor Rosch has called 'basic level' concepts, i.e., concepts at the highest level where elements still share a large number of properties, elicit similar motor programmes, and have similar figural characteristics (Rosch *et al.*, 1976). They also correspond to what Hoffmann (1982) calls 'primary concepts'. On the other hand, general concepts A subsume specific exemplars which are figurally highly discriminable. For instance, in the category of vehicles, the figural appearance of a car is very different from that of a motorcycle, a helicopter or a rubber raft. General concepts A correspond to higher taxonomic levels than general concepts B. The distinction between these two sorts of general concepts has been made by Segui and Fraisse (1968), and confirmed in an experiment on pictorialization of these two sorts of concepts: it takes longer to start drawing an illustration for general concepts A than B (Denis, 1979a). For each of the general terms A and B, a specific term was selected which in all cases was a high associate, non-ambiguous word, whose frequency was comparable to that of the general term (see Table 5.1).

Imagery values for this set of nouns were obtained on a rating scale whose anchors were 0 ('no image') and 6 ('very clear image'). The data show that these values in fact do not differentiate the two sets of items. This can be accounted for by the hypothesis above that the relatively high imagery value of general

Table 5.1 Experimental material. Source: Denis (1983) (original in French).

General Terms A	Specific Terms A	General Terms B	Specific terms B
Building	Church	Tree	Pine
Toy	Ball	Ring	Signet ring
Vegetable	Carrot	Knife	Penknife
Furniture	Chair	Flower	Daisy
Tool	Hammer	Ship	Liner
Container	Pail	Bird	Sparrow
Vehicle	Car	Fish	Trout
Clothes	Trousers	Snake	Viper

terms probably results from the fact that subjects select more specific terms, which are easier to represent figurally.

The next step consisted in drawing up a list of properties characterizing the class of objects subsumed by each of the terms, on the basis of responses by a group of subjects. The properties were either in the form of nouns (for instance, for SNAKE: it has *scales*, it has a *tongue*, it has *venom*), or adjectives (it is *elongated*), or verbs (it *crawls*). Only properties mentioned by at least 30 per cent of subjects were retained. Other examples of this procedure can be found in Ashcraft (1978), Hoffmann (1982), McNamara and Sternberg (1983), Rosch *et al.* (1976) and Tversky and Hemenway (1984). For instance, the seven properties below correspond to the subjects' listings for FLOWER, in decreasing order of frequency: PETALS, STEM, LEAVES, STAMENS, POLLEN, PISTIL, SMELL.

As predicted, the findings show that the mean number of features which characterize general concepts is lower than the number of features which characterize specific concepts (see Figure 5.2). In addition, although the mean number of features is very low for general concepts A in comparison to the corresponding specific concepts, there is almost no difference between general concepts B and corresponding specific concepts. Furthermore, the mean number of features is significantly lower for general concepts A than B.

These findings thus reinforce the contention that the cognitive status of general concepts A is distinct from that of general concepts B, which themselves are closer to the whole set of specific concepts. It supports the distinction introduced by Rosch

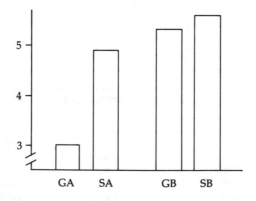

Figure 5.2 Mean number of features per concept.

et al. (1976) and confirms that the 'basic level' in subjects' cognitive segmenting of the world corresponds to the class, in a given taxonomy, where a high degree of figural similarity first appears between the elements. In the diagram in Figure 5.1, general concepts A are thus located at a higher level than general concepts B, which are very close to specific concepts A. Specific concepts B are, of all the concepts considered here, situated at the lowest level.

The next step consisted in defining to what extent each of the features referred to a figural property. Rather than trying to dichotomize this dimension, or to rely on intuition in order to classify features, we recruited a new group of subjects. Judgements were made on a seven-point rating scale similar to the imagery value rating scale. Since it seemed problematic to ask subjects to judge the 'figurativeness' of features as such, they were asked to estimate figurativeness by rating the capacity of an element to elicit a visual imaginal representation.

Ratings were obtained for the entire set of terms designating the features selected. These indices were assumed to reflect the figurativeness of each of the features. For example, Table 5.2 shows the index values for each feature defining the concept FLOWER (the extreme values of the index are 0 and 6).

This example is opportune since it highlights the factors likely to affect the figurativeness of the different aspects of an object. First, it is not surprising that some components of the FLOWER concept which are well defined figurally, such as PETALS, STEM, LEAVES, have high figurativeness indices. It is worth noting that a highly characteristic feature of this class of objects, the feature SMELL, has a low index, which is congruent with the fact that the rating instructions referred to visual imagery value. More interesting is the case of STAMENS, POLLEN and PISTIL, which correspond to highly characteristic properties of flowers, whose figural appearance is however not easy to evoke visually. The indices for these components are substantially lower than those of features

Table 5.2 Indices of figurativeness for features defining the
FLOWER concept.

PETALS	5.25
STEM	5.00
LEAVES	5.47
STAMENS	2.50
POLLEN	3.69
PISTIL	3.34
SMELL	2.47

which are easy to visualize. Similar cases where the imagery value of a word is relatively low in spite of the concreteness of the referent have been reported by Paivio, Yuille and Madigan (1968).

A mean index of figurativeness per feature was computed for each concept. The average indices for the four groups of items are presented in Figure 5.3. Statistical analyses show that mean figurativeness per feature is significantly lower for general concepts A than for the corresponding specific concepts, and that the means are lower for general concepts A than for general concepts B. General terms A contrast significantly with all the other terms, and the contrast is much more pronounced than the contrast based on the 'global' imagery values previously collected. General terms A indeed correspond to concepts defined by features whose figurativeness is overall less marked than that of the other concepts.

The findings so far support the basic assumption. In a taxonomy of physical objects, the transition from a general level to a more specific level is accompanied by an increase of the number of features describing the concept, and by an overall enrichment in the figurativeness of features. This, however, was only clear-cut for general concepts A and their subordinate specific concepts. The transition from general level B to a more specific level exhibits a different pattern: the number of features only increases marginally, and there is no increase of figurativeness of the features (it tends to decrease slightly). These data are compatible with the interpretation that general concepts A are situated at a higher level than the 'basic level', while general concepts B are at this level, or at a lower level.

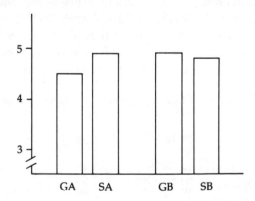

Figure 5.3 Mean index of figurativeness per feature.

Additional support comes from the significant positive correlation between the global imagery value of a word and the mean figurativeness of the features which define the corresponding concept. As expected, the index of figurativeness attached to the features describing a concept is predictive of the global imagery value of the corresponding word. This corroborates the notion of a determination of the imagery value of a word by the richness of the corresponding concept in figural features.

5.3.2 *Mental images and basic level*

The above findings are congruent with data on cognitive representations at different levels of taxonomies for physical objects (cf. Hoffmann, 1982; Rosch *et al.*, 1976; Tversky and Hemenway, 1984). These studies show that there is a 'critical' level in taxonomies, although authors tend to vary somewhat in terminology and cut-off point: 'basic level' for Rosch and Tversky, 'primary concept' for Hoffmann. All consider, however, that the critical level reflects basic cognitive segmentation of the environment. The definition of this level is the end-product of a compromise between demands of generality and demands of discriminability. As seen above, this level is the highest one in a hierarchy where the elements still possess similar figural characteristics. The basic level is thus the highest level of a taxonomy for which a visual image can be elaborated without recourse to specification (cf. Murphy and Smith, 1982).

Experimental arguments in favour of this notion are provided by data from an experiment conducted with Joachim Hoffmann and Michael Ziessler (cf. Hoffmann, Denis and Ziessler, 1983). One of the objectives of this experiment was to assess the relationship between the richness of a concept in figural features (i.e., the level of the concept in the taxonomy) and the process of formation of a visual image. In the part of the experiment which is relevant here, subjects were invited to form a visual image in response to nouns corresponding to various levels of several hierarchies. Subjects were required to depress a button to indicate when they had formed a clear and vivid visual image in response to the stimulus word.

Analysis of response latencies showed that the formation of a visual image was faster for words corresponding to concepts situated at the basic level (for instance, *car* or *aeroplane*). Image latencies were longer for words corresponding to concepts situated above the basic level (in this example, *vehicle*). Latencies were also longer for words which corresponded to concepts lower than the basic level (for instance, *jeep* or *jet*).

Forming the image of an object on the basic level of a hierarchy is thus a very specific cognitive activity. It consists in search and activation of the set of features which differentiate the concept figurally. Among the features defining a concept, figural features have particular cognitive saliency and as such are able to be tapped by the activating processes responsible for image-like cognitive events. The time required for this activation is likely to be minimal.

The increase in imagery latencies for concepts higher or lower than the basic level is probably due to different factors. Constructing the image of a concept located *higher* than the basic level is a demanding process inasmuch as this concept is poor in figural features. Some sort of imagery nevertheless remains possible provided that an instantiation process directed at a subordinate concept (governed by factors such as the familiarity or the typicality of the subordinate concepts) is implemented. In any case, the search for a more specific concept requires additional activity, as is reflected by the relative increase in image latency. On the other hand, constructing the image of a very specific concept, *lower* than the basic level, also requires additional cognitive activity, since a larger number of figural features must be activated to generate a differentiated image. However, another factor can also account for response times for highly specific concepts, namely the lesser cognitive availability of the figural features which differentiate the concepts from each other at the same level of specificity.

It is worth noting that in this image generation task, subjects' responses were highly affected by individual imagery capacities. On the basis of tests used in previous studies (Paivio and Ernest, 1971), we compared subjects who had either high or low capacities in visual imagery. On the whole, as is shown in Figure 5.4, imagery latencies for high imagers were shorter than those for low imagers. This difference probably reflects differential accessibility of figural features as a function of individual characteristics. Nevertheless, once an image has been formed, regardless of generation latency, the newly available representation can be used in a similar way by high and low imagers, for instance, when the image must be compared to a pictorial stimulus.

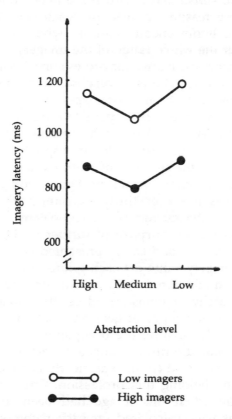

Figure 5.4 Mean imagery latencies as a function of the abstraction level of
designated concepts, for high and low imagers
Source: Hoffmann, Denis and Ziessler (1983).

Finally, there is a positive correlation between the imagery value
of the words used in this experiment and the richness of corresponding concepts in figural features. This finding corroborates
data from the experiment reported in the previous section.

5.3.3 *Figurativeness and semantic structure: Analysis of a corpus*

In analyzing the data in the experiment on the semantic structure
of general and specific terms, I pointed to the problem of the low
variability of imagery values between general and specific terms
since all were situated in the extremes of the rating scale. Materials
constructed from classic taxonomic hierarchies tend to restrict

terms to concrete verbal items, which are likely to elicit imagery activity. For these reasons, a new approach was devised for a larger and more homogeneous corpus, whose elements were expected to cover the whole range of the imagery rating scale.

The material used was names for professional occupations. The semantic world of occupations is very rich and its elements are distributed widely over the range of imagery values, from occupations having highly salient perceptual attributes (as *fireman* or *judge*) to occupations devoid of such attributes (as *publisher* or *manager*). This corpus was especially appropriate for testing the relationship between the number of features defining a concept and the richness of this concept in figural components. The material used was a set of thirty-six names of occupations, distributed all along the imagery scale. These items were classified into four subsets for the purpose of further analyses. The four groups of items, A, B, C and D, are presented in Table 5.3, along with the mean imagery value for each group of items.

As a control, an additional measure was obtained in order to validate the hierarchy of items based on their imagery values. This measure was the latency of generation of a visual image for each of the terms designating the occupations. A new group of subjects was presented with the names of each occupation on a screen and was instructed to form as clearly as possible a visual image of a person holding this profession. The subjects had to depress a button when this image had been formed. Mean imagery latencies were calculated for each name of occupation. Latencies appear in Table 5.4, with mean latencies for each group of items.

Table 5.3 Imagery values of the nouns selected. Source: Denis (1983) (original in French).

Group A		Group B		Group C		Group D	
Designer	0.33	Spokesman	1.75	Antiques dealer	3.46	Lumberjack	4.92
Intermediary	0.79	Wholesaler	1.88	Mayor	3.54	Typist	4.96
Collaborator	1.08	Researcher	2.04	Actor	3.71	Jockey	5.04
Manager	1.25	Businessman	2.42	Reporter	3.79	Judge	5.13
Creator	1.38	Engineer	2.79	Shopkeeper	3.96	Tennis player	5.17
Negotiator	1.42	Lawyer	2.83	Cashier	4.42	Butcher	5.25
Landlord	1.50	Manager	2.88	Animal trainer	4.67	Fireman	5.38
Consultant	1.63	Commentator	3.13	Car mechanic	4.71	Nurse	5.42
Author	1.67	Instructor	3.25	Rural policeman	4.75	Policeman	5.67
Means	1.23		2.55		4.11		5.22

Table 5.4 Imagery latencies (ms). Source: Denis (1983)

Group A		Group B		Group C		Group D	
Designer	3 919	Spokesman	1 909	Antiques dealer	1 218	Lumberjack	948
Intermediary	2 891	Wholesaler	1 926	Mayor	1 233	Typist	904
Collaborator	2 414	Researcher	1 606	Actor	998	Jockey	978
Manager	2 288	Businessman	2 099	Reporter	1 203	Judge	989
Creator	2 444	Engineer	2 031	Shopkeeper	1 006	Tennis player	1 129
Negotiator	2 533	Lawyer	1 868	Cashier	969	Butcher	942
Landlord	2 547	Manager	1 489	Animal trainer	1 162	Fireman	835
Consultant	1 991	Commentator	1 804	Car mechanic	1 073	Nurse	881
Author	1 923	Instructor	1 563	Rural policeman	1 407	Policeman	871
Means	2 550		1 811		1 141		942

Comparing Tables 5.3 and 5.4 clearly shows that nouns with the highest imagery values are also those which elicit visual images with shorter latencies, whereas low imagery values are associated with nouns eliciting longer latencies. This relationship, attested to by a high correlation coefficient value, validates the imagery values for the items used in the further steps of the experiment.

The next step consisted in drawing up the list of properties characteristic of each of the occupations selected. A new group of subjects were asked to provide such lists. All the properties (expressed in the form of nouns, adjectives or verbs) produced by all the subjects for the whole set of occupations were plotted. Only properties named by at least 25 per cent of the subjects were retained for further steps in the analysis.

Table 5.5 presents the list of properties retained for two occupations from Group A and two occupations from Group D.

Table 5.5 List of properties, in decreasing order of frequency of mention, and corresponding indices of figurativeness for two occupations from Group A and two occupations from Group D.

Group A	Manager		Creator	
	Manage	1.97	Create	3.78
	Business	3.06	Imagination	2.34
	In charge	2.53	Art	3.75
	Money	3.03	Invent	3.47
Group D	Butcher		Nurse	
	Meat	5.03	Care	4.81
	Sell	3.97	Hospital	5.25
	Apron	5.16	The sick	4.09
	Cut	4.84	White (clothes)	5.16
	Knife	4.66	Clinic	5.16
	White (clothes)	5.16	Injections	5.16
	Butcher shop	4.69	Doctor (works with)	5.25
			At home (can work)	4.44

Figure 5.5 shows the average number of properties used to define the occupations of the four groups. The higher the imagery value of the noun for an occupation, the larger the number of properties characterizing this occupation. This relationship is expressed by a positive significant correlation coefficient between imagery value and the number of properties for the whole set of thirty-six occupations.

The previous procedure was then repeated in order to evaluate the figurativeness of features. Using data from a new set of respondents, an index expressing the figurativeness of each feature was computed. Table 5.5 shows the indices for each feature for the four groups of occupations. It is clear that the values of these indices are lower for Group A than for Group D occupations.

A mean index of figurativeness per feature was then computed for each occupation. As shown in Figure 5.6, the mean index of figurativeness per feature gradually increases from Group A to Group D. This means that, from A to D, not only the concepts are composed of an increasingly higher number of features, but these features are themselves increasingly richer in figurativeness. Furthermore, the correlation between the number of features for an occupation and the mean figurativeness per feature is significant and positive.

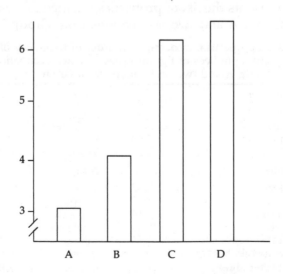

Figure 5.5 Mean number of properties per occupation.

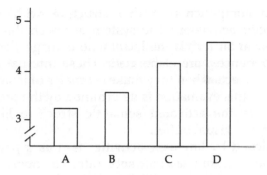

Figure 5.6 Mean index of figurativeness per feature.

These findings provide additional support to the assumption that (a) the imagery value of a word depends on the richness of the corresponding concept in semantic features (true aside from the contrast between general and specific terms); (b) the concepts richest in semantic features are also the richest in *figural* semantic features (true at least for the semantic worlds with physical referents, which these experiments were restricted to). Lastly, our model accounts for the correlation between the imagery value of nouns and their 'predicability' (that is, the number of descriptive statements in which nouns can serve as arguments) (cf. Jones, 1985, 1988).

5.4 Conclusion

The findings reported in this chapter show that the imagery value of a word is dependent on the richness of the corresponding concept in figural semantic features. The image of an object, when it is temporarily activated in an individual's cognitive system, reflects a piece of knowledge which itself is stored in conceptual abstract form. The visual image of an object, to use a metaphor, is the partial, transient embodiment of the concept of that object. It does not reflect an individual's total knowledge of that object, but only those pieces of knowledge referring to its figural components. The idea advocated here is that images are products of specific activating processes which electively apply to a subset of the units which compose the concept.

Estimating the imagery value of a word is secondary to the process which, starting from the activation of a semantic structure in a non-specific, amodal conceptual system, consists in providing some of the components of this structure with additional, modality-specific activation. The system in which this activation occurs (or 'visual buffer') is the locus where images, as analogue cognitive experiences, are elaborated. These internal events are evaluated by subjects when they make estimates of imagery value. The outcome of this evaluation is determined by the probability of finding units in the activated semantic structure likely to be transferred in the visual buffer.

Imagery elicited by linguistic activities is thus a psychological event constructed from a *semantic* substrate. The notion of images as 'surface representations', whose underlying structure needs to be accounted for, has received growing attention since the late 1970s (cf. Kosslyn, 1980; Shepard, 1978). Images can no longer be defined as global, non-analyzable mental events. There is a general consensus that images possess structural properties that can be described accurately, but that in the case of images associated with language, it is relevant to make hypotheses on the underlying structures from which these images are constructed.

In this respect, the componential approach is an appropriate tool. It can be used to study the relationships of imagery to language in a way that fulfils the demands of current analytical approaches of imagery. In addition, cogent arguments have been made in favour of the relevance of feature analysis of perceptual configurations (cf. Bower and Glass, 1976; Murray and Szymczyk, 1978; Smith and Nielsen, 1970; Thompson and Klatzky, 1978). Some authors contend that the salient features in these configurations are functional units in perceptual identification (cf. Pomerantz, Sager and Stoever, 1977).

The approach illustrated in this chapter probably requires some refinement. First, sets of features should certainly not be considered as simple lists. Rather, they need to be characterized in terms of their internal structure, i.e., the hierarchical organization of their elements. It is not enough to state that some features are more salient or more specific than others in a given conceptual structure. It is also necessary to make assumptions on the dependencies among these features and on the relationships between each feature and the conceptual structure to which it belongs.

In addition, it seems necessary to correct what might be construed as an 'atomistic' conception of mental images. Images are not mere juxtapositions of fragmentary components. A position which distances itself somewhat from the view that images are holistic, non-analyzable cognitive structures, is not automatically a solely atomistic one. Defining images as cognitive entities *composed* of elementary units does not entail that they are merely *composite* entities. Imagery, as modality-specific activation of figural components of concepts, develops within a schematic framework, i.e., within an analogue representation of the global shape of objects, or 'skeletal encoding' (Kosslyn, 1981). This framework enables individuals to reconstruct the global configuration of an object, and activate the features of the evoked object. The subjective vividness of an image is thus a function of the frequency with which features are activated in the configuration.

An appropriate validation of these assumptions consists in demonstrating that subjects can electively activate subsets of features which compose a concept. The experiments reported in the next chapter deal precisely with this issue.

6 Activation of Figural Features in the Processing of Sentences

Chapter 5 reports converging evidence for the hypothesis that conceptual representations are amenable to analysis, and for the relevance of the notion of figural features. This chapter goes one step further and explores a logical corollary to this hypothesis: the functional autonomy of the components of conceptual representations.

The assumption that conceptual representations can be analyzed implicitly postulates that the components of these representations are at least partially independent. This implies that activating processes can apply selectively to certain components or correlated subsets of them rather than to the entire configuration. The cognitive activation of a concept is total if all its components are activated simultaneously. The name of an object can theoretically elicit all the conceptual knowledge related to this object. Cognitive activation is 'partial' when a restricted number of these components are activated. This occurs if people centre their attention on a specific aspect of an object when presented with the name of this object. Selectivity is an inherent property of human attention. Evidence that partial cognitive activation takes place is an additional argument in favour of the hypothesis that concepts are analyzable, and will reinforce the hypothesis of the componential structure of conceptual representations.

6.1 Figural and non-figural properties in the analysis of concepts

The first experiment was planned to activate certain components of a conceptual representation experimentally and then test whether these components exhibited a higher state of activation than others. The hypothesis was that when semantic features, in particular figural features, of a concept have been activated in an individual's mind, transient 'traces' of this cognitive event should facilitate further processing of a stimulus exhibiting the corresponding figural properties.

In this experiment (Denis, 1984a), subjects were first involved in a task intended selectively to activate some components of the concepts they were to process. Specifically, subjects were asked to perform a classification task for a set of nouns designating members of a class. For instance, subjects were auditorily presented with twelve nouns of musical instruments (*piano, violin, accordion, cymbal*, etc.) and were asked to classify them into distinct categories. In one condition, the classification was to take figural properties into account. In particular, do the instruments mentioned have strings? Do they have keys? Each instrument was to be classified into one of four categories: has both strings and keys; has strings, and no keys; has keys, and no strings; has neither strings nor keys. In another condition, other subjects were required to take non-figural properties into account. In particular, is the instrument from before the twentieth century? Is it an instrument difficult (or purportedly difficult) to play?

The hypothesis was that each of these two types of classification would primarily activate the conceptual components relevant to the task. In other words, figural features would be activated in subjects' processing systems in one case, and non-figural features in the other case. It was expected that this activation would persist to some extent and that the amount of cognitive activation of the features would return to its initial state only after some delay. The main objective was to detect traces of the temporary persistence of figural features in subjects' cognitive systems when these subjects had previously activated these features in the classification task.

Measures were obtained in a subsequent task. Subjects were unexpectedly presented with drawings of musical instruments and required to recognize which instruments they had previously classified from distractors. Drawings in general depict the figural properties of objects. If a recognition response results from matching between the stimulus and a transient memory representation, matching will occur in optimal conditions if the memory representation has characteristics in common with the stimulus. In other words, when presented with the figural properties exhibited in a drawing, subjects should do better when the features recently activated in their cognitive system are figural features. On the other hand, subjects should do less well when these features are non-figural. Naturally, some matching can take place between non-figural features present in transient memory and figural properties in a drawing. But it is likely that this decision calls for additional processing steps. The prediction was that subjects required to recognize drawings would respond faster when they had previously made classification of figural rather than non-figural characteristics.

The findings show that when subjects initially activate figural features during the classification task, they subsequently respond to drawings faster than when classification is based on non-figural features. Although in both classification conditions the *same* lists of objects were processed (in comparable temporal conditions), recognition responses were significantly faster when classification previously elicited the activation of figural features (see Figure 6.1a).

One explanation is that after having activated figural features, subjects maintained a transient trace of this activation in memory, and were thus in a better position to respond to drawings that exhibited the figural properties of objects directly. On the contrary, when subjects initially activated non-figural features of the same concepts, they were in a more difficult cognitive situation when they later had to recognize stimuli (drawings) showing properties of another kind (figural properties). These findings

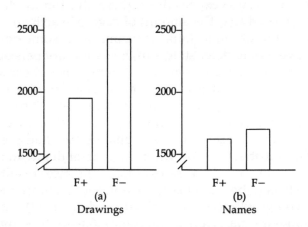

Figure 6.1 Mean recognition times for drawings or nouns (ms) as a function of type of properties, figural (F+) or non-figural (F−), in the classification task.

show that selective activation of figural features can be reflected in the speed of subsequent processing of pictorial material.

In another part of this experiment, subjects were to furnish recognition responses to written names rather than drawings of the musical instruments. This new condition was expected to have specific consequences on recognition. As stimuli, nouns do not have any of the (figural or non-figural) characteristics likely to have been activated previously. For the subjects, the fact of having processed figural characteristics should not particularly favour word recognition (whereas this was a facilitating factor in drawing recognition).

As expected, recognition times for nouns were not significantly different after one or the other classification condition (Figure 6.1b). Thus, the effects of the activation of figural features of a concept, demonstrated when recognition is executed on pictorial material, are no longer visible when recognition responses are given to nouns. Nouns, of course, have ties with conceptual representations, but it is likely that these ties are not stronger with the figural than with the non-figural part of these representations. In any case, as stimuli, nouns do not have characteristics which entail more elective access to one part of a concept or another. On the other hand, drawings, as pictorial signs for objects, contain immediately accessible representations of the figural part of concepts.

6.2 Figural and non-figural properties in the analysis of representations of singular objects

A further experiment examined whether selective activation of figural or non-figural features resulting from a subject's induced cognitive set could be evidenced not only for mental representations of classes of objects, as above, but also for the representations of singular objects. The singular 'objects' considered here were famous people, either real (such as Henri IV, Victor Hugo, Fidel Castro, etc.) or fictional (such as Asterix, Robin Hood, Zorro, etc.).

A classic issue in the psychology of semantics is whether there are distinct forms of memory representations for singular objects, on the one hand, and for classes of objects, on the other (cf. Le Ny, 1979). There are no compelling psychological arguments that proper names and category nouns are radically different. In a componential perspective, in particular, meanings attached to proper names can be approached by the same types of analyses as meanings of category nouns. Feature analyses of these two sorts of noun have been conducted, in particular by McNamara and Sternberg (1983). The structure of the lists of features are highly comparable for both types of items. However, McNamara and Sternberg's experiments show that the number of necessary and sufficient characteristics (or 'defining attributes') is higher in the case of proper names than for category nouns. Furthermore, distinctiveness is more pronounced within semantic representations of proper names than of common nouns (cf. Durso and O'Sullivan, 1983).

The 'specificity' of proper names, however, is relative and should not mask what they share with common nouns. In particular, to return to the representation of singular objects, the representation of a famous person, for instance, can be analyzed in terms of its figural features – physical appearance, for instance – and its non-figural ones. For example, our visual image of Zorro (but also the portrait an artist can make of him) calls for a number of figural features (MOUSTACHE, MASK, BLACK HAT, etc.), but probably does not directly imply such features as BRAVERY and GENEROSITY, although they are highly typical of Zorro.

In an experiment similar to the one described above, subjects were required to perform a classification task involving famous real and imaginary people. In one condition, classification was to take into account whether the person had or did not have two characteristics. Does he have a moustache? Does he typically wear a hat? This classification condition was expected to activate relevant figural features in subjects' working memory. In the other condition, subjects had to classify the same set of people, but as a function of two other characteristics: old (instructions specified that this meant: 'who lived before the twentieth century'); brave (especially famous for acts of bravery). This task was designed preferentially to activate non-figural features of corresponding representations.

In the recognition task, subjects were presented with portraits of the previously mentioned people interspersed with portraits of new ones. The findings showed that subjects had faster recognition responses when they had previously processed the figural aspects of the people. This difference was not observed when recognition was tested on written names of the people (Figure 6.2). Selective activation of figural features is thus reflected in the way subjects later processed pictorial material that displayed the corresponding properties.

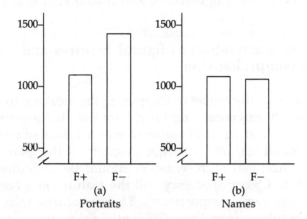

Figure 6.2 Mean recognition times for portraits or names (ms) as a function of type of properties, figural (F+) or non-figural (F−), in the classification task.

The findings provide arguments that *conceptual components* are dissociable, and more importantly that there can be selective activation of these components. The data are compatible with the idea that concepts can be activated partially, and thus that long-term conceptual representations are structured in such a way that selective activating processes can apply to them. Selective activating processes can be interpreted in terms of 'cognitive centration' on the property or properties subjects have to take into account in a given task. Conceptual representations may be first activated integrally and then undergo selective processing, centred on limited sets of properties.

In any case, the present findings also fit with data showing that semantic processing of a word may involve only some parts of its total meaning (cf. Eysenck, 1979; Johnson-Laird, Gibbs and de Mowbray, 1978), and that induced cognitive orientation during stimulus display (either on the object's physical appearance or functional characteristics) later affects recognition of this stimulus (cf. Emmerich and Ackerman, 1979).

The findings can also be paralleled to experiments showing that the classification of complex figural patterns implies the selection of certain features to the detriment of others, which subjects disregard (Frith and Frith, 1978). It is also well established that the processing of pictorial stimuli (e.g., judging the equivalence of drawings of familiar objects) generates representations that can be shaped by the instructions which define the aspects to be taken into account for judging object equivalence (Kelter *et al.*, 1984).

6.3 Selective activation of figural features and sentence comprehension

As mentioned at the outset of Chapter 5, the working hypothesis of the research programme reported here was that word meaning can be analyzed in terms of features, which I divided into figural and non-figural features. A major property of the features composing a conceptual representation should be underlined now, namely, their *differential saliency*. All the features of a concept do not have the same 'importance'. These features thus form a hierarchy resulting from their differential saliency.

For a given conceptual representation, this hierarchy can be operationally defined by presenting subjects with an isolated word and asking them to generate lists of predicative statements attributable to the objects referred to by the word (see Chapter 5). This procedure makes it possible to determine the frequency of mention of each statement for the sample of subjects. For instance, out of the entire set of responses given to the word *eagle*, the statement *'has claws'* is more frequent than *'has eyes'*. Furthermore, the order in which responses are generated is an indicator of their relative saliency. For instance, when both responses are given by the same subject, *'has claws'* is more frequently mentioned before *'has eyes'* than after. Such indications reflect the fact that in the representation that most people have of eagles, the feature HAS CLAWS is cognitively more salient than the feature HAS EYES (see also the examples given in Chapter 5).

Another very important aspect of the present model is the postulated flexibility of the hierarchy of features. The activation of a conceptual representation can be accompanied by a temporary reorganization of the hierarchy, through the influence of the linguistic context and, more generally, subjects' spontaneous or induced cognitive set. Evidence dates back to classic experiments demonstrating the effects of sentence context on the activation of some aspects of the concepts mentioned. Recall of the sentence *'The man tuned the piano'* is facilitated by the cue *'something with a nice sound'*, whereas recall of the sentence *'The man lifted the piano'* is facilitated by the cue *'something heavy'*. This differential effect suggests that different 'aspects' of a piano have been activated during reading of the two sentences (Barclay *et al.*, 1974). Subsequently, Tabossi and Johnson-Laird (1980) showed that subjects retrieve a relevant characteristic of a concept faster when this particular aspect of the concept is primed by a sentence. For instance, subjects respond faster to the question: *'Is a diamond hard?'* when it has been preceded by the sentence: *'The goldsmith cut the glass with the diamond'*, than by sentences referring to other properties of diamonds (*'The mirror dispersed the light from the diamond'*) or not referring to any particular aspect of diamonds (*'The film showed the person with the diamond'*). Thus, some aspects of word meaning can be activated during the comprehension of a sentence containing this word, and this selection is determined by the sentence context (cf. also Tabossi, 1982, 1988).

The experiments reported earlier in this chapter showed that figural or non-figural features composing a conceptual representation can be selectively activated. The next step consisted in showing that selective activating processes can also operate within the subset of figural features. These processes were investigated in the context of sentence comprehension.

The basic assumption here is that semantic processing of a sentence typically activates a bundle of semantic features in the reader's or listener's mind. These features are only a subset of the entire set of features that exhaustively define the concepts evoked in the sentence. The conceptual representation for the word *eagle* in the example above is assumed to be composed of features such as HAS WINGS, HAS CLAWS, IS BROWN, etc. However, when readers process a sentence like: *'Swooping down to the earth, with its feet forward, the eagle suddenly snatched the weasel'*, it is unlikely that they exhaustively activate their conceptual representations of eagles, earth and weasels (i.e., their total knowledge about these entities). Furthermore, as regards the EAGLE concept, it is likely that readers centre their cognitive processing on the feature HAS CLAWS, whereas the other features are activated to a lesser degree, or not at all.

This hypothesis was tested in a series of experiments based on a variant of the sentence–picture comparison paradigm (Denis and Le Ny, 1986). After having read a sentence such as the one in the example above, subjects were presented with a picture showing either a part of an eagle or a part of a totally unrelated object. Subjects were asked to judge whether the picture illustrated a part of an object mentioned in the sentence, by depressing one of two buttons. The results show that when subjects were presented with the picture of an eagle's claw, their (positive) responses were faster than when they were presented with a picture showing an eagle's wing. Symmetrically, when first presented with a sentence focusing on the feature HAS WINGS, such as: *'The eagle soared slowly and majestically into the heavens'*, subjects responded faster to the picture of a wing than to the picture of a claw (Figure 6.3).

One plausible interpretation is that semantic processing of descriptive sentences does not activate components of meaning to the same degree. The figural features focused on by the sentence are activated to the greatest extent, whereas other figural features are activated to a lower degree, or even not activated at all in some cases.

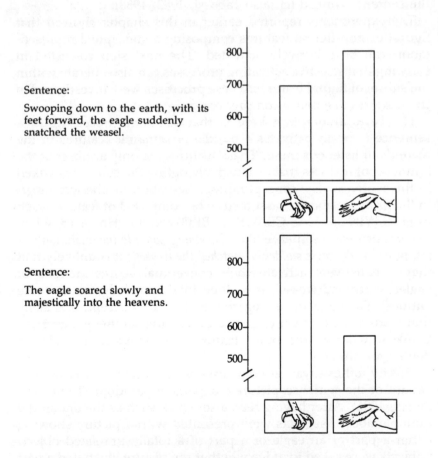

Sentence:

Swooping down to the earth, with its feet forward, the eagle suddenly snatched the weasel.

Sentence:

The eagle soared slowly and majestically into the heavens.

Figure 6.3 Mean response times (ms) for two drawings as a function of the sentence read previously (Eagle theme).

A further experiment was conducted to evaluate a purely 'linguistic' interpretation of the findings. According to this interpretation, after reading the sentence expected to activate the feature HAS CLAWS, subjects could implicitly complete the sentence with the word designating the part of the object on which the sentence was focusing: *'The eagle snatched the weasel . . . with its claws.'* When presented later with a picture, subjects would only decide whether the word they have just generated adequately denotes the picture. Response times to the pictures should thus be shorter when subjects are presented with an object part they had implicitly named than with any other object part.

The experiment was then replicated with pictures replaced by the nouns designating the object parts shown on the pictures. If the linguistic account of the findings in fact was true, the previously obtained effect should at least hold, or perhaps be enhanced. In addition, if an implicit verbal continuation of the sentence occurs, the implicit verbal response should be matched more readily against word probes than against picture probes. Thus, responses to words should be faster than to pictures.

In the experiment where subjects responded to nouns, response times for the items on which cognitive centration was highly likely were still shorter than response times for items on which it was unlikely, but this difference was no longer statistically reliable. Thus, substituting nouns for pictures did not abolish the effect, which indicates that selective activation is a rather general phenomenon. It should be recalled that this process has been reported in purely linguistic situations (cf. Barclay *et al.*, 1974; Tabossi and Johnson-Laird, 1980). However, the more clear-cut effect in the first experiment (with pictures) suggests that when selective activation operates on entities easy to figure, it is governed to a great extent by processes involving figural mental representations. This interpretation is itself compatible with the idea that in addition to the construction of a semantic representation of the sentence, subjects elaborate some non-linguistic 'model' of the described situation. As discussed in Chapter 4, visual imagery can serve such a function in the comprehension of sentences. These data, although they cannot resolve the issue of the nature of the model constructed by readers, lend themselves to an interpretation based on the notion of a 'mental model' of the described situation that serves as a ground for further cognitive operations (Johnson-Laird, 1983; Perrig and Kintsch, 1985; de Vega and Diaz, 1991).

Lastly, response times for word probes were consistently longer than for picture probes. This challenges the explanation of the previous main effect in terms of verbal continuation of the sentence. Implicit responses of this kind should have been matched more readily against word than picture probes, which is not the case here. In addition, the fact that pictures elicited faster responses than nouns is in line with the assumption that pictorial stimuli access mental representations of objects faster than verbal stimuli do (cf. Carr *et al.*, 1982; Irwin and Lupker, 1983; Nelson, Reed and McEvoy, 1977; Rosch, 1975; Snodgrass, 1984).

At this point of the investigation, the findings confirm that what is maintained in a reader's transient memory about an object mentioned in a sentence depends upon particular cognitive centration performed on the corresponding representation during reading. The transient mental representation of an eagle, after the processing of the first sentence, cannot be considered as equivalent to the representation subsequent to the processing of the second sentence. The data clearly suggest that when an individual reads a sentence about an object, the sentential context selectively 'shapes' the transient representation that the reader constructs of the object. This particular representation reflects the unequal rate of activation of the different features which compose a concept, at least in the reading conditions examined here.

This research has mainly focused on the selective activation of figural features. The last step consisted in examining to what extent the involvement of visual imagery affects differential saliency of features activated in transient memory. For instance, visually imagining the scene described by the sentence about an eagle snatching a weasel is expected to increase the rate of activation of those features which are central to the meaning of the sentence. This supplementary activation should consequently speed up the processes involved in the subject's response to the picture. Is this facilitation however homogeneous, with an equal increment of activation for all responses, or rather differential, depending on the rate of activation of features subsequent to semantic processing?

The third experiment of the series used the same kind of situation as previously (sentence reading, followed by judgement on a picture probe), except that the subjects were now explicitly required to form a visual image of the scene described in the sentence. The results showed that imagery instructions significantly affected response times. Imagining the scenes described by the sentences produced an overall speeding up of judgements. However, this facilitation was not equivalent for the two types of probe. Judgement times were shortened moderately for pictures illustrating the object part on which cognitive centration was expected to occur, while judgements were markedly sped up for pictures illustrating the other parts. This differential facilitation suggests that visual imagery which accompanies sentence processing does not substantially modify the rate of activation of features on which subjects already perform cognitive centration (the rate of activation being virtually at its maximum). On the other hand, imagery apparently increases the rate of activation of those features which were moderately activated in the absence of intentional imagery activity.

Finally, the difference observed in the initial experiment between responses to pictures illustrating the object part on which centring was likely to occur, and responses to the other pictures is no longer significant in the condition with imagery instructions. This suggests that the notion of differential activation during semantic processing of sentences must be complemented by the notion of differential facilitation through imagery, as a function of the initial rate of activation. However, the additional amount of activation resulting from imagery does not greatly favour those aspects of meaning on which the reader is already centring.

Obviously, in the reading condition without any imagery instructions, this experiment cannot evaluate the role of imagery in the centring process itself. It is likely that visualization of the scene is a spontaneous activity for individuals who are high imagers, and it can be assumed that for these subjects, the part of the image which corresponds to the feature on which centration is performed (the most activated part) has greater subjective vividness or clarity than the other parts. The notion of degree of 'resolution' of the different parts of a visual image is well documented (cf. Kosslyn, 1980). This reflects the subjective component resulting from differential activation applied to a mental representation.

What then is the incidence of instructions expressly inviting subjects to visualize the scene? It is likely that for subjects spontaneously inclined to elaborate images even in the absence of instructions, these instructions (which are expected to increase clarity or vividness of their images) have no such effects on the part of the image which is already at maximum activation. The 'peripheral' parts of the image – i.e., those which are activated less

– benefit from additional processing, and reach as high a level of activation (or almost as high) as the 'central' part of the image. In sum, the gains derived from imagery are only detectable for those parts of the representation which were the less actively processed initially. Lastly, this approach is compatible with the notion of some ceiling of activation: with imagery instructions, response times to both types of probes apparently attain their minimum values.

The above remarks do not imply that imagery only intervenes during comprehension when subjects are explicitly instructed to form images. Imagery, obviously, can be implemented by some readers without such instructions, and this is more likely the case when sentences have highly figural semantic content. However, imagery should be considered as an additional event that extends semantic processing. Semantic processing is governed by the principles of cognitive centration and differential activation. Additional imagery activity spontaneously produced by readers will be most likely brought to bear on the fraction of semantic information on which centration is performed. Imagery elicited by instructions extends activation to those parts which have only been activated slightly.

6.4 Figural information and the processing of descriptive sentences

In this last section, I return more specifically to a notion which was introduced in the previous section: the activation of figural components of representations constructed during semantic processing. The issue of how figural information is expressed in the representation of descriptive sentences was investigated in a series of studies (Dubois and Denis, 1988; see also Denis and Dubois, 1987). This series also touched on the issue of spontaneous instantiation of general terms in sentences, and aimed at relating the instantiation process with hypotheses on the organization of knowledge in memory. Here, I shall focus on the data relevant to the issue of how figural information is represented.

The experimental situation, as above, used a variant on the sentence–picture comparison paradigm. Subjects first read a sentence describing a scene in which several objects were interacting. After this sentence, subjects were presented briefly with a noun from the sentence. Then, the picture of an object was presented, and subjects were to judge whether it was an appropriate illustration of the noun. Responses were given by pressing one of two buttons (one for positive items, one for negative items). The hypothesis was that the time for responding to positive items depends on the similarity between the picture and the mental representation constructed by the reader. A picture whose figural content is congruent with the representation that the reader has constructed of the mentioned object should elicit faster responses than a picture having some characteristics which are discrepant with the representation constructed by the reader.

This is an example of a sentence used in this experiment: '*A majestic swan was gliding silently on the pond in the park*'. The picture presented after the sentence was designed to elicit positive responses for half of the subjects and negative responses for the other half. Two pictures were designed to elicit positive responses. In one case, the picture represented a typical instance of the object (a white swan; see Drawing A, Figure 6.4); in the other case, the picture represented a non-typical exemplar (a black swan, Drawing B). Both pictures were expected to elicit positive responses, since both were likely to illustrate the sentence presented previously.

A   B

C   D

Figure 6.4 Sample of the materials used in the experiments

For the whole set of materials used in this experiment, responses to A drawings were significantly shorter than responses to B drawings (Figure 6.5a). This finding is easy to interpret if it is assumed that in individuals' long-term memory, the representation of an object is composed of the features which characterize the most typical instances of this conceptual category (cf. Rosch, 1975). The representation that most individuals in our culture have of swans includes in particular the feature WHITE. When a subject activates the SWAN concept, the feature WHITE – which is likely to have a high rank in the hierarchy of the features composing the concept – is activated. When a subject is presented with a picture of a typical swan, matching is practically instantaneous between the features of the activated representation and the figural properties shown in the picture. In contrast, when the subject is presented with a picture of a black swan, matching is discrepant for one feature of the conceptual representation. Individuals' semantic memory, however, contains knowledge about the existence of black swans. Although we cannot hypothesize here on how this piece of knowledge is linked to the representation of typical swans (if this is the case), the additional processing required for deciding that, albeit black, a black swan has properties that make it a valid argument in the sentence is reflected by the significant increase in response times.

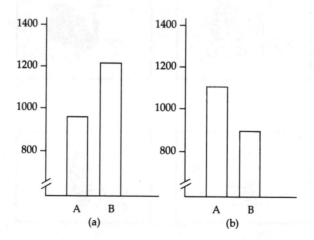

Figure 6.5 Mean correct response times (ms) for positive items (a) and negative items (b).

However, this increase might purely depend on the greater difficulty of *identifying* pictures of unfamiliar objects. Response times include a component which reflects the process of perceptual identification of the picture, and this process differs from the component reflecting the matching between the picture and the transiently activated mental representation. Control experiments consisted in measuring times for perceptual identification of pictures (without previous presentation of sentences). These controls show that perceptual recognition for B drawings tends to be slightly, but not significantly, longer than for A drawings (58 ms). This difference is far smaller than the difference between response times in the main experiment (245 ms). This shows that the longer time required for the processing of B drawings, in the task which consists in judging whether they can illustrate the sentence previously read, cannot be explained by their lesser identifiability, but essentially by the greater difficulty of their matching with mental representations reflecting typical instances of objects.

In this experiment, two other kinds of drawings were included to elicit negative responses. These drawings were selected to emphasize the figural components present in the representations activated during reading. In both cases, the subjects were given another exemplar of the category to which the object belonged, but this exemplar could not be a valid argument in the sentence for the target word. In one case, it was an object whose physical appearance was very close to that of the typical object illustrated by Drawing A. In the example we have been discussing, Drawing C in Figure 6.4 shows a goose, that is, a bird whose figural appearance is similar to that of the typical swan in many respects (white, long neck, etc.). In the other case, the object had a physical appearance which was totally dissimilar to that of Drawing A. In our example, Drawing D was that of a bird visually quite different from swans, namely, an owl.

For negative items, response times for C drawings were significantly longer than for D drawings (Figure 6.5b). This is coherent if when presented with a C drawing, subjects are assumed to process salient figural properties which belong to the representation constructed from the sentence and orient them towards a positive response. Actually, subjects must ignore this figural similarity and engage in further processing of the properties displayed in the C drawing. This additional processing is reflected in the increase of response times in comparison with the case where figural features in the representation constructed from the sentence are distinct from those from the processing of the D drawing. Here again, perceptual identification of C and D drawings is not responsible for the difference in response times. A control experiment shows that their identification times are highly comparable.

The fact that response times were overall longer for C than for D drawings clearly suggests that the representation constructed by subjects during sentence reading contains figural information related to the concepts mentioned. Transient activation of figural features of the SWAN conceptual representation is a process which must be assumed to exist to account for the differential processing of A and B drawings, as well as C and D drawings. Activation of figural features, as mentioned at the end of the previous section, may be 'prolonged' for some subjects by the generation of a visual image where these figural features are depicted. Such imagery activity, during sentence reading, is even more likely in that it is a strategy adapted to the demands of the situation. Visual images generated by readers when they wait for the target picture should be seen as an additional cognitive activity that enriches the semantic representation of the sentence and renders it optimal for comparison with the upcoming pictorial stimulus. It is therefore relevant to conjecture about the sensitivity of this spontaneous imagery activity to experimentally induced procedures designed either to increase or decrease the probability of its implementation.

In a further experiment, three conditions were examined: (*a*) in a visual distraction condition, during the interval preceding the presentation of the drawing, subjects were involved in a perceptual task expected to interfere with the imagery they might have implemented (this interfering task consisted in visual tracking of a line in a complex pattern); (*b*) in a visual imagery condition, subjects were explicitly asked to form a visual image of the scene described by the sentence (this requirement was expected to increase the probability that subjects would generate a visual representation of the semantic content of the sentence); (*c*) in a control condition, subjects were tested as in the previous experiment (only the interval preceding picture onset was modified to be adjusted to that of the other two conditions).

As concerns responses to both positive and negative items, response times were slightly shorter in the visual imagery condition than in the control condition, although not significantly. On the other hand, the visual distraction condition elicited much longer response times than the control condition. Overall, responses were faster for A than for B drawings, and slower for C than for D drawings, in similar proportions across conditions.

The close similarity of data in the control and imagery conditions strongly suggests that imagery is already operational in the control condition, even in the absence of imagery instructions. On the other hand, the distraction condition clearly shows the interference effect of visual distraction on imagery processes.

Overall, the findings from these experiments provide arguments for the assumption that in semantic processing of descriptive concrete sentences, the figural content of these sentences is expressed in the representation built up by the reader, and this is even more apparent when the upcoming task requires a decision which implies processing of figural information. In this respect, the sentence–picture comparison paradigm highlights the preparatory function of visual imagery, as a strategy facilitating the processing of upcoming figural information. The role of visual imagery in perceptual preparation has been demonstrated repeatedly (cf. Farah, 1985, 1989; Klatzky and Martin, 1983; Peterson and Graham, 1974). The present findings suggest that the semantic processing of descriptive sentences can generate cognitive events which possess a genuine figural content, and which can be implemented in the preparation of upcoming decisions on perceptual events.

6.5 Conclusion

The processing of descriptive sentences is the prime locus for evidencing some of the most interesting properties of conceptual representations hypothesized in the preceding chapter. What emerges is that the activation of a conceptual representation may only touch on a fraction of it. Selective activation, first shown in situations where isolated words are involved in 'oriented' semantic analysis, is also evidenced in situations where subjects process complex statements, and where their cognitive set towards one part of the representation is manipulated by sentential context. This part of the representation may show an extremely high level of activation, which is not significantly increased by additional imagery activity. On the other hand, imagery significantly increases the rate of activation of the other parts of the representation, those with initial lower activation.

Overall, there are valid reasons for believing that when readers process a sentence about an object with the expectation of further judging a picture illustrating this sentence, readers engage in selective activation of figural features of the conceptual representation for this object. The content of the transient representation activated by readers is partly determined by the organization of their knowledge in long-term memory. Thus, the figural components which are actually activated correspond to those belonging to the most typical instances of the concept. These assumptions regarding the activation of the figural part of the concept are supported by the fact that when readers are required to form images intentionally, their judgements on pictures are not strongly affected. Spontaneous imagery could thus play a significant role in the processing of descriptive sentences followed by a decision on pictorial material.

The analyses presented here were conducted in a 'general psychology' perspective. However, I mentioned that individual characteristics can orient some subjects towards more extensive processing of figural aspects. This brings us once again to the idea that in the absence of instructions, the implementation of imagery activity varies across individuals. Little mention has been made of individual differences in the relationships of imagery to language comprehension. These variables were taken into account in a further set of studies reported in the next chapter, which extends my approach of language processing to more complex linguistic materials, namely, texts.

7 Imagery and Text Processing

Since the late 1970s, considerable attention has been paid to the analysis of processes involved in the comprehension and memory for texts (e.g., van Dijk and Kintsch, 1983; Kintsch and van Dijk, 1978). Analysis of processing units and processes operating on these units has mainly been conducted through propositional approaches where the units composing the 'text-base' are seen as predicative semantic structures (or 'propositions'), which are usually chunked into higher-order structures (or 'macrostructures'). The issue of imagery activity concomitant to the semantic processing of texts remained marginal in these studies.

However, it is a matter of fact that many people report that they form visual representations of the characters, objects and events when reading texts. Is this activity inherent to the construction of text meaning? Or is it autonomous with respect to the processes which construct meaning? Is imagery a requisite process for elaborating the semantic (propositional) representation of text? Or is semantic processing first, and are images optional expressions of propositions?

These questions were foreign to research on comprehension and memory for texts for a long period of time. They basically were concerns for imagery researchers, who mainly investigated them in sentence comprehension paradigms. However, in the last few years, text processing research has been more inclined to examine how readers build representations of the 'situations' described by texts (distinct from the propositional text-base). Assumptions concerning the role of 'mental models' (Garnham, 1981; Johnson-Laird, 1983) or 'situation models' (Kintsch, 1986; Perrig and Kintsch, 1985) in text comprehension prompted renewed interest in activities such as visual imagery in text research. It is only very recently that the interactions between imagery research and text comprehension research have proved to be not only possible, but productive and mutually beneficial (see Denis, 1984b).

7.1 Imagery value and memory for narratives

One of the first methods for studying the role of imagery in the processing of texts consisted in varying the imagery value of words in texts. For instance, two versions of a narrative are constructed, which only differ for choice of adjectives. In one version, the adjectives modifying nouns refer to properties that are easy to express in a visual image. In the other version, these adjectives are replaced by others referring to abstract properties that are less easily expressed in a visual image. One version, for instance, uses the terms *'muscular longshoremen'* or *'bronze sunlight'*, the other refers to *'competent longshoremen'* or *'adequate sunlight'* in the corresponding sentences (Hiscock, 1976). The analysis then consists in comparing recall for the two sets of adjectives.

Experiments relying on this methodology typically show superior recall for versions with high imagery adjectives. In immediate recall, these versions elicit higher recall of the nouns to which these adjectives were associated (DeVito and Olson, 1973; Kirchner, 1969). High imagery adjectives are themselves better recalled than low imagery adjectives (DeVito and Olson, 1973; Hiscock, 1976; Morris and Reid, 1972). These experiments thus show the differential capacities of some lexical items to be coded imaginally during reading, which makes them more available at retrieval.

Another approach consists in testing memory for different paragraphs (or different passages in the same text) as a function of their concreteness. Recall is usually higher for concrete than for abstract passages (Johnson, 1974; Philipchalk, 1972; Yuille and Paivio, 1969). In addition, some other characteristics of paragraphs can combine with the effects of imagery, such as their specificity, comprehensibility or interest (Johnson, 1974).

7.2 Imagery activity and memory for texts

Another experimental paradigm used in research on imagery and text memory consists in eliciting some imagery activity on the part of readers, usually by instructions requiring them to visualize in a detailed fashion each piece of information in the text (in a narrative, this would be the scenes, the characters, what they are doing, where and how). Subjects are then tested for recall or recognition, and their scores are compared to those of control subjects who did not receive any imagery instructions. Bear in mind that use of this procedure does not imply that experimenters believe they are comparing a condition *with* and a condition *without* imagery. In the absence of imagery instructions, some subjects may spontaneously visualize the situations and events described in the text. Thus, the control condition is not free from effects attributable to imagery. Simply, in the condition with instructions, the experimenters strengthen the probability that subjects will implement an imagery strategy, whereas in the condition without instructions, this probability is assumed to be lower.

In general, implementation of imagery in reading, when induced by appropriate instructions, significantly favours text retention (Anderson and Kulhavy, 1972; Giesen and Peeck, 1984; Perrig, 1986; Rasco, Tennyson and Boutwell, 1975). Memory is usually tested in sentence verification tasks or tasks requiring the recall of specific information in the text. The effects of imagery are observed both when questions are about pieces of information explicitly presented in the text, and about information which was inferred by readers. Lastly, imagery activity facilitates responding to questions about concrete and spatial pieces of information, whereas recall of abstract information is not facilitated (Giesen and Peeck, 1984).

An especially interesting finding concerns the differential effects of visual imagery on text memory as a function of mode of presentation (written vs. oral). When subjects have been instructed to visualize the content of each episode of a narrative, the positive effects of these instructions are more marked when subjects *listened* to the text than when they *read* it (Levin and Divine-Hawkins, 1974; see also Maher and Sullivan, 1982). One plausible explanation is that visual imagery requires the implementation of the same part of the visual system that is also tapped during reading. When subjects listen to a text, their visual processing system is fully available for translating verbal information into visual images. On the other hand, simultaneous management of the two activities by the same system increases cognitive load, and restricts system efficiency in the encoding of information (cf. Brooks, 1970).

Although the positive effects of imagery on text memory are well documented, interpretation of these effects remains open to discussion. Two main factors are thought to account for imagery efficiency. First, as was mentioned before, imagery is a process which enables supplementary encoding of semantic information extracted from texts by readers. Semantic processing, which is responsible for storage of abstract, propositional representations, is 'extended' by the activity which consists in forming representations having structural properties similar to those of perceptual events. Thus, the readers not only store the end-product of semantic processing in a propositional format, but also store the end-product of additional processing, in the form of imaginal representations.

Furthermore, images are representations which rather than collections of disparate objects generally reflect structured sets displaying the interactions among these objects. The images formed by readers of narrative or descriptive texts combine meaningful elements into highly integrated configurations with high internal organization. There is a number of experimental arguments that visual imagery as a mode of representation is especially suited to the combination of meaningful units and the encoding of complex scenes which reflect the interactions among a set of objects (cf. Beech and Allport, 1978; Begg, 1978; Bower, 1971; Paivio and Begg, 1981). In as much as imagery is a process that makes it possible to integrate units of information and maintain them in highly organized structures, it is a factor for increased efficiency of mnemonic encoding, since retrieval of one unit is likely to direct subjects to other associated units in the configuration.

Another critical question also calls for examination. Do some aspects of text-processing benefit more from imagery than others? The facilitating effects of imagery have been demonstrated primarily for rather short texts containing a small number of episodes. However, one of the core concepts in the literature on text processing is that of hierarchized structural levels of text meaning. Has imagery any role to play at levels situated higher than the episode level?

Perrig (1986) collected data showing that during the processing of a narrative, visual imagery contributes highly to the encoding of 'microstructures' (such as sentences), but that it has no direct connection with the processes responsible for thematic storage of text. It is likely that the macrostructure of a text, which only contains the more general ideas of the text, is essentially made up of elements with low figural value, such as those expressing causal relationships, motives, mental states, etc., which cannot be directly expressed in visual images. Hence, imagery is not assumed to contribute significantly to the building of the macrostructure. On the other hand, the encoding of text microstructures (for instance, the particular action of an agent on a given object, as described in one sentence of the text) benefits greatly from visual imagery, inasmuch as imagery provides figuration of topological or functional relationships among persons and objects in an integrated visual form. These ideas can be paralleled to Marschark's (1985) claim that in memory for prose, imagery has the most potent effects when context is at a minimum (as in word or sentence lists). On the contrary, the effects of imagery are less pronounced when the linguistic units to be processed are presented in context (e.g., sentences in paragraphs) (see also Marschark *et al.*, 1991).

7.3 Individual imagery differences

Another method for investigating the effects of imagery on text-processing consists in taking individual imagery differences into account. The experimental situation is the same for all subjects. All receive the same reading instructions, which do not refer to imagery. The experiment then consists in comparing performance of subjects who have a strong tendency to form visual images in the course of their cognitive activities and subjects who are not inclined to visualize.

Chapter 2 referred to psychometric techniques for the measurement of individual imagery differences. Research in this field shows that individual characteristics have an effect on the execution of tasks requiring the formation and manipulation of visual images (cf. Denis, 1990a; Ernest, 1977). Within the range of studies where subjects have to memorize verbal information, several experiments have shown that subjects with high imagery capacities perform better than other subjects (Ernest, 1977; Ernest and Paivio, 1971; Hishitani, 1985). Individual imagery differences are thus worth being considered in the investigation of complex verbal materials. They can shed light on the role of imagery in comprehension and memory for texts.

A few studies have explored the effects of individual imagery characteristics on memorization of texts. Two studies were conducted by Riding and Taylor (1976) and Riding and Calvey (1981) on children aged seven to eleven. A distinction was made along a dimension considered by the authors as bipolar between subjects mainly oriented towards visual imagery and those more prone to encode information verbally. When subjects were invited to read concrete prose passages that were extremely likely to elicit visual images, recall scores were higher for visualizers than for verbal coders. Conversely, verbal coders surpassed visualizers in recall of abstract passages. These findings suggest that as early as seven, and perhaps before, there are differentiated 'cognitive styles' in children, which are likely to be reflected in the ways subjects process text information.

My investigations in this field are presented below. These were conducted with adult subjects. In these studies, individual imagery characteristics were evaluated with Marks' (1973) Vividness of Visual Imagery Questionnaire (VVIQ). This questionnaire has been widely used in imagery research. While the findings of some studies based on the VVIQ remain inconclusive (Berger and Gaunitz, 1979; McKelvie and Rohrberg, 1978), responses to this questionnaire have been found to predict performance in a number of tasks designed to tap visual imagery (Finke and Kosslyn, 1980; Finke and Schmidt, 1978; Gur and Hilgard, 1975; Hishitani, 1985; McKelvie and Demers, 1979; Marks, 1973, 1977).

The questionnaire consists in verbal descriptions of scenes that the respondents must evoke in the form of visual images. Subjects are then required to report the vividness of their images on a five-point rating scale. The expectation is that subjects who tend to report more vivid imagery on the questionnaire (or 'high imagers') will be more likely to generate visual images of text content than subjects reporting non-vivid imagery (or 'low imagers').

7.4 Imagery and the recognition of words from a narrative

The general aim of the experiments reported below was to identify differences in the processing of texts resulting from readers' individual imagery characteristics. In the first experiment (Chaguiboff and Denis, 1981), subjects who had read a narrative were involved in a recognition task for words which had been presented in the text. The two measures were the number of correct responses and the recognition latencies. An item that is efficiently encoded in memory is not only likely to be recognized correctly, but also more rapidly. For this reason, we expected that readers who formed visual images for some lexical units in the text and therefore had a memory representation of these units that was more 'available' after reading, should show better recognition of these units than subjects who did not activate these units in the form of visual images while reading.

In this experiment, items were presented for recognition either in the form of written words or in the form of drawings. Our first expectation was to confirm the typical phenomenon of longer recognition latencies for pictures than for words when learning involved verbal material (cf. Denis and Colonelli, 1976). Moreover, a specific hypothesis concerned the magnitude of this difference as a function of individual imagery characteristics. If a recognition response results from perceived similarity between the stimulus proposed for recognition and a memory representation for the corresponding stimulus, recognition of an item presented in the form of a drawing should be easier, and thus faster, for subjects who activated an imaginal representation of this unit during learning. For this reason, we expected subjects with most vivid imagery to be at less of a disadvantage than the other subjects in the recognition of pictures.

Adult subjects read a 2,000-word narrative at their own pace, and were only informed that they would subsequently have to answer questions about the text. The text told the story of a car ride, with numerous episodes describing various characters, scenes and events. Sixteen subject–verb–object sentences were inserted in the text. For half, the target word – that is, the word that would be later tested for recognition – was the grammatical subject; for the other half, it was the grammatical object. All the target words were concrete, high imagery nouns.

After reading, subjects were visually presented with thirty-two items, either in the form of written nouns for half of the subjects or outline drawings for the other half. These items included the sixteen target items (i.e., words which were in the text, therefore calling for positive recognition responses) and sixteen distractors (calling for negative responses). During the recognition task, subjects were required to respond by pressing one of two buttons ('yes' or 'no'), which interrupted a timer that was started at the onset of the item. At the end of the experiment, subjects had to complete the VVIQ, which served to distinguish 'high' from 'low' imagers' above and below the median of the VVIQ scores.

For the whole set of subjects, recognition scores were roughly similar for nouns and pictures. However, recognition latencies appeared to be very sensitive to the experimental variables. Overall, recognition for nouns was faster than recognition for pictures.

Figures 7.1 and 7.2 show the mean number and mean latencies for correct recognitions, respectively, distinguishing high and low imagers' responses. Overall, high imagers gave more correct responses than low imagers, and their recognition latencies were significantly shorter for both positive and negative items. This finding suggests that imagery spontaneously developed by high imagers during reading may have activated representations which remained available for the processing of a further task (the recognition task).

Furthermore, in low imagers, correct recognition for nouns elicited significantly shorter latencies than pictures, whereas high imagers did not exhibit this noun–picture difference. This finding reveals that the relative difficulty of recognizing a picture as compared to the recognizing of a noun is greatly reduced in the most vivid imagers. These subjects are thus in a better position than the others for maintaining representations which are easily accessed by a pictorial stimulus in memory. The representations constructed by low imagers, on the contrary, are likely to have lesser figural content. Our findings thus strengthen the assumption

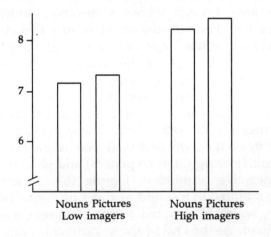

Figure 7.1 Mean correct recognition scores for positive items, for high and low imagers.

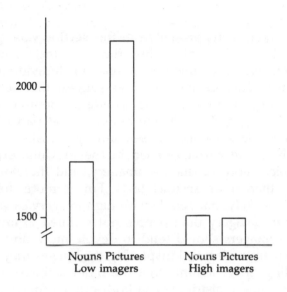

2000 –

1500 –

| Nouns Pictures | Nouns Pictures |
| Low imagers | High imagers |

Figure 7.2 Mean correct recognition latencies for positive items (ms), for high and low imagers.

that there are differences in the encoding processes implemented by high and low imagers during reading, the former being more prone than the latter to elaborate visual images for narrative episodes.

The assumption of additional processing on the part of high imagers was confirmed by the analysis of subjects' reading times. During the experiment, the time spontaneously devoted by subjects to reading the text was recorded. It turned out that high imagers devoted significantly longer times to reading than low imagers (with a difference of about +10 per cent). Moreover, the correlation between imagery characteristics (as reflected by VVIQ scores) and reading times was positive and significant. This result can be accounted for by assuming that total reading time includes a component that is devoted to elaborating and maintaining visual images (in fact, the sum of microcomponents distributed all along the reading period), and that high imagers spend longer on these processes than low imagers when they read texts likely to elicit imagery. The difference between high and low imagers' reading times suggests a relationship between the availability of memory representations at recognition and the formation of visual images during the processing of text.

7.5 Imagery, reading time and memory for narratives

The set of experiments presented in this section was specifically devoted to the analysis of reading times for texts conducive to imagery activity, as a function of readers' individual imagery characteristics. The previous findings suggest that between the beginning and end of text reading, a certain amount of activity is devoted to imaging. Even if one assumes that part of imagery activity takes place parallel to semantic processing, some text types, such as the narrative used in the previous experiment, probably elicit more substantial imagery, and therefore call for more time, than more abstract texts. Furthermore, for a given narrative, it is likely that people with high imagery capacities will develop more imagery than people not inclined to image. As a result, high imagers should tend to devote more time than low imagers to maintaining and inspecting the images they construct while reading. If we assume that the other abilities involved in reading are equally distributed in both groups (perceptual abilities, visual decoding of letter strings, abilities in semantic analysis, previous knowledge, etc.), then the longer time devoted to imagery activity should be reflected in longer total reading times for high imagers.

In this new set of experiments (Denis, 1982c) a new narrative was used. Its length was approximately the same as the previous one. It told the story of a farmer who rides to a village to sell his crops and then meets with a series of incidents travelling home. After reading, subjects completed a two-alternative forced-choice test on characters and events discussed in the text. Following the experiment, subjects completed the VVIQ.

When high and low imagers were compared, the former spontaneously took significantly longer to read than the latter (for this text, on the order of +14 per cent, and even +24 per cent when analysis was restricted to subjects in the most extreme quartiles). In addition, high imagers also obtained significantly higher scores on the memory test of text content (Figure 7.3). This result provides support for the inference that high imagers did in fact spontaneously engage in more imagery activity during reading than low imagers, and that the extra time devoted to reading by high imagers at least partly reflects the extra imagery processing they developed when reading highly imageable material. Further arguments in favour of this interpretation come from the studies reported in Chapter 4 on differential strategies implemented for comparing sentences and pictures. Subjects who compare the picture to a visual representation of the content described by the sentence are those who both devote longer than the others to the reading of sentences and exhibit the highest visuospatial capacities (cf. MacLeod, Hunt and Mathews, 1978).

A control experiment was devised in order to evaluate the potential claim that high imagers have longer reading times simply because they are slow readers in general. If this was the case, then high imagers should systematically tend to devote longer times than low imagers to reading any text, and a difference in reading times should still be observed even for texts unlikely to elicit any images.

The experiment was thus repeated, but subjects now read an abstract text instead of the previous one. The text was on objective vs. subjective approaches in psychology. It consisted only of abstract sentences that were unlikely to elicit any visual images. Results showed that high and low imagers did not differ in their reading times for this highly abstract, non-imageable text. Furthermore, there was no difference between both groups on the retention test administered after reading (Figure 7.4). Thus, the differences in reading times for the narrative text genuinely reflect differences in the time devoted to imagery activity. On the whole,

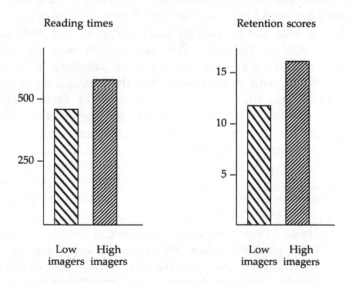

Figure 7.3 Reading times (s) and retention scores for high and low imagers (narrative text).

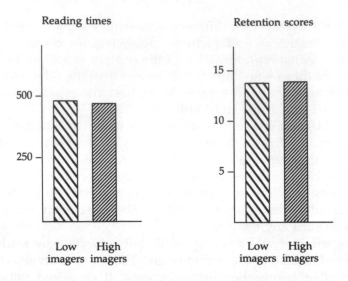

Figure 7.4 Reading times (s) and retention scores for high and low imagers (abstract text).

it seems warranted to conclude that individual imagery charac-teristics affect the processing of verbal material only in so far as this material is likely to elicit visual imagery.

Additional experiments were performed with the purpose of influencing imaginal processing during text reading through very simple instructional manipulations, and observing their effects on both reading times and memory for text. A new sample of subjects was presented with the previously used narrative and instructed to read it as fast as possible. The assumption was that such instructions would create special cognitive constraints on the processing of text, and in particular that they would incite high imagers to decrease the amount or frequency of their imagery activity. On the other hand, the shortening of reading times should be less marked, and perhaps should not occur, in low imagers, who spontaneously devote little time to imaging.

The findings were in line with expectations. Whereas low im-agers' reading times were not significantly shortened, high imagers 'gained' 26 per cent of reading time in comparison with the self-paced reading condition, and their reading times were even slightly shorter than those of low imagers. This result, however, does not allow us to infer precisely *when* high imagers save time in fast reading conditions. One may assume that if they still construct images, they tend to decrease the time spent constructing them. In addition, they may shorten the length of time that they maintain images. However, because the time to generate images is typically much shorter than the time spent maintaining them (cf. Cocude and Denis, 1988), it is likely that decreased time in maintaining images is the main factor behind the decrease in total reading times in high imagers in this experiment.

Perhaps the most interesting finding in this fast reading condition emerged from the analysis of retention scores. High imagers obtained higher scores than low imagers, as in the experiment with normal reading conditions. This was true even though high imagers had significantly shorter reading times. Further, their scores did not differ from those following the self-paced reading condition. Thus, a sizeable part of imagery activity can be eliminated in high imagers without any apparent detrimental effects on text memory. This may be due to the fact that at least some portion of imagery activity developed during reading by high imagers is not specifically directed towards information encoding. Further, it suggests that memory superiority of high over low imagers, as demonstrated in the first experiment, is not simply a consequence of high imagers' longer reading times. Lastly, the similarity in high imagers' recognition scores despite presumed lowering of their imagery activity is compatible with the hypothesis of better mnemonic 'productivity' in these subjects as compared with low imagers.

The final experiment of this series explored the effects of instructing subjects to read while constructing visual images of characters and events for every sentence of the text. Imagery instructions produced an overall increase in total reading times, attributable to the increase in time devoted to imaging proper. However, while this increase was only 19 per cent for high imagers (as compared with the self-paced reading times), the increase was 40 per cent for low imagers. The reading behaviour of high imagers, who bring imagery into play considerably even in the absence of instructions, was thus affected by these instructions in much lower proportions than the reading behaviour of low imagers. For the latter subjects, who spontaneously image little, imagery instructions had the most impact. Finally, the total reading times of low imagers were overall very close to those of high imagers. Furthermore, imagery instructions significantly improved retention scores, primarily in low imagers, who reached a performance level comparable to that of high imagers.

To conclude, in conditions that simulate spontaneous reading, individual imagery characteristics significantly influence the temporal course of text processing. High imagers seem to be inclined to use their imagery abilities when they read a text likely to elicit images, and this imagery activity is reflected in extra reading times. Several interpretations of this effect remain possible. One interpretation mentioned earlier is that although all subjects construct images equally frequently, high imagers tend to maintain their images longer than low imagers do. An alternative and compatible interpretation is that high imagers build more complex images, or images richer in detail, thus requiring further elaboration, which would be reflected by extra time. A third possibility, which contrasts with the first interpretation, is that low imagers simply do not construct images as often as high imagers. Further research is needed in order to test the relative validity of these explanations.

Individual differences in imagery abilities also have significant effects on memory for information extracted from the text, with high imagers having higher retention scores. However, the relationship between imagery abilities and memory is not a simple one since high imagers are able to eliminate a sizeable part of their imagery activity without significant impairment of retention. This means that imagery activity developed by high imagers in spontaneous reading conditions can be reduced without severely affecting memorization. This result raises the question of the role of spontaneous imagery in mnemonic encoding. At least some part of imagery activity developed during prose reading is not specifically directed toward memorization. This makes sense, given that in daily psychological life there are imagery activities whose functions are not easy to characterize, unless they are related to a kind of homeostasis of the mind (as is the case for daydreaming) (see also Kosslyn *et al.*, 1990b). These activities are distinct from imagery activities with definite cognitive purposes (e.g., imagery that accompanies perceptual anticipation, search in memory for figural information, spatial problem solving, etc.). Probably some part of imagery elicited by narratives is not clearly 'goal-directed'.

However, imagery is not simply a free-running process. Imagery remains a prime instrument for encoding figural information and therefore must be considered as one of the *cognitive strategies* aimed at maximizing the probability of information encoding and storage. This role is evident in the very last experiment, in which individuals who are not inclined to produce images spontaneously are able to develop an imagery activity when instructed to do so (which is clear from the lengthening of reading times) and thereby benefit from this since their retention scores reach the same high level as high imagers' scores.

7.6 Imagery and the processing of descriptive texts

The first generation of cognitive research on text-processing focused on narratives. This state of affairs resulted from the initial specific interest of text linguistics in narration, for instance folk-tales. Narratives inevitably became the first type of text which attracted psychologists dealing with text comprehension and memorization. There are, however, a number of other text types, and many which are likely to elicit imagery during reading. The first text type examined below is character description.

In this set of studies (Denis, 1987), subjects were invited to read four texts describing imaginary characters (Adrien, a lumberjack, Sylvia, an air hostess, etc.). Each text was two pages long. The descriptions contained highly concrete as well as less concrete passages. The highly concrete passages described the physical features of the characters and were expected to elicit substantial imagery. The moderately concrete passages were about the psychological and moral features of the characters, and were not likely to evoke images. The order of presentation of both types of passages was counterbalanced across texts and across subjects.

As in the previous experiments, reading times were recorded. Contrary to the previous set of experiments, a within-subject design was used. All subjects were first tested in self-paced reading conditions for two texts. They were instructed to read in an ordinary fashion, at their own pace, without rereading. When the subjects had finished reading these two texts, they received one of three sets of instructions. One group of subjects was simply told to read the two other texts as before. The second group was instructed to read the texts as fast as possible, so as to reach the end of each text in as short a time as possible. The third group of subjects was instructed to elaborate as detailed and vivid visual images as possible for characters, actions, and scenes presented in the texts. At the end of the experiment, all subjects completed a test designed to assess their memory of text content.

The subjects who participated in this experiment were classified as high or low imagers (above and below group median on the VVIQ). On the whole, high imagers' spontaneous reading times were significantly longer than low imagers' times (+9 per cent when considering the whole sample; +20 per cent when contrasting the VVIQ scorers in the most extreme quartiles). This finding confirms results from previous experiments. It supports the assumption that extra processing is implemented by readers who are prone to elaborate visual images from verbal descriptions.

After fast reading instructions, subjects on the average showed a significant decrease in their reading times. The decrease was significantly greater in high than in low imagers. As a result, with fast reading instructions, both high and low imagers had extremely comparable reading times (Figure 7.5a). This finding, which replicates the effect found in the previous experiment, holds for both highly and moderately concrete passages.

After visual imagery instructions, subjects on the average showed a significant increase in their reading times. High and low imagers did not significantly differ from each other in reading times (Figure 7.5b). Detailed analysis showed that this increase was greater in low than in high imagers, but this was essentially due to times for the most concrete passages. While the reading time increase was similar for all passages in high imagers, the increase was much more pronounced for the most concrete

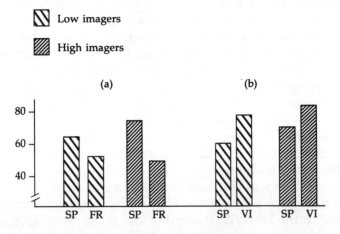

Figure 7.5 Mean reading times per page (s) of high and low imagers first involved in self-paced (SP) reading conditions, then either submitted to fast reading (FR) instructions (a) or visual imagery (VI) instructions (b)
Source: Denis (1987)

passages in low imagers. These findings suggest that people who are not inclined to form images spontaneously are nevertheless able to implement imagery when they are instructed to do so, but that this implementation is easier for them when it concerns materials that are conducive to visual imagery.

Analysis of retention scores shows that overall high imagers had higher scores than low imagers in the self-paced reading condition. As in the previous experiment, a likely explanation is that high imagers' higher memory performance results from additional processing while reading (additional processing which is at least partially reflected by reading times).

When subjects read with fast reading instructions, there was an overall decrease in retention scores. However, as in the previous set of experiments, retention scores remained substantially higher in high as compared to low imagers (Figure 7.6a). This finding suggests that although they are placed under temporal constraints which limit the implementation of imagery, high imagers remain able to perform memory encoding more efficiently than low imagers.

Visual imagery instructions resulted overall in significantly higher retention scores (Figure 7.6b). More detailed analysis,

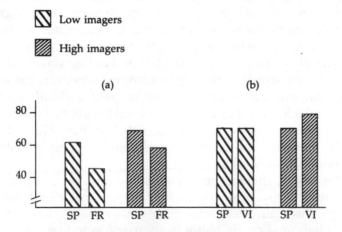

Figure 7.6 Mean retention scores (percentage correct) of high and low imagers first involved in self-paced (SP) reading conditions, then either submitted to fast reading (FR) instructions (a) or visual imagery (VI) instructions (b)
Source: Denis (1987)

however, reveals that this effect was essentially concentrated in the highly concrete passages. For these passages, both high and low imagers had the highest retention scores. When these scores are compared against those in the self-paced reading condition, the score increase is significant for high imagers, but not for low imagers. In other words, high imagers reveal through their retention scores that they indeed responded to imagery instructions. In contrast, low imagers, who also responded to these instructions (as attested to by their increased reading times) did not derive the same benefit from the additional processing they engaged in. As concerns the items corresponding to moderately concrete passages, high imagers showed a slight increase in their retention scores, whereas a slight decrease was observed in low imagers. The effect of imagery instructions on encoding was thus mainly found for those parts of the texts which lent themselves best to visualization.

To sum up, these experiments show that (a) in naturalistic reading conditions (as natural as possible in the context of an experiment), high imagers are involved in extra processing (presumably imagery) as compared with low imagers; this extra processing favours the encoding of additional information, as is revealed by retention scores, which are higher for high imagers; (b) in conditions where constraints are imposed in order to lower the degree of implementation of visual imagery, memory encoding is impaired in both groups, but high imagers show a greater capacity to overcome the effects of these constraints; (c) in conditions where subjects are explicitly encouraged to use visual imagery, both groups show through their reading times that they indeed take these instructions into account; however, the effects on retention scores are clearer in high imagers, and only for those passages which were the easiest to visualize; slight facilitation is shown for low imagers, who apparently are less able to benefit from the imaginal processing developed to comply with the instructions.

On the whole, these experiments show that low imagers draw only limited gain from processing based on visual imagery (although this gain was more clear-cut in the previous experiments). High imagers do better in comparison to low imagers not only in spontaneous reading conditions, but also in conditions with strong constraints (such as fast reading). They also perform better when they are invited to use the reading strategy that they would in any case have implemented spontaneously.

7.7 The processing of texts describing spatial configurations

More recently, research has focused on another type of descriptive text, i.e., texts describing spatial configurations. Descriptive texts are structurally different from narratives, and have been shown to elicit different types of processing (cf. Einstein *et al.*, 1990; Kintsch and Young, 1984; McDaniel *et al.*, 1986). The role of visual imagery in the processing of spatial descriptions, however, has not received a great deal of empirical interest. Nevertheless, assumptions regarding this role are substantiated by a number of observations and experimental studies. For instance, subjects who use a visual imagery strategy when they process auditorily presented spatial descriptions are apparently able to compensate for the detrimental effects of non-systematic descriptive sequences (cf. Foos, 1980; Levine, Jankovic and Palij, 1982). It is easy to see that imagery is especially suited to the construction of this type of representation, in that it is the prime mode of representation for expressing the topological relations among a set of elements in an analogue fashion. When subjects have to build and temporarily store the mental representation of a spatial configuration, they are likely to tap those representational capacities of their repertory which are the best suited for this construction. This being said, other sorts of representations, such as procedural representations, may contribute to the processing of spatial environments, especially in the early phases of learning (cf. Perrig and Kintsch, 1985; Thorndyke and Hayes-Roth, 1982).

To remain within the framework of imaginal aspects of representations, an important issue is that of the relationship between an essentially linear structure (that of descriptive discourse) and a non-linear structure in two or three dimensions (the described space, but most likely, the mental representation of that space). How do subjects' cognitive systems build up a non-linguistic representation distributed over a coordinate representational space step by step from a linear sequence of sentences? This raises the complementary issue regarding the production of descriptive discourse: How will people confronted with a two- or three-dimensional spatial entity 'linearize' information in order to produce descriptive discourse? The generation of discourse describing space is a domain where it is easy to show that linguistic production is largely influenced by cognitive factors (cf. Levelt, 1982, 1989; Robin and Denis, 1991; Shanon, 1984; Ullmer-Ehrich, 1982; Wunderlich and Reinelt, 1982).

These issues were addressed in a set of experiments. The facets presented below are the most directly related to the issue of the contribution of imagery to comprehension and memory for texts describing geographical configurations (Denis, 1988; Denis and Denhière, 1990).

In the first experiment, we compared two modes of 'linearization' of information in texts describing a geographical configuration, in this case an island which included six geographical features (Figure 7.7). One version (Version 1) described the features according to a sequence resulting from the repeated horizontal scanning of the configuration (Figure 7.8a). This order of presentation corresponds to the dominant descriptive strategy in the sample from which subjects for this experiment were taken. It reflects a high degree of systematicity. Another version of the text (Version 2) described the same features according to a non-systematic order, deviating from linearity and violating the principles of referential continuity (Figure 7.8b).

Prior to reading one of these two texts, subjects were first presented with a blank map of the island, with each feature location represented by an X. Then, the map was removed from subjects' visual field. Subjects read the text on a screen in a sentence-by-sentence presentation, by keying for sentence onset. The subjects were informed at the start of the experiment that their final task would consist in completing the blank map and writing the words for the corresponding features below each X.

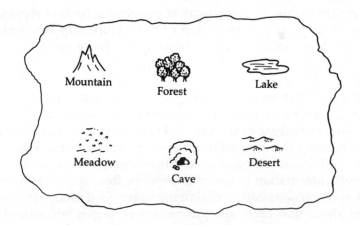

Figure 7.7 Geographical configuration used in the experiment

(a)

Version 1

1. In the extreme north-west part, there is a mountain.
2. To the east of the mountain, there is a forest.
3. To the east of the forest, there is a lake.
4. In the extreme south-west part, there is a meadow.
5. To the east of the meadow, there is a cave.
6. To the east of the cave, there is a desert.

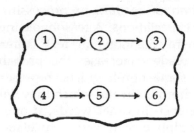

(b)

Version 2

1. In the extreme north-west part, there is a mountain.
2. To the east of the mountain, there is a forest.
3. To the south of the mountain, there is a meadow.
4. In the extreme south-east part, there is a desert.
5. To the west of the desert, there is a cave.
6. To the north of the desert, there is a lake.

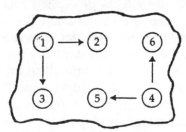

Figure 7.8 Two versions of the description

Each subject was presented with the two types of text (each text described a set of six different landmarks). The hypothesis was that Version 2 would result in an increase in cognitive load, which would be reflected in particular by longer reading times, as compared with those for Version 1.

Results showed that processing times were longer in the case of Version 2. This effect, however, appeared selectively, i.e., as of the third sentence, the first statement which contained information on a location the reader did not expect. This finding suggested that the construction of a 'cognitive map' of the configuration is rendered more difficult when it is based on a text which does not follow a sequencing that matches readers' expectations. Moreover, recall (labelling the blank map) was better after Version 1 than after Version 2. Longer processing times did not result in more efficient storage of information, but in fact reflected the cognitive adaptation of readers to processing constraints that contradicted their expectations. A reasonable interpretation is that this situation where violations in text coherence are rapidly identified by the readers increases the probability that readers have recourse to some non-linguistic representation, in which they can inscribe information and which they will store in memory at lesser cognitive cost. In other words, if one assumes that the processing of descriptive texts serves to elaborate a model-like representation, involving mental imagery, the usefulness of this model should be even greater when readers have to process a text which presents more extensive structural deficiencies.

The data from this experiment are not directly informative on the role of visual imagery in the processing of descriptive texts, nor on the usefulness of images depending on text structure (although subjects' reports reflect the high availability of imagery-based strategies during reading). Therefore, in a second experiment, we examined the effects of explicit imagery instructions. When subjects were instructed to visualize the configuration while reading the texts and to enter each detail as the text is processed, processing times did not differ substantially from those of the first experiment. While it is generally difficult to interpret the absence of a difference, this finding is highly compatible with the interpretation that subjects in the first experiment (without imagery instructions) spontaneously developed some imagery activity (evidence of which can be found in the initial processing time data). Finally, recall scores increased in a slight but not significant way when subjects were given imagery instructions.

In a further experiment (see Denis, 1991), the original condition of reading without imagery instructions was used again, and individual differences were investigated. We differentiated subjects in terms of their visuospatial abilities as measured by an objective spatial test (the Minnesota Paper Form Board). Subjects

with the highest visuospatial abilities had overall shorter processing times than the other subjects. Furthermore, the increase in
processing times from Version 1 to Version 2 was much less
marked than for subjects with poor visuospatial abilities. This
result suggests that high spatial visualizers are better equipped
cognitively to process a poorly structured text. The low spatial
visualizers are relatively more handicapped in a situation where
visuospatial imagery is an appropriate strategy. Finally, recall
performance tends to be higher for subjects with the highest
visuospatial abilities, although the effect is not significant. Thus,
for a comparable (or not significantly different) performance level,
the cognitive cost of processing is apparently higher for subjects
who are less inclined to elaborate visual models.

These findings provide additional evidence that the processing
of texts describing configurations is facilitated by the elaboration
of non-linguistic representations which analogically encode the
spatial relationships among the components of the configuration,
that is, representations which entertain a relationship of structural
resemblance with those derived from perception (cf. Ehrlich and
Johnson-Laird, 1982; Mani and Johnson-Laird, 1982; Morra, 1989;
Saariluoma, 1989). This being said, if visuospatial models of
configurations can be constructed from linguistic inputs, the
question remains whether these models possess structural and
functional properties similar to those of models derived from
perceptual processing. For instance, will cognitive computations
performed on a visual image be as valid when this image derives
from a verbal description as when it derives from perceptual
experience?

A new set of experiments was conducted in order to compare
cognitive operations implemented on these two kinds of representations: on the one hand, images derived from perceptual processing of a spatial configuration and, on the other hand, images
constructed from the processing of a verbal description of this
configuration (Denis and Cocude, 1989). The mental scanning
paradigm was used (cf. Kosslyn, Ball and Reiser, 1978; see
Chapter 3). Our reasoning was that if images constructed from
discourse have structural characteristics similar to those of images
constructed from perceptual processing, we should in both cases
obtain the same linear relationship between mental scanning
times and scanned distances. Thus, the Kosslyn paradigm was
extended to a condition where the elaboration of the mental image
of an island resulted from the processing of a verbal description of

that island. For this experiment, we designed new material which could be presented perceptually or in the form of a non-ambiguous verbal description, enabling subjects to locate the geographical details (a lighthouse, a beach, etc.) accurately.

In the condition where the visual image resulted from perceptual learning of the map, a linear relationship between scanning times and distances was found ($r = 0.90$). In the new condition, where subjects only processed a verbal description, a significant correlation between times and distance was found as well ($r = 0.91$). This finding supports the contention that mechanisms governing mental scanning are valid for both types of images, and that both possess quite similar structural properties. However, the similarity between images derived from texts and images derived from perception is dependent upon the rate of learning of the text. In a variant of this experiment, another group of subjects processed the text for a learning period reduced by half as compared with the previous group (three presentations instead of six). We assumed that these subjects would not have the same possibility to create as coherent and integrated images as the other subjects. In fact, the correlation between scanning times and distances was somewhat lower for them ($r = 0.65$). Furthermore, their absolute scanning times were longer than previously. These indications suggest that for a moderate rate of learning, an image constructed from text does not attain the coherence of an image derived from perception, with the consequence that a certain amount of 'error' contaminates the scanning process. With additional learning, the image derived from text reaches a structural coherence and resolution which make it cognitively exploitable in conditions practically identical to those of perceptually-based images.

Similar conclusions have been reached in situations where subjects who built the representation of a spatial configuration from text are required to perform comparisons of distances between landmarks. In particular, symbolic distance effects are found which are very similar to those observed in situations involving perceptual comparisons, in that the smaller the difference between two distances to be compared, the longer the comparison process (cf. Denis, 1990b). On the whole, texts apparently can form the basis for building representations that are structurally isomorphic to the described objects, as is the case of visual images resulting from perceptual processing of these objects. Equally important, the representations constructed from texts not only contain those pieces of information which were explicitly stated (for instance, that there is a harbour at a given location), but they also contain metric information which was not made explicit at any time in the texts (such as information regarding the relative distances between landmarks).

7.8 Conclusion

The views expressed above are congruent with those developed during the 1980s on the notion of 'mental model' (Johnson-Laird, 1980, 1983), or the very similar notion of 'situation model' advocated by van Dijk and Kintsch (1983; Perrig and Kintsch, 1985). The basic idea is that in addition to the processing of 'surface' aspects of a text, comprehension involves two distinct levels of processing: one level corresponds to the elaboration of meaning in the form of a text-base; this processing level generates propositional representations maintaining a discursive structure, and where some have a special status (in particular, those which constitute the macrostructure); the second processing level corresponds to the elaboration – not of the 'representation of the text' (strictly speaking), – but of the 'representation of the state of affairs' (or 'situation') the text is about. The representation built at this level of processing has characteristics which are no longer discursive, but which are those of a 'model' of the described entities. In particular, when these entities are spatial in nature, the model possesses characteristics which reflect the spatial properties of the object. The cognitive advantage of this form of representation is that it provides readers with a non-linguistic model of the text, whose structure as well as access rules are similar to those of perceptual events. The major property of a model is that it allows readers to make inferences without necessary recourse to computations based on formal logic.

The two processing levels postulated need to be differentiated as regards another characteristic. The elaboration of a propositional text-base is considered as an obligatory step in the construction of text meaning. On the other hand, the elaboration of a model is an optional addition to the processes which construct meaning. This processing level can theoretically be eliminated without hindering the elaboration of a propositional representation. Our data on the differential processing of narratives by high and low imagers provide arguments in favour of this conception. Model-like representations, however, need a semantic base (the text-base) in order to be elaborated. It is the figurable part of this base which is expressed in models, provided appropriate transformational operations are implemented.

8 Imagery, Problem-Solving and Reasoning

The area which has been explored most fully as regards the role of imagery processes is that of comprehension and memorization of sentences and texts. This chapter turns to tasks involving problem-solving situations and reasoning activities, in which the role of imagery has received much less attention.

Our knowledge of reasoning and problem-solving has increased dramatically in recent years. One of the most notable developments has been the incorporation of the notion of representation in conceptualizations. Analyses of problem-solving processes all include and sometimes formalize the representation subjects build of the problem situation, the specified goal, the means required to reach this goal, and the constraints on implementation of these means (cf. Newell and Simon, 1972; Richard, 1990). Although many problem-solving investigators have acknowledged the potential role of imagery in these representational processes, no systematic and coordinated works comparable in scope to that of works on language comprehension and memorization have emerged. The main exception is a set of experiments presented below on the resolution of three-term syllogisms.

This chapter reviews recent experimental approaches to imagery in its relationships with reasoning and problem-solving, and examines assumptions on the functional properties of visual images when implemented in these activities. Interested readers may consult several other overviews on imagery and problem-solving (cf. Denis, 1991; Kaufmann, 1985; Kosslyn, 1983, ch. 10; Richardson, 1983).

8.1 Visual imagery and problem-solving

As in Chapter 4, the main techniques used to demonstrate imagery effects on problem-solving are reviewed first.

155

The first technique consists in measuring the performance of subjects when asked to process problems containing wording that is more or less likely to generate imaginal representations. This characteristic of verbal statements is highly relevant in language comprehension and memory. Understanding a problem calls first of all for understanding of the problem statement. Problem statements can be subject to semantic analysis by the researcher, but are also worth examining in terms of the imagery activity they elicit and the role of images in the elaboration of the representation subjects construct of the problem data.

The concreteness of the material in the problem statement apparently has considerable impact on the ease with which subjects proceed to apply problem-solving strategies. A good illustration can be found in an experiment by Carroll, Thomas and Malhotra (1980), who compared resolution of two isomorphic versions of the same problem, one dealing with data easy to figure, the other with less figurable data. The problem was an 'ill-structured' (or 'ill-defined') problem, that is a problem for which there is not a single optimal solution, but rather a plurality of more or less satisfactory solutions. Specifically, the problem consisted of organizing a set of seven entities, while taking into account several criteria (dependencies or incompatibilities between these entities). In the 'spatial' isomorph of the problem, the entities were the offices of seven employees, located in such a way down a corridor that respective ranks of the employees in the firm were taken into account. In the 'temporal' isomorph, the entities were the successive steps in a manufacturing process, and the sequence had to obey several constraints. The two problems were structurally equivalent, but one was likely to elicit spatial representations, while the other, which stressed temporal dependencies, was expected not to do so. The results show that subjects performed better on the spatial office layout problem (in terms of the number of functional requirements satisfied) and had shorter solution times than on the temporal scheduling problem.

It is worth noting that all the subjects who processed the spatial problem spontaneously produced graphic representations over the course of problem-solving (which was not the case for subjects who solved the temporal problem). The fact that subjects were authorized to consolidate their thinking through a graphic activity precludes explanations that are solely based on a *mental* imagery interpretation. However, what emerges from this study is that there are some problems whose content is especially conducive to figural representation, and that this factor is of major importance in problem-solving.

The second technique, rather than varying the figurability of the data, consists in maintaining these data constant for the whole set of subjects, and modifying the probability that subjects will implement imagery activity. For a given type of material and a given task, the probability for subjects to use images spontaneously during problem-solving is not maximal. But it can reach or tend towards a maximum if explicit instructions are given to subjects to generate figural mental representations of the data and use them in problem-solving. The experimenter then compares performance for two equivalent groups of subjects administered the same task. One group (the control group) is simply invited to solve the problem, whereas the other (the experimental group) receives visual imagery instructions in addition. In many kinds of situations, subjects in the experimental group perform faster or make fewer errors than those in the control group.

This is the case, for instance, for spatial deduction problems. Take the following problem for instance: *'There are four roads here. I have come from the south and want to go to Jacksonville. The road to the right leads somewhere else. Straight ahead it leads to a ranch. In which direction is Jacksonville: (a) south, (b) west, (c) east, (d) north?'* Subjects who are prompted to visualize the problem data (either through explicit instructions or demonstrations based on graphics) perform overall better than subjects in the control condition (Frandsen and Holder, 1969). Use of imagery can then be considered as a *strategy* which optimizes the conditions for elaboration of a representation of the data.

The third technique used to evaluate the effects of imagery activity on problem-solving consists of giving the same problem and instructions to all subjects (i.e., neutral instructions, without any reference to visualization). What is investigated are the differences among subjects as to their visuospatial capacities. Typically, spatial problems such as in the above example are solved more rapidly, or as quickly with fewer errors by subjects characterized as high visuospatial imagers. On the other hand, poor visualizers have overall more difficulty in finding solutions. However, when the latter subjects receive instructions to visualize, they show a significant increase of performance, which sometimes reaches the level of spontaneous performance of high visualizers (Frandsen and Holder, 1969).

Higher performance of high visuospatial imagers has been

found for the processing of many other sorts of problems. This is the case for perceptual problems, in which subjects have to compare spatial configurations, analyze their properties, judge whether they match, or anticipate the effects of some transformation (cf. Barolo, Masini and Antonietti, 1990; Shepard and Cooper, 1982). This is also the case for problems where visualization, rather than serving to represent spatial data, helps depict non-spatial data through some symbolic format. This is typically the case of problems where durations (and more generally all types of continuous dimensions) can be figured by lengths. This is also the case of class inclusion problems, where data can be represented in the form of circles inscribed in one another. High spatial visualizers in general perform more accurately than low visualizers when solving problems of this kind (Frandsen and Holder, 1969).

8.2 Spatial representations and deductive reasoning

Transitive inference problems have been the main focus in recent years for the investigation of the role of imagery in deductive reasoning. This area was the locus of heated theoretical debate at the end of the 1960s. Without reporting the details of the controversy, it may be helpful to recall that the debate was over the nature of mental representations used to solve the classic three-term syllogism: *'Paul is taller than Peter. James is shorter than Peter. Who of the three is the tallest?'*

An 'imagist' interpretation of resolution was advocated by Huttenlocher (1968), who posited that the strategy developed during the processing of a syllogism relies on the elaboration and use of symbolic spatial images. The subjects are supposed to map symbolic representations of the terms presented in the premises in a 'mental space', along a vertical axis corresponding to the dimension *taller–smaller*, and to base their responses on the inspection of the relative positions of the three terms in the image (cf. also DeSoto, London and Handel, 1965; Handel, DeSoto and London, 1968). This interpretation was criticized by Clark (1969), who argued against assigning this role to images and claimed that representations stemming from the processing of premises were abstract and non-imaginal. Clark emphasized several linguistic principles, in particular the principle of 'lexical marking' of adjectives in the premises. He argued that imagery cannot be the basis for a theory of reasoning, and that only the deep structure of statements can account for their processing by subjects.

Studies by Shaver, Pierson and Lang (1974–5) shed new light on this problem. Shaver and his colleagues investigated the effects of several imagery variables, corresponding to the three techniques described above. The results show that a relation which directly describes a spatial arrangement ('*above-below*') is processed more easily than non-spatial relations, and that among the latter, those which can nevertheless be expressed through some spatial metaphor (as is the case for '*better-worse*') are easier to process than the others. Furthermore, visual presentation of the syllogisms, which is supposed to interfere with the production of visual images, gives rise to more errors than auditory presentation. The difference is more pronounced for non-spatial problems. Lastly, performance in syllogistic reasoning is positively correlated with subjects' visuospatial abilities (at least for male subjects, whose abilities in spatial reasoning are overall higher than those of female subjects). This set of findings as a whole is indicative of the facilitatory effect of spatial imagery in syllogistic reasoning, although they suggest a more modulated interpretation of the role of imagery in reasoning. The findings imply that without being a necessary component of processes involved in reasoning, imagery is nevertheless likely to contribute effectively to the solving of syllogisms.

In a second experiment, Shaver, Pierson and Lang (1974–5) showed that subjects encouraged to use a spatial imagery strategy made fewer errors than control subjects. Imagery-based strategies thus enhance problem-solving, although imagery is not seen as a necessary and sufficient component of the problem-solving process. Note that some subjects who were not instructed to generate images and who did not report any spontaneous imagery activity had a performance level as high as subjects who received instructions (cf. also Wetherick, 1991). Some of these subjects, in addition, reported having been disturbed by the instructions to use imagery.

Imagery cannot account for the resolution of all problems, since some are clearly more permeable than others to imagery-based strategies. Further experiments have confirmed that the resolution of three-term syllogisms is faster and more accurate for syllogisms rated as evoking high imagery (Williams, 1979). Similarly, the concreteness of the terms is a factor which improves performance in the testing of conditional rules (cf. Gilhooly and Falconer, 1974). Furthermore, in the Shaver, Pierson and Lang (1974–5) studies, analysis of within-session order effects indicates that the imagery-based strategy tends to develop progressively (see also Quinton and Fellows, 1975). Johnson-Laird (1972) has suggested that in deductive reasoning, subjects' strategies change as a function of their familiarization with the task. 'Spatial' strategies dominate initially but can be replaced by 'linguistic' strategies later on. In a similar vein, Kaufmann (1980) has claimed that imagery has greater impact in the initial phase of the problem-solving process. With increasing familiarity, linguistic strategies subsequently become more economical and take on increasing importance. As a whole, these conceptions and data suggest that 'imagistic' and 'linguistic' theories of reasoning are potentially compatible.

As a matter of fact, at the start of the 1980s, there was an upsurge of models combining features of both theoretical approaches. In Sternberg's (1980a, 1980b, 1981) 'mixed' model of resolution of linear syllogisms, premises are first coded as propositions reflecting the deep structure of the linguistic input, and are then recoded in the form of spatial arrays. The theory gives special importance to the term common to the two premises (the 'pivot term'), which is thought to play an essential role in the combination of the two initially constructed spatial arrays (each containing two terms) into a single array containing the three terms. Subjects' responses are thought to result from the inspection of this three-term array. In some cases, if the terms of the premises have not been coded in a sufficiently well-defined spatial image, subjects may rely on the information contained in the propositional representations.

Sternberg's model also has the merit of taking the notion of individual strategies into account, as measured by subjects' processing capacities and cognitive styles. Some people seem to be more inclined to rely on spatial imagery when resolving syllogisms, while others tend to have more spontaneous recourse to linguistic strategies (cf. Sternberg and Weil, 1980). The emphasis on the adjustment between problem-solving strategies and subjects' cognitive capacities has profoundly modified the theoretical approach, in the same way as an individual differences perspective affected the sentence–picture comparison paradigm in language comprehension (see Chapter 4).

The notion of a dual representational system is also present in Kosslyn's (1983) analysis of the processing of transitive inferences. The idea here is that subjects use whichever of the two forms of representation that is accessed first. There are numerous circumstances in which imaginal representations are the most readily used. However, if conditions are created which facilitate the retrieval of information stored in a propositional form, the probability that subjects will use imagery is lowered.

In an experiment reported by Kosslyn (1983), subjects memorized the names of five people and associated a different intelligence category (for instance, *'very smart', 'very dumb', 'average smart'*, and so on) with each. Next, subjects were asked to answer questions of the type: *'Is Herman smarter than Stanley?'* Before the question, subjects were required to form the image of a line on which dots symbolized the relative positions of the five people as regards intelligence. On half the trials, the subjects were to form the images of dots at the 'centre' of their visual field, just in front of their imaginary point of view. On the other half, the dots were to be imaged way to the right, at the 'periphery' of their visual field. This latter manipulation was expected to lessen the subjective 'clarity' of the image and to make the image more difficult to maintain. If an image is actually used as a symbolic representation of the hierarchy of the five people, it should be more effective when it is formed in the 'centre' than in the less resolved 'periphery' of the visual buffer. It was found that subjects' responses were faster when the dots were imaged in the centre than in the periphery. This suggests that imagery can indeed be used as a medium for reasoning.

Another group of subjects was involved in extensive over-learning of the five people and their status as regards intelligence. Not only were subjects asked to memorize their names and positions along the intelligence dimension, but when the associations were perfectly memorized, learning continued to the point where, given a name, subjects could instantly snap back with that person's status on the dimension. This over-learning was intended to increase the probability of storage of information in a propositional form. When these subjects were later presented with questions, they were required, like the subjects in the first group, to form an image of dots either at the centre or at the periphery. Results show that in this group response times did not differ in the two imagery conditions. The subjects were apparently able to recall the characteristics associated with the names so fast that they could compare them and make a decision before they finished inspecting the image.

In short, Kosslyn's findings provide grounds for the assumption that imagery demonstrates its efficiency in transitive inference tasks, but that it loses its efficiency when a problem can be solved more rapidly on the basis of propositional representations. To be complete, however, one should also mention the existence of negative or equivocal results regarding the role of imagery in syllogistic reasoning and transitive inference (cf. Fuchs, Goschke and Gude, 1988; Newstead, Manktelow and Evans, 1982; Richardson, 1987; for a recent reappraisal, see Mohr and Engelkamp, 1991).

Transitive inference problems were also one of Johnson-Laird's (1983) best sources for his theory of 'mental models' (see Chapter 7). In problems of the following type: '*In a troupe of performers, all dancers are singers and none of the dancers are jugglers. Can it be that some singers are jugglers?*', the claim is that resolution will be facilitated if subjects create a symbolic representation of the different possible combinations by visualizing all the possible nestings of classes mentioned. Here, images are privileged instruments for the creation of such models. They provide subjects with representations where the response is readily available, such that solving the problem does not necessarily imply making use of rules of formal logic (rules which are necessarily involved when computation is performed on propositions). However, a specific model elaborated during the processing of a problem may not be able to incorporate a newly presented piece of information. In this case, the model is no longer useful and is discarded and replaced by a propositional representation. Johnson-Laird argues that one of the major advantages of propositional representations is to provide subjects with a parsimonious way of storing and processing indeterminate pieces of information (cf. also Byrne and Johnson-Laird, 1989).

The lesson to be drawn from these theoretical arguments is that the 'exclusive' approaches to mental representations which were developed in the early works on deductive reasoning are unsound. The fact that the original theoretical debate on the spatial or propositional nature of representations has remained unresolved may well reflect that in fact these two sorts of representations are actually both used in the processing of transitive inferences, but at different phases of processing.

8.3 Functional properties of visual images in problem-solving

Which properties of visual images are the most directly relevant to problem-solving? Probably the first relevant property is the *structural similarity* of images to perceptual representations, and by extension the substitute role that images play when percepts cannot be elaborated (either because of the absence of stimuli in the perceptual field, or because of some transient or permanent impairment in the individual's perceptual system). This role of imagery is decisive when subjects are presented with descriptive statements of a set of non-present data and operations applied to them, and build up representations that have a structural organization similar to that of perception. Subjects, then, are in a position to generate mental entities that can be used as models, which have to be maintained at a sufficiently high level of activation for the duration that operations are applied to them.

The processing of many sorts of problems has been shown to be facilitated by the construction and manipulation of representations with a figural content. One of the most famous problems of this kind is the following: *'Think of a cube, all six surfaces of which are painted red. Divide the cube into twenty-seven equal cubes by making two horizontal cuts and two sets of two vertical cuts each. How many of the resulting cubes will have three faces painted red, how many two, how many one, and how many none?'* (Skinner, 1953, p. 273). Subjects' reports indicate high availability of some mental depiction, which they use to visualize the twenty-seven small cubes and count the number of each type. Here, imagery provides a representation of a cube where counting operations closely *simulate* those which would be performed on an actual cube cut into smaller ones. Operations are performed on the representation with minimal delay and without real world physical restrictions (manipulating twenty-seven real cubes, for instance). These advantages, however, are counterbalanced by the additional load on subjects' working memory, which may reach the limits of its processing capacities.

Can imagery alone help solve this type of problem? Processing problems of this type is possible indeed without recourse to visual imagery. To decide how many cubes have three faces painted red, subjects can, for instance, tap available information in their knowledge base, indicating that a cube has eight corners, and that since a corner is defined by the intersection of three faces, there will be eight cubes with three red faces. In fact, the vast majority of subjects tend to develop imagery strategies when they have to process this type of problem, especially when its novelty value is maximal. Imagery is a highly available form of representation. Even if subjects have mastered other more sophisticated algorithms, they spontaneously make use of imagery, which a majority of them know to be an efficient strategy for thinking and memory (cf. Denis and Carfantan, 1985; Katz, 1987).

Another relevant property of imagery is its *integrative potential*. Images are mental representations which are sometimes termed 'economical', in that the elements making up images are organized into highly integrated structures. By contrast with an enumerative list of object properties, images maintain a large number of informational units together as a unified whole. This integrative feature of images may minimize memory load. A number of studies have shown that imagery is efficient in learning and memory (e.g., Paivio, 1971; Richardson, 1980). This is due not only to additional coding of information made possible through imagery, but also to the integrative nature of the products of this coding, which reduces interference. Imagery can thus be seen as a process which increases the availability and manipulability of information currently processed in working memory (cf. Baddeley, 1986; Logie, 1989).

Lastly, images can be manipulated in a way that realistically simulates *transformations* on physical objects, thus making the successive states resulting from these transformations cognitively available. Manipulations of images have the advantage of being performed in a flexible and swift manner, enabling on-line inspection of current hypotheses (by contrast with the cost implied by actual creation of successive states on which subjects must reason). As a result, the processing of a problem whose components can be readily implemented in a picture-like representation may be favoured by a well-conducted imagery process that capitalizes on the representational properties of these components. To re-utilize the line of reasoning applied to language comprehension, the propositional representation constructed of the data of a problem can be expressed additionally in a form that makes symbolic manipulations possible. These manipulations are functionally analogous to real manipulations, and provide subjects with symbolic equivalents of physical states resulting from actual manipulations.

These considerations lead to the distinction between two functions of images in thinking. The first function is to *depict* the data of the problem to be processed (either directly or through some symbolic notation). The second is the role of imagery in the *manipulation* of the data once these have been depicted. This brings us back to the classic distinction between (*a*) the *content* of the representation constructed from a statement, which is expressed figurally in a visual image, and *(b)* the *processes* that apply to this content, i.e., the operations through which this content undergoes the transformations required by the statement: these processes serve at once or by successive steps to shift the figural content from an initial state to a terminal state in accordance with the instructions in the statement. An extremely interesting line of research in this respect consists of investigating the capacities of subjects to use their imagery in a productive manner to mentally assemble parts of patterns. Recent studies indicate that people are able to mentally combine geometric forms in a visual image and make unexpected discoveries of resulting patterns (cf. Finke, Pinker and Farah, 1989; Finke and Slayton, 1988; Helstrup and Anderson, 1991).

Note as well that although there are cases in which the solution to a problem can be directly 'read' off an image (as in Skinner's cube problem), there are others where the solution can be found easily without it explicitly appearing in an image. Rather than a decisive functional role, imagery here plays a role of transient *support* to the development of thinking. Consider a sharing problem expressed in a statement starting with a set of forty-two marbles. It is unlikely that the visual image of this set really contains the cardinal characteristics of the set, as would be the case for a perceptual representation, and it is hard to imagine that counting operations identical to those applied to a set of real objects are indeed implemented on this representation. Hence, the mental representation of this piece of information, even if imagery plays a role, contains exploitable informational units which are not expressed *as such* in the image, but are nevertheless activated in some more abstract form, and used in problem-solving.

On the other hand, there are cases where the image, as a mental experience, contains *more* information than is strictly necessary for the solution. Here the functional components of an image formed in the course of thinking need to be partialled out from those which are not critical to the solution. For instance, a well-known phenomenon is the variety of ways a given concept is figurally represented in different individuals. If students are required to form the image of an apple pie, the descriptions each subject will make of his or her image will vary considerably. Suppose that these images are formed in the context of problem-solving, and that the statement of this problem requires the sharing of this pie. Obviously, the specific (idiosyncratic) features of each of these images is quickly relegated to the background, and what is important is not the surface features, sources of differentiation among subjects' mental experiences, but a more basic feature, i.e., that all images share a critical structural characteristic: their circular shape. This property characterizes the most typical pies, and in any case the vast majority of their representations (either graphic or mental). Thus, if these different images are tapped for problem-solving, not all the features which characterize them, but one feature in particular which constitutes the critical figural component to be exploited in problem-solving is being sought. This reveals the importance for subjects who use imagery in problem-solving to exert efficient cognitive control on their imaginary productions, and to rely exclusively on the relevant components of images.

For imagery processes to be brought into play, the first condition is that the data to be processed *can* indeed be depicted mentally. This condition is clearly met when the problem statement describes physical objects and physical operations to be performed on them. Images, in this case, are essentially *denotative*. Even in a highly schematic manner, images are cognitive reflections of a real world. Their efficiency depends on how accurately they denote the relevant parts of the data to be manipulated. Transformations applied to images thus mimic the transformations which could be applied to real objects. The best examples of such types of problems are those which require the processing of spatial information.

However, there are problems which have no such properties, such as linear syllogisms on dimensions which cannot be directly pictured, or problems of class inclusion. The problems, nevertheless, can be *made pictorial*, provided imagery is used for its symbolic value. For instance, as suggested above, a vertical line can represent any sort of dimension, even a highly abstract one. Dots along this line can characterize the objects classified on this dimension (cf. Kosslyn, 1983; Shaver, Pierson and Lang, 1974–5). The image, in this case, is a *notation*. It serves as a kind of *visual cognitive aid* in the development of abstract reasoning (cf. Kirby and Kosslyn, 1990).

One very important point then consists in determining *how* to picture the data of an abstract problem. I have mentioned above some roundabout ways to translate non-spatial information in the form of spatial metaphors. However, before undertaking such coding or translation, it is opportune for subjects to ask whether it is really worth the effort to picture not readily picturable problems. In the affirmative, will some pictorial techniques be more effective than others?

In certain cases, efforts to depict the data of a problem may prove to be detrimental to thinking, and imagery, for lack of appropriate control, may result in fallacious representations. A typical example can be found when a person is required to calculate ½ − ⅓. Suppose that a child has been strongly encouraged to rely on visualization of circles or parts of circles (or parts of apple pies) when making numerical computations of this kind. This child will be inclined to visualize the quantity '½' as a half-circle. With this representation mentally foregrounded, there is a risk that the quantity '⅓ to be subtracted from ½' will be biased towards '⅓ of the currently available representation' (that is, ⅓ of ½), and not '⅓ of 1'. Inappropriately controlled imagery may thus create misleading sets.

There are cases where the formation of a 'realistic' model of the situation described by the problem statement creates an obstacle to reasoning. This is especially true of problems in which objects in motion occupy different portions of space at different times. Most people tend to visualize the successive stages of the situation, whereas in most cases 'abstract' reasoning relying on the equation linking time, distance and speed, is enough to reach the solution easily. Appropriate use of imagery in problem-solving thus first consists in detecting whether processing will be facilitated by such a procedure, or whether processing should preferentially rely on some alternate non-imaginal computational strategy.

A good example is the monk problem originally reported by Duncker (1945) and further discussed by Kosslyn (1983) and Glass and Holyoak (1986): *'A monk begins to climb a path up a mountain at 8:03 on Monday morning. The path is very tortuous, twisting and turning, becoming steep and rocky at times. The monk makes it to the top at 4:30, having stopped for a fifteen-minute lunch of dried bread and water at noon sharp. The monk then spends the entire night in meditation on the mountain top. At 8:03 the next morning he begins to descend the same path he used the previous day. Invigorated by his meditation, he makes very good time on his descent and arrives at the bottom at 1:05 in the afternoon.'* The question is: *'Was there any time of day (you need not say when) when the monk was at exactly the same point on the path on Monday and Tuesday?'* (Kosslyn, 1983, p. 180).

This is obviously the sort of problem where any attempt at representing realistically what happens on this mountain at every stage of the story is of poor heuristic value. On the contrary, a certain form of imaginal *simulation* may be favourable to reasoning. For instance, subjects can imagine *two* monks, on the same day at the same hour, one climbing up, and the other climbing down the mountain. This representation should help to realize that the two monks will pass each other at a given time, at a given point on the path.

Symbolic, more abstract imagery can also be used in the same way as simulation imagery. For instance, on a graph where time is represented on the abscissa and height on the ordinate, an ascending line will represent the trip up, and a descending line will represent the trip down. This makes it obvious that the two lines will cross, and that the intersection represents the time and the point common to the two trips. This is a good example of how imagery can work efficiently with different modes of visual representation. The critical issue for the problem-solver is to identify the most appropriate type of visualization for the problem at hand.

8.4 Conclusion

Evidence suggests that the intentional use of an imagery strategy has an impact on the solving of various types of problems and reasoning. Any account of this efficiency must entertain the 'reality model' role that imagery plays in thinking, provided that the 'realism' of images is monitored appropriately. There is an obvious value in encouraging, for instance, in educational contexts, the use of imagery in situations where subjects undergo constraints which limit their perceptual access to objects (or graphic substitutes) and their possibilities to manipulate them.

Most of the studies reported in this chapter point to the strong tendency for the human mind to mentally *picture* situations which require reasoning. At the same time, there is also a consensus that images are not the only vehicles for thinking. However, the cognitive primacy of imagery in the processing of many sorts of situations is widely acknowledged. Recent theoretical and experimental developments lend additional support to hypotheses which incorporate the notions of 'model' and 'simulation' in the analysis of situations where people have to reason from verbal descriptions of data that are not directly available to visual perception.

9 Imagery and Action

There is nothing *a priori* further removed than imagery and action. One is mostly an inner experience; the other is oriented towards the outside world. One belongs to the class of private events; the other is public in nature. Most approaches to mental imagery consider images to be internal events which serve other internal events (such as those involved in memorization, comprehension, reasoning, and so on), whose 'outputs' essentially consist in verbal responses which do not change the state of the outside world. The present chapter aims at extending the issue of imagery by examining its role when it accompanies or prepares an individual's action on the world.

9.1 Imagery, resolution of practical problems and creative thinking

Images, as noted earlier, are tools for the evocation of the past. They can also orient people towards the future. A typical example is imaginal anticipation of perceptual events which have yet to occur. Anticipatory imagery is frequently involved in situations where people expect upcoming perceptual events to take place and prepare to react to them. The experimental data reviewed in Chapter 3 show that in many cases the reactions of a person placed in such a situation are facilitated by imaginal anticipation of the to-be-detected event.

There is also a broad class of situations where imagery acts as an anticipatory representation in the course of *actions* involved in the creation of objects or configurations. Images play this role in the elaboration of industrial or art objects which are shaped in successive steps by their creators. Some good examples are artists, when they start to compose a new colour combination on the canvas, architects, when designing new relations between shapes, or craftsmen, when shaping raw material to create an object. Here, images are privileged instruments for anticipating the *outcome* of a creative act. Their function is to instantiate hypotheses. Each image elaborated in the course of creation illustrates one of the set of possible outcomes. The images individuals use to anticipate the shape of an object during manufacture, in particular prior to the execution of irreversible steps, illustrate the operational role of a considerable part of mental imagery.

Imagery makes it possible to examine hypotheses without the cost of actual execution of these hypotheses. Here, imagery draws its potential from the fact that it is a form of mental representation which has maximal structural similarity to the physical situations it reflects. The flexibility of imagery also plays a decisive role in that it enables rapid transformations of current representations, and hence examination of various hypotheses at minimal temporal cost.

A series of experiments by Kaufmann (1979) was devoted to the contribution of mental imagery to the processing of 'practical' construction problems in which subjects were required to find an adequate solution for a novel concrete situation. For instance, they were asked how they could transfer a number of peas from a glass on one table to an empty glass on another table, two metres away, without being allowed to move from the first table. The subjects were asked to solve the problem with specific material: some newspapers, a short piece of string and a pair of scissors. In another problem, subjects were asked how to attach two ropes hanging from the ceiling, which were too far away for the subject to hold one without letting go of the other. In order to solve this problem, the suggested materials were a screwdriver, a pair of pliers and a box of drawing pins. In these experiments, the subjects responded verbally, but these responses described individuals' *actions* on physical objects.

Kaufmann's experiments show that subjects who solve these sorts of problems correctly are those who bring visualization processes into play the most actively. These same subjects are also capable of imagining the greatest number of alternative solutions when presented with one solution. Analysis of verbal reports confirms that the majority of subjects generate visual images during their attempts to find solutions that are analogous to the main solution.

Kaufmann also compared the resolution of practical problems as a function of mode of presentation of data. If visual imagery plays a role, resolution should be facilitated by procedures that tap visual perception directly, for instance, in situations where data are presented figurally. The results show that when the problem statement and the objects to be used for its resolution are presented pictorially, the subjects perform better than with a verbal presentation. Figural presentations (either concrete or pictorial) enable subjects to apprehend directly the properties of objects that are relevant for the processing of the problem. In addition, visualization apparently plays a heuristic role in productive thinking. This derives from the fact that imagery is a flexible mode of representation which allows for rapid anticipation of transformations in the situations being processed (cf. Antonietti, 1991).

On the whole, as anticipatory simulations of possible outcomes of action, images seem to play an important role in the regulation of behaviours by which individuals act on the world and perform transformations (see also Kaufmann, 1980, 1985). In this respect, the concept of 'operative image', as proposed by Ochanine (1978), stresses the regulatory function of imagery in human action. Imagery is considered to be a privileged form of representation in that it provides individuals with an internal model of the world, a model that is built up from action and is designed to organize action. Imagery is close to the concept of 'schema', as a cognitive instrument for action planning and guidance.

Beyond the manipulation of physical or pictorial objects, images also intervene in activities resulting in the elaboration of more abstract entities. Extreme types of these abstract objects are, for instance, scientific theories. Einstein stated that visual imagery played a major role in the elaboration of his theory of relativity (cf. Patten, 1973). Another frequently cited example is the discovery of the molecular structure of benzene by Kekule during his daydreams on atoms joining and forming chain-like molecules, and his famous dream about writhing chains curled like a snake swallowing its tail. These individual examples can be paralleled to claims about the role of metaphors in the elaboration of scientific conceptions (cf. Miller, 1984; Shepard, 1978, 1988). There are many instances showing that when images intervene in the course of a process of invention or discovery, they frequently take the form of visual metaphors, or analogue representations from other areas of sensory experience.

9.2 Mental imagery and the construction of cognitive maps

One basic form of human activity is movement within spatial environments, and specifically moving from one point to another. Point-to-point movement obviously depends on how people plan to reach their objectives. Planning itself is dependent on the quality of the representation people have of the space in which they must move or travel (not only proximal environments that are accessible to direct perception, but also remote environments, out of the perceptual field at the time of planning).

In recent years, there has been increased interest in the concept of 'cognitive maps', as internal representations of the environment, its metric properties, and the topological relations between landmarks. A great deal of research has consisted in showing that when people have no access to symbolic materials such as maps, the cognitive map of a territory is a representation which can serve as a basis for cognitive computations (comparison of distances, determination of relative positions of landmarks, etc.), which allow people to orient themselves. The validity of these computations obviously depends on the isomorphism of the cognitive map to the represented space, and in particular to its capacity of preserving the Euclidean properties of physical space (Hirtle and Jonides, 1985; Hirtle and Mascolo, 1986; McNamara, 1986; McNamara *et al.*, 1989; McNamara, Ratcliff and McKoon, 1984; Moar and Bower, 1983; Ramey, Péruch and Pailhous, 1982; Sholl, 1987).

To access the representations individuals have constructed of environmental spaces, researchers use an indirect approach, consisting of either observing actual navigation of these individuals or requiring them to externalize their representations in the form of a map. In a classic study on Parisian taxi-drivers' representation of the city, Pailhous (1970) used both methods. The analysis of the findings showed a high positive association between drivers' real performance (their choice of appropriate routes) and the accuracy of the maps they draw. If drawn maps are assumed to reflect at least some aspects of subjects' cognitive maps, the correlation obtained suggests that programming routes depends to a great extent on subjects' use of their spatial representation of the area. This representation is likely to be the basis for computing directions.

However, the representation that taxi-drivers have of a city probably involves two components: first, drivers have some 'conceptual' view of the city, which is similar to a two-dimensional survey map; second, they have a direct, more concrete view of the city, corresponding to what they actually see on the ground. Pailhous's studies indicate that these two forms of representation contribute differentially to the implementation of route strategies. The 'survey' map is thought to be the basis for the operations performed when taxi-drivers determine routes, i.e., when they set up global action programmes, whereas ground cues are believed to play a more important role in local decision-making, which calls on the 'secondary network' of urban space.

Research on representation of space and cognitive maps of real geographical environments expanded in the 1970s. The major assumption is the isomorphism of the representation to the represented geographical information. This stress on isomorphism, however, is tempered by the existence of systematic 'distortions', which places restrictions on the postulate of strict metric isomorphism. For instance, it has been shown that subjects overestimate distances containing obstacles, whether these are artificial (cf. Kosslyn, Pick and Fariello, 1974) or parts of naturalistic settings: certain environmental features which normally increase the effort of moving between locations, such as hills, lead to systematic overestimations of distances, whereas the lengths of straight routes tend to be underestimated (cf. Cohen, Baldwin and Sherman, 1978). Difficulties along a route thus distort the representation that people have of this route.

The factors which bias the estimation of distances in naturalistic settings are also operational in urban environments. For instance, Byrne (1979) showed that for the residents of a city, routes in the town centre are overestimated in comparison to routes of similar lengths out of town. Furthermore, routes which include several bends are judged longer, compared with predominantly straight routes. These sources of bias can be accounted for if one assumes that subjects tend to use cognitive maps which do not generally encode vector information, but that the number of locations remembered to be on the route is the main basis for judging its length (see also Thorndyke, 1981). In addition, the estimation of angles between intersecting roads is systematically biased towards the approximation of a right angle (on this point, see also Moar and Bower, 1983; Pailhous, 1970). In general, distortions in cognitive maps apparently occur in the direction of increased 'systematicity' or 'schematization' of the representation (cf. Holyoak and Mah, 1982; Stevens and Coupe, 1978; Tversky, 1981).

Thus, there are representations which can be qualified as 'fallacious', in that they contain a certain amount of error. Fallacious representations can also result in incoherencies to which, however, the cognitive system is apparently able to adjust. In his classic study on the image of the city, Lynch (1960) showed that for many Boston residents, the main park of their city is a square with . . . five right-angled corners! These 'representational biases', which can be detected in the descriptions people make of their environmental space (verbally or graphically), do not prevent these people from navigating in this space in an adequate way. With additional navigational experience and, more importantly, with inspection of physical maps, fallacious representations can be rectified. Byrne (1979) suggested that it is mainly by the use of published maps that people acquire vector information of large-scale space.

Researchers have been increasingly interested in the processes by which people construct internal representations of their environments, either from direct experience (including perception and navigation) or from the processing of symbolic information, such as maps or schemas (cf. Presson, DeLange and Hazelrigg, 1989). Both sources of information can be used for learning purposes, but each has its own advantages, which are related to the types of decisions subjects make when using their cognitive maps. For instance, what a person acquires from a map is survey knowledge which encodes *spatial relations* between landmarks. This knowledge resides in memory in the form of mental images, which subjects subsequently use to perform scanning and distance measurements as they would on physical maps. In contrast, knowledge acquired from navigation is procedural in nature and bears mainly on routes connecting landmarks. Mental simulation of travel along these routes is then used by subjects for computing spatial judgements. Thorndyke and Hayes-Roth (1982) compared subjects who acquired spatial knowledge either from studying the map of an environment or from actual navigation in this environment. Results showed that map learning is superior for judgements of relative location and straight-line distances among landmarks. Learning from navigation is superior when people have to orient themselves with respect to unseen objects and to estimate route distances. These differential effects, however, are only obtained in the early steps of learning.

The great majority of studies on the construction of cognitive maps have been conducted in situations where subjects have direct perceptual experience of the environment to learn, or experience of symbolic (map) representations. It is also possible to acquire knowledge about a spatial environment from verbal descriptions of this environment. Imagery research attests that subjects are capable of processing linguistic descriptions of objects they have never perceptually experienced, and to elaborate representations of these objects with a satisfactory level of accuracy with respect to the model. Learning from descriptions in general requires longer processing times than learning from maps (cf. Perrig and Kintsch, 1985; Tversky, 1991). Furthermore, the order in which pieces of information are presented in a description significantly affects the processes of elaboration of the cognitive map (cf. Denis and Denhière, 1990; Foos, 1980). Lastly, texts describing an environment can either orient subjects towards the elaboration of a map-like or a procedural representation. These two sorts of texts have differential effects on the computations performed later by subjects on their mental representation of the environment (cf. Perrig and Kintsch, 1985).

An important topic in this area is the specific role of visual imagery in the elaboration of mental representations of spatial configurations. The findings reviewed in Chapter 3 show that given sufficient amount of learning, the mental image of a geographical configuration preserves the relative distances among the critical points of the configuration (cf. Kosslyn, Ball and Reiser, 1978). The structural properties of visual imagery make it a prime mode of representation for encoding spatial information.

When subjects are required to elaborate cognitive maps from linguistic descriptions, imagery is likely to be involved. Images have been shown to be the mode of representation which is best suited for maintaining information in working memory in order to incorporate subsequent pieces of information. Thus, imagery is a major instrument for coding, in that it enables subjects to enter new pieces of information by successive additions. When learning is based on a map, imagery is here again the most appropriate means for creating representations that are isomorphic to the configurations being processed (Thorndyke and Hayes-Roth, 1982). In addition, subjects' visual memory ability has been shown to facilitate learning of spatial information (cf. Thorndyke and Stasz, 1980).

When cognitive maps are used, they frequently exhibit characteristics which are those of visual images. Operations performed on them are highly similar to those performed on graphic

materials in perceptual situations. In particular, mental exploration is capable of taking shortcuts as efficiently as when it takes
originally learned path segments (cf. Levine, Jankovic and Palij,
1982). Furthermore, mental scanning of the visual image of a
territory seems to be used by subjects in order to estimate
distances between points of this territory (cf. Thorndyke, 1981; see
also Denis and Cocude, 1989).

On the whole, all these indications converge on the privileged
role of mental imagery in the elaboration and use of cognitive
maps. Individuals' abilities to act in the world are extended by
enriched representations of space. In this respect, imagery is a
valuable cognitive tool for the planning and the regulation of
individuals' actions in their spatial environments. However, when
people build mental models of three-dimensional environments
from verbal descriptions, results show that different spatial locations (for instance, above vs. below, or ahead vs. behind) are
differentially accessible (cf. Franklin and Tversky, 1990). This
suggests that although mental models are 'spatial' in the sense
that they represent relative spatial directions, they may not have
all the analogue, quasi-perceptual qualities of visual images. Thus,
to understand how cognitive maps are used, accounts in terms of
simple perception-like analogues are not sufficient, but obviously
need to be supplemented by accounts based on how space is
conceived (cf. Tversky, 1991).

9.3 Imagery and mental practice in the acquisition of motor skills

The third facet of human activities to which imagery is likely to
contribute is the acquisition of motor skills, in particular through
the technique of 'mental practice'. The phrase 'mental practice'
applies to situations in which an individual mentally evokes a
motor pattern without concomitant production of the muscular
activity normally involved in the execution of this pattern.

The basic paradigm of mental practice studies involves the
comparison of three conditions: a physical practice condition,
where subjects are required to actually perform a given motor skill
for a set period of time; a mental practice condition, where
subjects are invited to perform symbolic (mental) rehearsal of the
to-be-learned skill; and a control condition, where subjects perform a task which is neutral with respect to the target skill. For

each of the groups assigned to these conditions, a pre-test measure of subjects' performance in the target skill is made before the experiment, and a post-test measure is made at the end. Most studies in this area show that in comparison with the control condition, mental practice has positive effects on final performance. In some cases, these effects remain somewhat lower than those resulting from the physical practice condition, but in some other cases, they are not significantly different from those effects. Lastly, experiments in which mental and physical practice are combined typically show effects which are more marked than those of physical practice alone.

Motor activities calling for muscular endurance are generally insensitive to mental practice. On the other hand, the efficiency of mental practice is clear-cut in the acquisition of skills with a strong cognitive component and requiring fine visuo-motor coordination (for instance, dart-throwing, basketball free throws, ball striking, etc.) (for more detailed reviews, see Denis, 1985; Denis, Chevalier and Eloi, 1989; Feltz and Landers, 1983).

There are two major classes of theoretical explanations for mental practice effects. 'Neuromuscular' theories mainly rely on experimental data on subliminal neuromuscular activity which is generated during the imagination of movements. In mental practice, subliminal activation of neuromuscular units, as detected by electromyography, is thought to excite kinesthetic feedback, and hence produce a kinesthetic 'image' of the actual movement (cf. Wehner, Vogt and Stadler, 1984). This 'image' is stored in memory and activated later in the context of the execution of the movement. 'Symbolic' theories, on the other hand, emphasize the cognitive aspects of mental practice. These theories base their claims on the effects of mental practice in the early phase of learning, that is during the purportedly 'cognitive' stage of learning (cf. Marteniuk, 1976; Schmidt, 1982). Mental practice thus would essentially allow subjects to build a *representation* of the situation and of performance. Facilitation would result mainly from the implementation of a 'central' activity, rather than from use of peripheral feedbacks. An important argument in favour of this class of hypotheses is that bilateral transfer occurs even when the training task (which involves the contralateral limb) is performed through mental practice (Kohl and Roenker, 1980, 1983). Heuer's (1985) 'programming hypothesis' is that peripheral effects concomitant to imagination of movements are not essential to mental practice. Rather, what is essential is the central process that is reflected by these peripheral side effects. The same central process is thought to be implemented whether subjects imagine or actually perform a movement. Mental practice effects thus result from the addition of such central programming activities (see also Annett, 1988; Savoyant, 1988).

In general, mental practice instructions call to a great extent on imagery, which is the most appropriate form of representation to figure the objects involved in the motor skill, their locations, the distances separating them from the subject, etc. A certain form of imagery is involved as well for evoking kinesthetic sensations, relative positions of limbs, etc. Kinesthetic imagery probably plays an important role in the representation subjects have of their own motor activities (cf. Hale, 1982; Mahoney and Avener, 1977). It is well established in particular that imagined movements closely mimic actual movements in their temporal organization, thus suggesting that both are driven by the same planning programmes (cf. Decety, Jeannerod and Prablanc, 1989; Decety and Michel, 1989).

More information is available on the contribution of visual imagery to mental practice. Analysis of works in this field suggests that in order for visual imagery to be efficient in mental practice, it must have three important properties. The first property is image *vividness*, which is believed to reflect the rate of activity of the mental processes underlying the experience of imagery. As discussed above, visualization is the end-product of the transient activation of representational units in a specialized processor. This activation has a phenomenological counterpart, the experience of imagery, which is accessible to conscious inspection. Vividness is a characteristic of the mental experience connected to this inspection. It is assumed to vary as a function of the level of activation of the representational units recruited for image generation.

Some experimental findings suggest that the vividness of visual imagery involved in mental practice has positive effects on motor learning. Marks (1977) reported that during the learning of a rotary pursuit tracking task, subjects classified as vivid imagers (on the basis of self-report measures in response to the VVIQ) benefited more from mental practice than poor imagers. Similarly, Ryan and Simons (1982) demonstrated that subjects who described themselves as 'imagers' showed greater improvement in mental practice of a balancing task than 'non-imagers'. Furthermore, when both groups of subjects were explicitly encouraged to use imagery, they both benefited from such instructions, but the greatest improvement was in the group of imagers. These findings suggest that people with a spontaneous proclivity to elaborate vivid images are also in a position to make profitable use of these images in a learning procedure calling upon imagery.

The second relevant property of images in mental practice is their *controllability*. If generating vivid images is a requirement for making best use of them, it is important for images to remain under some control from the system which elaborates them. As discussed in Chapter 3, the assumption is that once an image has been generated in the visual buffer, 'refreshing' processes are applied to the image in order to maintain it at a sufficiently high level of activation. These refreshing processes are assumed to be partially under subjects' control. Subjects are able to decide whether additional activation should be given to the image or whether the image should be interrupted in order to generate another one. The utility of an image thus depends on the subject's capacity to generate images that are not only vivid and persistent, but persistent only for the time they are needed.

Another aspect of controllability aside from the persistence of unmodified images is the different kinds of operations that are performed on images once they have been generated. For instance, excessive vividness of imagery places limits on appropriate 'handling' of the images being processed. Several kinds of processes likely to operate on images are involved in the representation of motor skills in sport contexts. For instance, mental rotation can be involved in the representation that players have of their own movements, as these are perceived by an opponent on the field. Subjects' control of this cognitive operation seems to be an important condition for the efficiency of visual imagery in mental practice (cf. Richardson, 1969).

The third property is the *accuracy of reference* of images. It is not only indispensable for images to be vivid and under the subject's cognitive control during mental practice. It is also necessary that the figural content of the image accurately depicts what it is supposed to refer to, for instance, the dimensions of objects, the direction of movement, its magnitude, etc. If the learner generates images which contain systematic distortion, it is reasonable to question whether mental practice using such imagery will be as efficient as when images realistically refer to the correct target movement.

A study by Johnson (1982) provides arguments for the significance of this factor. In this experiment, subjects were submitted to a linear positioning task in which they moved a slide along a track until it reached a stop. All subjects received fifteen acquisition trials and later had to recall the movement by moving the slide along the track with the stop removed. This recall phase was preceded by an interpolated activity. In a control condition, the interpolated activity consisted in counting backwards. This condition, not surprisingly, did not result in any significant constant error at recall. In two other conditions, the interpolated activity consisted in *imagining* performing the same task. Some subjects were instructed to imagine they were moving the slide to the same position as in the initial learning phase, while others were to imagine they were moving it to another position (for instance, if they initially learned a 30-centimetre movement, the novel, imaginary movement was 60 centimetres, or vice versa).

Results showed that after imagery of the same movement, constant error was virtually zero, whereas it reached a significant value after imagery of a novel movement. Furthermore, the direction of the error was affected by the length of the imaginary movement. For instance, when a subject initially performed actual 30-centimetre movements, and then imagined 60-centimetre movements, the final test on the standard 30-centimetre movement revealed a systematic tendency towards *longer* movements, and vice versa. A further result in this experiment was observed in a condition where the interpolated activity consisted in actually rehearsing a movement either half or twice the original movement. Direction and magnitude of constant error were highly comparable to those observed in the condition with imaginary interpolated movements.

Johnson's experiment shows that images of movements can affect the subsequent production of movements, and that biasing effects on the movement to be recalled are similar to those resulting from actual movements. Thus, in the recall of a previously learned movement, 'incorrect' images (that is, images whose referents are different from the original movement) can systematically have biasing effects on performance.

These notions were confirmed in the context of the acquisition of a sport motor skill (cf. Eloi and Denis, 1987). The aim of this study was to determine to what extent learning of a movement which normally benefits from mental practice can be hindered when subjects are led to build an 'erroneous' (or 'irrelevant') image of the movement. The experiment was on a motor skill which is sensitive to mental practice, namely, basketball free throws. In the first part of the experiment, a comparison was drawn between a physical and a mental practice condition, where instructions in both cases centred subjects on the aspects generally considered by experts as calling for prime perceptual processing. Positive effects on performance were observed after learning in both conditions, in comparison with a control condition. In the second part of the experiment, a physical and a mental practice condition were compared again, but in both cases, subjects were invited to process primarily other (purportedly not relevant) aspects of the situation. The results showed that not only after physical practice, but also after mental practice, the final level of performance remained lower than the level attained in the first part of the experiment. This finding confirms that when an image illustrates a situation, but its content does not reflect the relevant aspects of the situation, the usefulness of this image may be undermined (see also Budney and Woolfolk, 1990). This research also provides support for the claim that in mental practice, visual images have genuine *referential* functions, as cognitive substitutes for non-available perceptual information.

On the whole, not only imagery *activity*, but the figural *content* of representations generated by this activity have a true functional value in the development of skills that enhance the individual's repertory of activities.

9.4 Conclusion

Examples from three domains testify to the significant role that imagery plays in several forms of human action. The studies reviewed illustrate the importance of cognitive aspects in human behaviour. At the crossroads of cognition and action, images enter into planning and management of individual behaviour. While fulfilling its role of *representation*, imagery is at the same time a *guide for action* and an *instrument for the acquisition of skills* used in action.

Conclusion Perspectives for Imagery Research

A retrospective look at imagery research over the last twenty years in cognitive psychology shows that focus has been on two major classes of issues. The first class of issue approaches the *nature* of images as psychological events, their structure, their internal organization. The second examines their *functioning*, their role when they are implemented in other psychological activities such as memorization, reasoning and language processing. My aim in this book has been to present the major findings on the structure of images, and the processes governing their generation, maintenance, and transformations. I have also stressed the specific usefulness of images in many forms of cognitive functioning. It is important, in this respect, to underline that demonstrating the efficiency of imagery in cognition does not authorize the claim that imagery is the only efficient mode for processing information. Imagery, in general, furnishes individuals who must deal with some absent entity with the possibility of performing computations on a mental representation which realistically mimics the absent entity. But obviously, imagery is not the sole form of representation that can undergo cognitive computations.

Although cognitive research provides responses about what images are and how they affect individuals' psychological activity, much remains unresolved in the field of imagery research. The third, and still very open, issue in contemporary cognitive psychology is where images 'come from'. In other words, what accounts for the genesis and articulation in the repertory of human cognitive skills, of the system which elaborates, stores, and transforms mental images? Interested readers will find a thoughtful discussion of theories accounting for the development of mental imagery in children in Lautrey and Chartier (1991).

All these questions have emerged within the field of cognitive psychology, where the current answers, and most probably the future responses, are likely to be found. However, it is obvious that imagery researchers are now dealing with issues which go beyond psychology proper and overlap with other fields. This concluding chapter examines some of the directions in which imagery is now investigated in an interdisciplinary fashion with other cognitive sciences.

Data base for imagery and neuropsychological structures

The first locus of convergence concerns the cognitive 'data base' from which mental images are generated. It is generally accepted that images do not arise *ex nihilo* in the mind. At a given point in psychological functioning, an image results from transient activation of a representation available in long-term memory. This representation remains dormant until processes access it and cause it to undergo some kind of activation by transfer to a specialized processor, whose end-product is a mental image.

A fundamental distinction is thus made between *permanent* and *transient representations*. Transient representations are expressed in the form of mental events which show structural similarity with perceptual events, as seen above. Most of empirical approaches reviewed in this book deal primarily with these transient representations, their intrinsic properties, and the hypothetical properties of the mental medium on which they are inscribed. However, imagery research needs to explore levels prior to image formation, namely, the infrastructure from which images are generated. This calls for hypotheses on the data base necessary for visual imagery, its organization, the nature and format of its components, and the relations of these components to the lexicon. A number of conceptualizations have been put forward, some of which have been presented in this volume. Most remain at a certain level of generality, but there is a need for more empirical work on the cognitive equipment underlying imagery activity. Another set of hypotheses, coordinated with the previous ones, concerns the repertory of processes which contribute to imagery activity. A distinction should then be made between the processes which operate on the data base and those which operate on the transient representations elaborated from this base.

Of the empirical approaches currently being tested, the most promising ones are correlational analyses of tasks assumed to involve a given set of processes, and pathological case studies evidencing elective impairments of imagery processes. As a consequence, a new field of research has opened up, whose objective is to characterize those parts of the neural architecture responsible for the storage of the data base (i.e., where the 'precursors' of mental images are stored) and for the implementation of imagery processes (i.e., the repertory of procedures).

The host of current biological models of mental processes has prompted cognitive psychology to evaluate the compatibility of its own data with these models. Detailed assumptions have been made on the nervous structures which are activated and the sorts of connections which are involved when the brain generates images and performs operations on them (e.g., Farah, 1988; Kosslyn *et al.*, 1990a; Kosslyn 1991). The neuropsychology and neurophysiology of mental imagery, which have a long history, may be on the verge of a renaissance of research perspectives, given the degree of development and precision of current theoretical hypotheses on imagery processes. In addition, better understanding of visual object representation is likely to be one outcome of the combination of computational and neuroscientific constraints. Integrative approaches such as these have been applied to low-level processing, and there are new perspectives for high-level vision as well, in which computational frameworks arising from computer vision research are used to interpret human neurophysiology (cf. Plant and Farah, 1990).

Imagery research and computer science

There are a number of areas for joint encounters between imagery research and computer science, in particular artificial intelligence. One noteworthy attempt in this field is computer simulation of the functioning of the human information processing system. The design of programs that simulate imagery processes, for instance, their use in reasoning, are viewed as a step towards the understanding of naturalistic functioning of imagery. Simulation obviously is not an end in itself, but rather is a heuristic tool or empirical constraint researchers adopt to achieve explicitness and precision in each component of their theories. Rather than allowing scientists to formulate vague questions about the role of images in cognition, simulation constrains them to formulate sets of specific questions on the nature of symbols activated in mental images and the processes manipulating these symbols.

At another level, the computer is not only a tool for explicitation of a theory, but also a model for psychological functions. The human mind and the computer share the ability, and probably the ultimate purpose, of processing information and manipulating symbols. Both are able to process configurations or sets of signals describing objects. In the example of mental scanning, the psychologist postulates the existence of internal representations and formulates questions on the mental operations applied to these representations. Allusion is sometimes made, in a metaphorical way, to some 'inner eye' (or 'mind's eye') which scans over these representations. In fact, the 'mind's eye' which 'looks' at the image cannot be compared to the eye which performs perceptual exploration of external objects. It can be more validly compared to the processes by which a computer interprets configurations of points which are presented to it. Processes operating on mental images can be viewed as sets of tests which evaluate and interpret the data entered into a computer.

Imagery is also the highly stimulating locus of convergence in the domain of natural vs. artificial comprehension of language. In this book, I have referred to the conceptions which consider the human processor as a system equipped with multiple forms of representation, open to a variety of types of exploitation. Theories assuming the joint implementation of propositional and model-like representations in text comprehension consider that a given entity processed by a subject is represented in duplicate, under differentiated symbolic forms. While there are arguments in favour of the utility for the human cognitive system to have alternative forms of representation at its disposal, it is not readily apparent to perceive the advantages of entertaining such redundancy in artificial comprehension systems. Artificial intelligence tools can indeed serve to construct 'economical' comprehension systems based on the implementation of a single form of representation, typically, propositional representations. Today, however, new conceptions reflect the need to enhance the propositional text-base in comprehension systems with analogical forms of representation, to which functions similar to those of imaginal representations in the human processor are assigned. Wouldn't computers, then, generate images designed to serve their own heuristics and computations? Recent work in this area suggests that there may be new prospects for inscribing figural representations in artificial systems which not only depict the meaning of the verbal messages they process, but also are exploited by the system in order to make decisions, for instance judge message coherence by detecting contradictions which would be less readily detected in a propositional text-base (cf. Janlert, 1985).

There are other domains where imagery research can usefully interact with computer science. Many psychological experiments have evidenced the limitations of the human information processing system. For instance, there is a limitation in the number of units likely to be processed simultaneously by subjects. Such limitations are well documented in the domain of visual imagery. To generate and maintain images is more difficult when these images are more complex and contain more elements. This clearly points to the value of procedures aiming at reducing such limitations and, in particular, procedures which allow for the externalization of images and their production in graphic form.

Computerization offers such possibilities for transient production of configurations. It extends the visualization function by providing it with a perceptual substrate, which momentarily frees the processor and allows it to perform cognitive operations on the actual physical configuration which could not be executed on the image (for instance, comparing several design configurations). But mainly, in addition to the possibility to perform cognitive processing on permanent material traces (which other media also make possible), the computer is capable of making this trace evolve. Provided transformation procedures are implemented, images generated on a screen can be affected by dimensional or structural modifications, again showing their value in the computer-assisted generation of configurations. Architecture, technical drawing and the fields of ergonomics and art devoted to design can benefit from joint examination of issues in cognitive psychology and computer-assisted design.

Automatic pattern recognition is another field for potential encounters. People who design expert systems in this domain can gain from better knowledge on how experts segment the objects that they deal with perceptually and how they build figural mental representations of them. The processes which construct representations to be used later in the classification of actual patterns can be taken into account by designers of such systems.

Imagery and human engineering

In the creative activities mentioned above, a major function of imagery is to instantiate hypotheses, i.e., to mentally anticipate on the potential issues of a creative act. Here, images are not used for their capacity to evoke past events, but rather in the context of action planning. One chapter of this book was devoted to analyzing the role of images in human action: resolution of practical problems, creative thinking, orientation in space, preparation for movement and acquisition of motor skills. The works which were reviewed show how mental imagery can serve action. Images, as anticipatory representations of future states of the world, enter naturally into the economy of behaviours by which people act on reality and transform it.

It is not far-flung in this respect to identify links between imagery and the concerns of human engineering. To take a single example, many pictorial aids (maps, schemas, diagrams, etc.) are designed by their creators to be used directly, but it is also likely that users will have to draw on the information from this aid without having direct access to it. It is clear that the conception and design of this aid will determine the ways users exploit the information they acquired from it.

These new developments testify to the significant place of imagery in a number of current cognitive issues. Through its ability to generate in the human mind a form of representation which provides specific possibilities of processing, through the flexibility of this form of representation, which can be subjected to a range of transformational processes, through its capacity to both prolong perceptual events and to anticipate on future states of the world, and to guide creative forms of human action, imagery merits greater attention and renewed efforts in cognitive research.

References

Anderson, J. R. (1978) Arguments concerning representations for mental imagery. *Psychological Review*, 85, 249–77.

Anderson, J. R. (1990) *Cognitive Psychology and its Implications* (3rd edn.). New York: W. H. Freeman.

Anderson, J. R. and Bower, G. H. (1973) *Human Associative Memory*. Washington, DC: Winston.

Anderson, J. R. and Paulson, R. (1978) Interference in memory for pictorial information. *Cognitive Psychology*, 10, 178–202.

Anderson, R. C. and Kulhavy, R. W. (1972) Imagery and prose learning. *Journal of Educational Psychology*, 63, 242–3.

Annett, J. (1988) Imagery and skill acquisition. In M. Denis, J. Engelkamp and J. T. E. Richardson (eds.), *Cognitive and Neuropsychological Approaches to Mental Imagery*, Dordrecht, The Netherlands: Martinus Nijhoff, 259–68.

Antonietti, A. (1991) Why does mental visualization facilitate problem-solving? In R. H. Logie and M. Denis (eds.), *Mental Images in Human Cognition*, Amsterdam: North-Holland, 211–27.

Ashcraft, M. H. (1978) Property norms for typical and atypical items from 17 categories: A description and discussion. *Memory and Cognition*, 6, 227–32.

Baddeley, A. (1986) *Working Memory*. Oxford: Clarendon Press.

Bagnara, S., Simion, F., Tagliabue, M. E. and Umiltà, C. (1988) Comparison processes on visual mental images. *Memory and Cognition*, 16, 138–46.

Banks, W. P. and Flora, J. (1977) Semantic and perceptual processes in symbolic comparisons. *Journal of Experimental Psychology: Human Perception and Performance*, 3, 278–90.

Barclay, J. R., Bransford, J. D., Franks, J. J., McCarrell, N. S. and Nitsch, K. (1974) Comprehension and semantic flexibility. *Journal of Verbal Learning and Verbal Behavior*, 13, 471–81.

Barolo, E., Masini, R. and Antonietti, A. (1990) Mental rotation of solid objects and problem-solving in sighted and blind subjects. *Journal of Mental Imagery*, 14 (3–4), 65–74.

Barrett, J. and Ehrlichman, H. (1982) Bilateral hemispheric alpha activity during visual imagery. *Neuropsychologia*, 20, 703–8.

Basso, A., Bisiach, E. and Luzzatti, C. (1980) Loss of mental imagery: A case study. *Neuropsychologia*, 18, 435–42.

Baylor, G. W. (1971) *A Treatise on the Mind's Eye.* Unpublished doctoral thesis, Carnegie-Mellon University.

Beech, J. R. (1980) An alternative model to account for the Clark and Chase picture verification experiments. *Journal of Mental Imagery*, 4 (2), 1–10.

Beech, J. R. and Allport, D. A. (1978) Visualization of compound scenes. *Perception*, 7, 129–38.

Begg, I. (1978) Imagery and organization in memory: Instructional effects. *Memory and Cognition*, 6, 174–83.

Begg, I. and Paivio, A. (1969) Concreteness and imagery in sentence meaning. *Journal of Verbal Learning and Verbal Behavior*, 8, 821–7.

Belmore, S. M. (1982) The role of imagery in recognition memory for sentences. *Acta Psychologica*, 50, 107–15.

Belmore, S. M., Yates, J. M., Bellack, D. R., Jones, S. N. and Rosenquist, S. E. (1982) Drawing inferences from concrete and abstract sentences. *Journal of Verbal Learning and Verbal Behavior*, 21, 338–51.

Bennett, G. K., Seashore, H. G. and Wesman, A. G. (1963) *Differential Aptitude Tests.* New York: Psychological Corporation.

Berger, G. H. and Gaunitz, S. C. B. (1979) Self-rated imagery and encoding strategies in visual memory. *British Journal of Psychology*, 70, 21–4.

Binet, A. (1886) *La Psychologie du raisonnement.* Paris: Alcan.

Bisiach, E. and Luzzatti, C. (1978) Unilateral neglect of representational space. *Cortex*, 14, 129–33.

Bower, G. H. (1971) Imagery as a relational organizer in associative learning. *Journal of Verbal Learning and Verbal Behavior*, 9, 529–33.

Bower, G. H. and Glass, A. L. (1976) Structural units and the redintegrative power of picture fragments. *Journal of Experimental Psychology: Human Learning and Memory*, 2, 456–66.

Brain, R. W. (1954) Loss of visualization. *Proceedings of the Royal Society of Medicine*, 47, 288–90.

Brooks, L. R. (1970) An extension of the conflict between

visualization and reading. *Quarterly Journal of Experimental Psychology*, 22, 91–6.

Bruner, J. S. (1964) The course of cognitive growth. *American Psychologist*, 19, 1–15.

Bruyer, R. (1982) Neuropsychologie de l'imagerie mentale. *L'Année Psychologique*, 82, 497–512.

Budney, A. J. and Woolfolk, R. L. (1990) Using the wrong image: An exploration of the adverse effects of imagery on motor performance. *Journal of Mental Imagery*, 14 (3–4), 75–86.

Byrne, R. M. J. and Johnson-Laird, P. N. (1989) Spatial reasoning. *Journal of Memory and Language*, 28, 564–75.

Byrne, R. W. (1979) Memory for urban geography. *Quarterly Journal of Experimental Psychology*, 31, 147–54.

Carpenter, P. A. and Just, M. A. (1975) Sentence comprehension: A psycholinguistic processing model of verification. *Psychological Review*, 82, 45–73.

Carr, T. H., McCauley, C., Sperber, R. D. and Parmelee, C. M. (1982) Words, pictures, and priming: On semantic activation, conscious identification, and the automaticity of information processing. *Journal of Experimental Psychology: Human Perception and Performance*, 8, 757–77.

Carroll, J. M., Thomas, J. C. and Malhotra, A. (1980) Presentation and representation in design problem-solving. *British Journal of Psychology*, 71, 143–53.

Cave, K. R. and Kosslyn, S. M. (1989) Varieties of size-specific visual selection. *Journal of Experimental Psychology: General*, 118, 148–64.

Chaguiboff, J. and Denis, M. (1981) Activité d'imagerie et reconnaissance de noms provenant d'un texte narratif. *L'Année Psychologique*, 81, 69–86.

Changeux, J.-P. (1983) *L'Homme neuronal*. Paris: Fayard.

Chase, W. G. and Clark, H. H. (1972) Mental operations in the comparison of sentences and pictures. In L. W. Gregg (ed.), *Cognition in Learning and Memory*. New York: Wiley, 205–32.

Chew, E. I. and Richardson, J. T. E. (1980) The relationship between perceptual and memorial psychophysics. *Bulletin of the Psychonomic Society*, 16, 25–6.

Clark, H. H. (1969) Linguistic processes in deductive reasoning. *Psychological Review*, 76, 387–404.

Cochran, E. L., Pick, A. D. and Pick, H. L., Jr (1983) Task-specific strategies of mental 'rotation' of facial representations. *Memory and Cognition*, 11, 41–8.

Cocude, M. (1988) Generating and maintaining visual images: The incidence of individual and stimulus characteristics. In M. Denis, J. Engelkamp and J. T. E. Richardson (eds.), *Cognitive and Neuropsychological Approaches to Mental Imagery*, Dordrecht, The Netherlands: Martinus Nijhoff, 213–22.

Cocude, M. and Denis, M. (1986) The time course of imagery: Latency and duration of visual images. In D. G. Russell, D. F. Marks and J. T. E. Richardson (eds.), *Imagery 2*, Dunedin, New Zealand: Human Performance Associates, 57–62.

Cocude, M. and Denis, M. (1988) Measuring the temporal characteristics of visual images. *Journal of Mental Imagery*, 12 (1), 89–101.

Cocude, M. and Denis, M. (1990) *Visualizing Dynamic Events: A study of image duration*. Paper presented at the Third European Workshop on Imagery and Cognition, Aberdeen, Scotland, August.

Cohen, R., Baldwin, L. M. and Sherman, R. C. (1978) Cognitive maps of a naturalistic setting. *Child Development*, 49, 1216–18.

Cooper, L. A. (1975) Mental rotation of random two-dimensional shapes. *Cognitive Psychology*, 7, 20–43.

Cooper, L. A. (1976) Demonstration of a mental analog of an external rotation. *Perception and Psychophysics*, 19, 296–302.

Cooper, L. A. and Shepard, R. N. (1973) Chronometric studies of the rotation of mental images. In W. G. Chase (ed.), *Visual Information Processing*, New York: Academic Press, 75–176.

Cooper, L. A. and Shepard, R. N. (1975) Mental transformations in the identification of left and right hands. *Journal of Experimental Psychology: Human Perception and Performance*, 1, 48–56.

Corballis, M. C. and McLaren, R. (1982) Interaction between perceived and imagined rotation. *Journal of Experimental Psychology: Human Perception and Performance*, 8, 215–24.

Cornoldi, C. and Paivio, A. (1982) Imagery value and its effects on verbal memory: A review. *Archivio di Psicologia, Neurologia e Psichiatria*, 43, 171–92.

Costermans, J. (1980) *Psychologie du langage*. Brussels: Pierre Mardaga.

D'Agostino, P. R. and Small, K. G. (1980) Cross-modality transfer between pictures and their names. *Canadian Journal of Psychology*, 34, 113–18.

Davies, G. M. and Proctor, J. (1976) The recall of concrete and abstract sentences as a function of interpolated task. *British Journal of Psychology*, 67, 63–72.

De Beni, R. and Cornoldi, C. (1988) Imagery limitations in totally congenitally blind subjects. *Journal of Experimental Psychology: Learning, Memory, and Cognition*, 14, 650–5.

Decety, J., Jeannerod, M. and Prablanc, C. (1989) The timing of mentally represented actions. *Behavioural Brain Research*, 34, 35–42.

Decety, J. and Michel, F. (1989) Comparative analysis of actual and mental movement times in two graphic tasks. *Brain and Cognition*, 11, 87–97.

Denis, M. (1975) *Représentation imagée et activité de mémorisation.* Paris: Editions du CNRS.

Denis, M. (1979a) Latence d'une réponse graphique à des termes généraux et spécifiques. *L'Année Psychologique*, 79, 143–55.

Denis, M. (1979b) *Les Images mentales.* Paris: Presses Universitaires de France.

Denis, M. (1982a) On figurative components of mental representations. In F. Klix, J. Hoffmann and E. van der Meer (eds.), *Cognitive Research in Psychology*, Amsterdam: North-Holland, 65–71.

Denis, M. (1982b) Images and semantic representations. In J.-F. Le Ny and W. Kintsch (eds.), *Language and Comprehension*, Amsterdam: North-Holland, 17–27.

Denis, M. (1982c) Imaging while reading text: A study of individual differences. *Memory and Cognition*, 10, 540–5.

Denis, M. (1983) Valeur d'imagerie et composition sémantique: analyse de deux échantillons de substantifs. *Cahiers de Psychologie Cognitive*, 3, 175–202.

Denis, M. (1984a) Propriétés figuratives et non figuratives dans l'analyse de concepts. *L'Année Psychologique*, 84, 327–45.

Denis, M. (1984b) Imagery and prose: A critical review of research on adults and children. *Text*, 4, 381–401.

Denis, M. (1985) Visual imagery and the use of mental practice in the development of motor skills. *Canadian Journal of Applied Sport Sciences*, 10, 4S-16S.

Denis, M. (1987) Individual imagery differences and prose processing. In M. A. McDaniel and M. Pressley (eds.), *Imagery and Related Mnemonic Processes: Theories, individual differences, and applications*, New York: Springer-Verlag, 204–17.

Denis, M. (1988) Imagery and prose processing. In M. Denis, J. Engelkamp and J. T. E. Richardson (eds.), *Cognitive and Neuropsychological Approaches to Mental Imagery*, Dordrecht, The Netherlands: Martinus Nijhoff, 121–32.

Denis, M. (1990a) Approches différentielles de l'imagerie mentale. In M. Reuchlin, J. Lautrey, C. Marendaz and T. Ohlmann (eds.), *Cognition: L'individuel et l'universel*. Paris: Presses Universitaires de France, 91–120.

Denis, M. (1990b) Comparing Distances in Images Generated from Verbal Descriptions. Paper presented at the Third European Workshop on Imagery and Cognition, Aberdeen, Scotland, August.

Denis, M. (1991) Imagery and thinking. In C. Cornoldi and M. A. McDaniel (eds.), *Imagery and Cognition*. New York: Springer-Verlag, 103–31.

Denis, M. and Carfantan, M. (1985) People's knowledge about images. *Cognition*, 20, 49–60.

Denis, M. and Carfantan, M. (1986) What people know about visual images: A metacognitive approach to imagery. In D. G. Russell, D. F. Marks and J. T. E. Richardson (eds.), *Imagery 2*. Dunedin, New Zealand: Human Performance Associates, 27–32.

Denis, M. and Carfantan, M. (1990) Enhancing people's knowledge about images. In P. J. Hampson, D. F. Marks and J. T. E. Richardson (eds.), *Imagery: Current developments*. London: Routledge, 197–222.

Denis, M., Chevalier, N. and Eloi, S. (1989) Imagerie et répétition mentale dans l'acquisition d'habiletés motrices. In A. Vom Hofe (ed.), *Tâches, traitement de l'information et comportements dans les activités physiques et sportives*. Issy-les-Moulineaux, France: EAP, 11–37.

Denis, M. and Cocude, M. (1989) Scanning visual images generated from verbal descriptions. *European Journal of Cognitive Psychology*, 1, 293–307.

Denis, M. and Colonelli, C. (1976) Mémorisation de dessins ou de noms selon le matériel utilisé lors de la reconnaissance. *L'Année Psychologique*, 76, 39–53.

Denis, M. and Denhière, G. (1990) Comprehension and recall of spatial descriptions. *European Bulletin of Cognitive Psychology*, 10, 115–43.

Denis, M. and Dubois, D. (1987) Sentence–picture comparison: A paradigm for identifying knowledge structures and comprehension processes. In E. van der Meer and J. Hoffmann (eds.), *Knowledge Aided Information Processing*. Amsterdam: North-Holland, 101–18.

Denis, M. and Le Ny, J.-F. (1986) Centering on figurative features during the comprehension of sentences describing scenes. *Psychological Research*, 48, 145–52.

DeSoto, C. B., London, M. and Handel, S. (1965) Social reasoning and spatial paralogic. *Journal of Personality and Social Psychology*, 2, 513–21.

Desrochers, A. (1988) Imagery, memory, and prose processing. In M. Denis, J. Engelkamp and J. T. E. Richardson (eds.), *Cognitive and Neuropsychological Approaches to Mental Imagery*. Dordrecht, The Netherlands: Martinus Nijhoff, 155–64.

De Vega, M. and Diaz, J. M. (1991) Building referents of indeterminate sentences in the context of short narratives. In R. H. Logie and M. Denis (eds.), *Mental Images in Human Cognition*. Amsterdam: North-Holland, 153–68.

DeVito, C. and Olson, A. M. (1973) More on imagery and the recall of adjectives and nouns from meaningful prose. *Bulletin of the Psychonomic Society*, 1, 397–8.

Dijk, van, T. A. and Kintsch, W. (1983) *Strategies of Discourse Comprehension*. New York: Academic Press.

Dubois, D. and Denis, M. (1988) Knowledge organization and instantiation of general terms in sentence comprehension. *Journal of Experimental Psychology: Learning, Memory, and Cognition*, 14, 604–11.

Duncker, K. (1945) On problem solving. *Psychological Monographs*, 58 (Whole no. 270).

Durso, F. T. and Johnson, M. K. (1979) Facilitation in naming and categorizing repeated pictures and words. *Journal of Experimental Psychology: Human Learning and Memory*, 5, 449–59.

Durso, F. T. and O'Sullivan, C. S. (1983) Naming and remembering proper and common nouns and pictures. *Journal of Experimental Psychology: Learning, Memory, and Cognition*, 9, 497–510.

Eagle, M., Wolitzky, D. L. and Klein, G. S. (1966) Imagery: Effect of a concealed figure in a stimulus. *Science*, 151, 837–9.

Eddy, J. K. and Glass, A. L. (1981) Reading and listening to high and low imagery sentences. *Journal of Verbal Learning and Verbal Behavior*, 20, 333–45.

Ehrlich, K. and Johnson-Laird, P. N. (1982) Spatial descriptions and referential continuity. *Journal of Verbal Learning and Verbal Behavior*, 21, 296–306.

Ehrlichman, H. and Barrett, J. (1983) Right hemispheric specialization for mental imagery: A review of the evidence. *Brain and Cognition*, 2, 55–76.

Einstein, G. O., McDaniel, M. A., Owen, P. D. and Coté, N. C. (1990) Encoding and recall of texts: The importance of material appropriate processing. *Journal of Memory and Language*, 29, 566–81.

Eley, M. G. (1981) Distinguishing imagery from propositional recoding processes in sentence–picture verification tasks. *Canadian Journal of Psychology*, 35, 254–69.

Eloi, S. and Denis, M. (1987) Imagerie et répétition mentale dans l'acquisition d'une habileté sportive. In A. Vom Hofe and R. Simonnet (eds.), *Recherches en psychologie du sport*. Issy-les-Moulineaux: EAP, 45–53.

Emmerich, H. J. and Ackerman, B. P. (1979) The effect of orienting activity on memory for pictures and words in children and adults. *Journal of Experimental Child Psychology*, 28, 499–515.

Engelkamp, J. (1986) Motor programs as part of the meaning of verbal items. In I. Kurcz, G. W. Shugar and J. H. Danks (eds.), *Knowledge and Language*, Amsterdam: North-Holland, 115–38.

Engelkamp, J. and Krumnacker, H. (1980) Imaginale und motorische Prozesse beim Behalten verbalen Materials. *Zeitschrift für experimentelle und angewandte Psychologie*, 27, 511–33.

Erdelyi, M. H. (1982) A note on the level of recall, level of processing, and imagery hypotheses of hypermnesia. *Journal of Verbal Learning and Verbal Behavior*, 21, 656–61.

Erdelyi, M. H., Finkelstein, S., Herrell, N., Miller, B. and Thomas, J. (1976) Coding modality vs. input modality in hypermnesia: Is a rose a rose a rose? *Cognition*, 4, 311–19.

Ernest, C. H. (1977) Imagery ability and cognition: A critical review. *Journal of Mental Imagery*, 1, 181–215.

Ernest, C. H. (1987) Imagery and memory in the blind: A review. In M. A. McDaniel and M. Pressley (eds.), *Imagery and Related Mnemonic Processes: Theories, individual differences, and applications*, New York: Springer-Verlag, 218–38.

Ernest, C. H. and Paivio, A. (1971) Imagery and verbal associative latencies as a function of imagery ability. *Canadian Journal of Psychology*, 25, 83–90.

Eysenck, M. W. (1979) The feeling of knowing a word's meaning. *British Journal of Psychology*, 70, 243–51.

Farah, M. J. (1984) The neurological basis of mental imagery: A componential analysis. *Cognition*, 18, 245–72.

Farah, M. J. (1985) Psychophysical evidence for a shared representational medium for mental images and percepts. *Journal of Experimental Psychology: General*, 114, 91–103.

Farah, M. J. (1988) Is visual imagery really visual? Overlooked evidence from neuropsychology. *Psychological Review*, 95, 307–17.

Farah, M. J. (1989) Mechanisms of imagery-perception interaction.

Journal of Experimental Psychology: Human Perception and Perform-ance, 15, 203–11.

Farah, M. J., Gazzaniga, M. S., Holtzman, J. D. and Kosslyn, S. M. (1985) A left hemisphere basis for visual mental imagery? *Neurop-sychologia*, 23, 115–18.

Farah, M. J., Hammond, K. M., Levine, D. N. and Calvanio, R. (1988a) Visual and spatial mental imagery: Dissociable systems of representation. *Cognitive Psychology*, 20, 439–62.

Farah, M. J., Levine, D. N. and Calvanio, R. (1988) A case study of mental imagery deficit. *Brain and Cognition*, 8, 147–64.

Farah, M. J., Péronnet, F., Gonon, M.-A. and Giard, M.-H. (1988b) Electrophysiological evidence for a shared representational me-dium for visual images and visual percepts. *Journal of Experimental Psychology: General*, 117, 248–57.

Farah, M. J., Weisberg, L. L., Monheit, M. and Péronnet, F. (1989) Brain activity underlying mental imagery: Event-related poten-tials during mental image generation. *Journal of Cognitive Neuro-science*, 1, 302–16.

Farrell, J. E. and Shepard, R. N. (1981) Shape, orientation, and apparent rotational motion. *Journal of Experimental Psychology: Human Perception and Performance*, 7, 477–86.

Feltz, D. L. and Landers, D. M. (1983) The effects of mental practice on motor skill learning and performance: A meta-analysis. *Jour-nal of Sport Psychology*, 5, 25–57.

Finke, R. A. (1980) Levels of equivalence in imagery and percep-tion. *Psychological Review*, 87, 113–32.

Finke, R. A. (1985) Theories relating mental imagery to perception. *Psychological Bulletin*, 98, 236–59.

Finke, R. A. (1989) *Principles of Mental Imagery*. Cambridge, MA: The MIT Press.

Finke, R. A., Johnson, M. K. and Shyi, G. C.-W. (1988) Memory confusions for real and imagined completions of symmetrical visual patterns. *Memory and Cognition*, 16, 133–7.

Finke, R. A. and Kosslyn, S. M. (1980) Mental imagery acuity in the peripheral visual field. *Journal of Experimental Psychology: Human Perception and Performance*, 6, 126–39.

Finke, R. A. and Kurtzman, H. S. (1981) Mapping the visual field in mental imagery. *Journal of Experimental Psychology: General*, 110, 501–17.

Finke, R. A. and Pinker, S. (1982) Spontaneous imagery scanning in mental extrapolation. *Journal of Experimental Psychology: Learning, Memory, and Cognition*, 8, 142–7.

Finke, R. A. and Pinker, S. (1983) Directional scanning of remembered visual patterns. *Journal of Experimental Psychology: Learning, Memory, and Cognition*, 9, 398–410.

Finke, R. A., Pinker, S. and Farah, M. J. (1989) Reinterpreting visual patterns in mental imagery. *Cognitive Science*, 13, 51–78.

Finke, R. A. and Schmidt, M. J. (1977) Orientation-specific color aftereffects following imagination. *Journal of Experimental Psychology: Human Perception and Performance*, 3, 599–606.

Finke, R. A. and Schmidt, M. J. (1978) The quantitative measure of pattern representation in images using orientation-specific color aftereffects. *Perception and Psychophysics*, 23, 515–20.

Finke, R. A. and Shepard, R. N. (1986) Visual functions of mental imagery. In K. R. Boff, L. Kaufman and J. P. Thomas (eds.), *Handbook of Perception and Human Performance: Vol. II. Cognitive Processes and Performance*, New York: Wiley, 37/1–37/55.

Finke, R. A. and Slayton, F. (1988) Explorations of creative visual synthesis in mental imagery. *Memory and Cognition*, 16, 252–7.

Flores d'Arcais, G., Schreuder, R. and Glazenborg, G. (1985) Semantic activation during recognition of referential words. *Psychological Research*, 47, 39–49.

Fodor, J. A. (1975) *The Language of Thought*. New York: Thomas Y. Crowell.

Foos, P. W. (1980) Constructing cognitive maps from sentences. *Journal of Experimental Psychology: Human Learning and Memory*, 6, 25–38.

Fraisse, P. (1970) La verbalisation d'un dessin facilite-t-elle son évocation par l'enfant? *L'Année Psychologique*, 70, 109–22.

Fraisse, P. (1974) Mémoire de dessins et de phrases en fonction de la durée de présentation. *L'Année Psychologique*, 74, 145–56.

Frandsen, A. N. and Holder, J. R. (1969) Spatial visualization in solving complex verbal problems. *Journal of Psychology*, 73, 229–33.

Franklin, N. and Tversky, B. (1990) Searching imagined environments. *Journal of Experimental Psychology: General*, 119, 63–76.

Freyd, J. J. and Finke, R. A. (1984) Facilitation of length discrimination using real and imaged context frames. *American Journal of Psychology*, 97, 323–41.

Friedman, A. (1978) Memorial comparisons without the 'mind's eye'. *Journal of Verbal Learning and Verbal Behavior*, 17, 427–44.

Friedman, A. and Bourne, L. E., Jr (1976) Encoding the levels of information in pictures and words. *Journal of Experimental Psychology: General*, 105, 169–90.

Frith, C. D. and Frith, U. (1978) Feature selection and classification: A developmental study. *Journal of Experimental Child Psychology*, 25, 413–28.

Fuchs, A., Goschke, T. and Gude, D. (1988) On the role of imagery in linear syllogistic reasoning. *Psychological Research*, 50, 43–9.

Garnham, A. (1981) Mental models as representations of text. *Memory and Cognition*, 9, 560–5.

Giesen, C. and Peeck, J. (1984) Effects of imagery instruction on reading and retaining a literary text. *Journal of Mental Imagery*, 8 (2), 79–90.

Gilhooly, R. J. and Falconer, W. A. (1974) Concrete and abstract terms and relations in testing a rule. *Quarterly Journal of Experimental Psychology*, 26, 355–9.

Glass, A. L., Eddy, J. K. and Schwanenflugel, P. J. (1980) The verification of high and low imagery sentences. *Journal of Experimental Psychology: Human Learning and Memory*, 6, 692–704.

Glass, A. L. and Holyoak, K. J. (1986) *Cognition*. New York: Random House.

Glass, A. L., Millen, D. R., Beck, L. G. and Eddy, J. K. (1985) Representation of images in sentence verification. *Journal of Verbal Learning and Verbal Behavior*, 24, 442–65.

Goldenberg, G. (1989) The ability of patients with brain damage to generate mental visual images. *Brain*, 112, 305–25.

Goldenberg, G., Podreka, I., Steiner, M., Suess, E., Deecke, L. and Willmes, K. (1988) Pattern of regional cerebral blood flow related to visual and motor imagery: Results of Emission Computerized Tomography. In M. Denis, J. Engelkamp and J. T. E. Richardson (eds.), *Cognitive and Neuropsychological Approaches to Mental Imagery*. Dordrecht, The Netherlands: Martinus Nijhoff, 363–73.

Goldenberg, G., Podreka, I., Steiner, M. and Willmes, K. (1987) Patterns of regional cerebral blood flow related to memorizing of high and low imagery words – An emission computer tomography study. *Neuropsychologia*, 25, 473–85.

Gordon, I. E. and Hayward, S. (1973) Second-order isomorphism of internal representations of familiar faces. *Perception and Psychophysics*, 14, 334–6.

Green, D. W. (1977) The immediate processing of sentences. *Quarterly Journal of Experimental Psychology*, 29, 135–46.

Grossi, D., Modafferi, A., Pelosi, L. and Trojano, L. (1989) On the different roles of the cerebral hemispheres in mental imagery: The 'o'Clock Test' in two clinical cases. *Brain and Cognition*, 10, 18–27.

Guenther, R. K. (1980) Conceptual memory for picture and prose episodes. *Memory and Cognition*, 8, 563–72.

Guilford, J. P. (1967) *The Nature of Human Intelligence*. New York: McGraw-Hill.

Gur, R. C. and Hilgard, E. R. (1975) Visual imagery and the discrimination of differences between altered pictures simultaneously and successively presented. *British Journal of Psychology*, 66, 341–5.

Hale, B. D. (1982) The effects of internal and external imagery on muscular and ocular concomitants. *Journal of Sport Psychology*, 4, 379–87.

Handel, S., DeSoto, C. B. and London, M. (1968) Reasoning and spatial representations. *Journal of Verbal Learning and Verbal Behavior*, 7, 351–7.

Harris, P. L., Morris, P. E. and Bassett, E. (1977) Classifying pictures and words: Implications for the dual-coding hypothesis. *Memory and Cognition*, 5, 242–6.

Haynes, W. O. and Moore, W. H. (1981) Sentence imagery and recall: An electroencephalographic evaluation of hemispheric processing in males and females. *Cortex*, 17, 49–62.

Hebb, D. O. (1968) Concerning imagery. *Psychological Review*, 75, 466–77.

Helstrup, T. and Anderson, R. E. (1991) Imagery in mental construction and decomposition tasks. In R. H. Logie and M. Denis (eds.), *Mental Images in Human Cognition*, Amsterdam: North-Holland, 229–40.

Heuer, H. (1985) *Mental Practice of Motor Skills*. Report 44/1985, Research Group on Perception and Action, Center for Interdisciplinary Research, University of Bielefeld, Germany.

Hirtle, S. C. and Jonides, J. (1985) Evidence of hierarchies in cognitive maps. *Memory and Cognition*, 13, 208–17.

Hirtle, S. C. and Mascolo, M. F. (1986) Effect of semantic clustering on the memory of spatial locations. *Journal of Experimental Psychology: Learning, Memory, and Cognition*, 12, 182–9.

Hiscock, M. (1976) Effects of adjective imagery on recall from prose. *Journal of General Psychology*, 94, 295–9.

Hishitani, S. (1985) Imagery differences and task characteristics in memory. In D. F. Marks and D. G. Russell (eds.), *Imagery 1*, Dunedin, New Zealand: Human Performance Associates, 5–13.

Hoffmann, J. (1982) Representation of concepts and the classification of objects. In F. Klix, J. Hoffmann and E. van der Meer (eds.), *Cognitive Research in Psychology*, Amsterdam: North-

Holland, 72–89.

Hoffmann, J., Denis, M. and Ziessler, M. (1983) Figurative features and the construction of visual images. *Psychological Research*, 45, 39–54.

Holmes, V. M. and Langford, J. (1976) Comprehension and recall of abstract and concrete sentences. *Journal of Verbal Learning and Verbal Behavior*, 15, 559–66.

Holt, R. R. (1964) Imagery: The return of the ostracized. *American Psychologist*, 19, 254–64.

Holyoak, K. J. (1974) The role of imagery in the evaluation of sentences: Imagery or semantic factors? *Journal of Verbal Learning and Verbal Behavior*, 13, 163–6.

Holyoak, K. J. (1977) The form of analog size information in memory. *Cognitive Psychology*, 9, 31–51.

Holyoak, K. J. and Mah, W. A. (1982) Cognitive reference points in judgments of symbolic magnitude. *Cognitive Psychology*, 14, 328–52.

Huttenlocher, J. (1968) Constructing spatial images: A strategy in reasoning. *Psychological Review*, 75, 550–60.

Intons-Peterson, M. J. (1983) Imagery paradigms: How vulnerable are they to experimenters' expectations? *Journal of Experimental Psychology: Human Perception and Performance*, 9, 394–412.

Intons-Peterson, M. J. and McDaniel, M. A. (1991) Symmetries and asymmetries between imagery and perception. In C. Cornoldi and M. A. McDaniel (eds.), *Imagery and Cognition*, New York: Springer-Verlag, 47–76.

Intons-Peterson, M. J. and Roskos-Ewoldsen, B. B. (1989) Sensory-perceptual qualities of images. *Journal of Experimental Psychology: Learning, Memory, and Cognition*, 15, 188–99.

Intons-Peterson, M. J. and White, A. R. (1981) Experimenter naiveté and imaginal judgments. *Journal of Experimental Psychology: Human Perception and Performance*, 7, 833–43.

Irwin, D. I. and Lupker, S. J. (1983) Semantic priming of pictures and words: A levels of processing approach. *Journal of Verbal Learning and Verbal Behavior*, 22, 45–60.

Janlert, L.-E. (1985) *Studies in Knowledge Representation*. University of Umea, Institute of Information Processing, Report UMINF-127.85.

Johnson, M. K., Bransford, J. D., Nyberg, S. E. and Cleary, J. J. (1972) Comprehension factors in interpreting memory for abstract and concrete sentences. *Journal of Verbal Learning and Verbal Behavior*, 11, 451–4.

Johnson, M. K. and Raye, C. L. (1981) Reality monitoring. *Psychological Review*, 88, 67–85.

Johnson, M. K., Raye, C. L., Wang, A. Y. and Taylor, T. H. (1979) Fact and fantasy: The roles of accuracy and variability in confusing imaginations with perceptual experiences. *Journal of Experimental Psychology: Human Learning and Memory*, 5, 229–40.

Johnson, M. K., Taylor, T. H. and Raye, C. L. (1977) Fact and fantasy: The effects of internally generated events on the apparent frequency of externally generated events. *Memory and Cognition*, 5, 116–22.

Johnson, P. (1982) The functional equivalence of imagery and movement. *Quarterly Journal of Experimental Psychology*, 34A, 349–65.

Johnson, R. E. (1974) Abstractive processes in the remembering of prose. *Journal of Educational Psychology*, 66, 772–9.

Johnson-Laird, P. N. (1972) The three-term series problem. *Cognition*, 1, 57–82.

Johnson-Laird, P. N. (1980) Mental models in cognitive science. *Cognitive Science*, 4, 71–115.

Johnson-Laird, P. N. (1983) *Mental Models: Towards a cognitive science of language, inference, and consciousness*. Cambridge: Cambridge University Press.

Johnson-Laird, P. N. (1989) Mental models. In M. I. Posner (ed.), *Foundations of Cognitive Science*, Cambridge, MA: The MIT Press, 469–99.

Johnson-Laird, P. N., Gibbs, G. and de Mowbray, J. (1978) Meaning, amount of processing, and memory for words. *Memory and Cognition*, 6, 372–5.

Jolicoeur, P. and Kosslyn, S. M. (1985) Is time to scan visual images due to demand characteristics? *Memory and Cognition*, 13, 320–32.

Jones, G. V. (1985) Deep dyslexia, imageability, and ease of predication. *Brain and Language*, 24, 1–19.

Jones, G. V. (1988) Images, predicates, and retrieval cues. In M. Denis, J. Engelkamp and J. T. E. Richardson (eds.), *Cognitive and Neuropsychological Approaches to Mental Imagery*, Dordrecht, The Netherlands: Martinus Nijhoff, 89–98.

Jones-Gotman, M. (1979) Incidental learning of image-mediated or pronounced words after right temporal lobectomy. *Cortex*, 15, 187–97.

Jones-Gotman, M. and Milner, B. (1978) Right temporal-lobe contribution to image-mediated verbal learning. *Neuropsychologia*, 16, 61–71.

Jorgensen, C. C. and Kintsch, W. (1973) The role of imagery in the evaluation of sentences. *Cognitive Psychology*, 4, 110–6.

Katz, A. N. (1978) Differences in the saliency of sensory features elicited by words. *Canadian Journal of Psychology*, 32, 156–79.

Katz, A. N. (1981) Knowing about the sensory properties of objects. *Quarterly Journal of Experimental Psychology*, 33A, 39–49.

Katz, A. N. (1987) Individual differences in the control of imagery processing: Knowing how, knowing when, and knowing self. In M. A. McDaniel and M. Pressley (eds.), *Imagery and Related Mnemonic Processes: Theories, individual differences, and applications*, New York: Springer-Verlag, 177–203.

Kaufmann, G. (1979) *Visual Imagery and its Relation to Problem Solving*. Bergen: Universitetsforlaget.

Kaufmann, G. (1980) *Imagery, Language and Cognition: Toward a theory of symbolic activity in human problem-solving*. Bergen: Universitetsforlaget.

Kaufmann, G. (1985) A theory of symbolic representation in problem solving. *Journal of Mental Imagery*, 9 (2), 51–69.

Keenan, J. M. and Moore, R. E. (1979) Memory for images of concealed objects: A re-examination of Neisser and Kerr. *Journal of Experimental Psychology: Human Learning and Memory*, 5, 374–85.

Kelter, S., Grötzbach, H., Freiheit, R., Höhle, B., Wutzig, S. and Diesch, E. (1984) Object identification: The mental representation of physical and conceptual attributes. *Memory and Cognition*, 12, 123–33.

Kintsch, W. (1974) *The Representation of Meaning in Memory*. Hillsdale, NJ: Lawrence Erlbaum Associates.

Kintsch, W. (1986) Memory for prose. In F. Klix and H. Hagendorf (eds.), *Human Memory and Cognitive Capabilities: Mechanisms and performances*, Amsterdam: North-Holland, 841–50.

Kintsch, W. and van Dijk, T. A. (1978) Toward a model of text comprehension and production. *Psychological Review*, 85, 363–94.

Kintsch, W. and Young, S. R. (1984) Selective recall of decision-relevant information from texts. *Memory and Cognition*, 12, 112–7.

Kirby, K. N. and Kosslyn, S. M. (1990) Thinking visually. *Mind and Language*, 5, 324–41.

Kirchner, E. P. (1969) Vividness of adjectives and the recall of meaningful verbal material. *Psychonomic Science*, 15, 71–2.

Klatzky, R. L. and Martin, G. L. (1983) Categorical and idiosyncratic imagery as preparation for object perception. *Journal of Mental Imagery*, 7 (1), 1–17.

Klee, H. and Eysenck, M. W. (1973) Comprehension of abstract and concrete sentences. *Journal of Verbal Learning and Verbal Behavior*, 12, 522–9.

Kohl, R. M. and Roenker, D. L. (1980) Bilateral transfer as a function of mental imagery. *Journal of Motor Behavior*, 12, 197–206.

Kohl, R. M. and Roenker, D. L. (1983) Mechanism involvement during skill imagery. *Journal of Motor Behavior*, 15, 179–90.

Kosslyn, S. M. (1973) Scanning visual images: Some structural implications. *Perception and Psychophysics*, 14, 90–4.

Kosslyn, S. M. (1975) Information representation in visual images. *Cognitive Psychology*, 7, 341–70.

Kosslyn, S. M. (1976) Can imagery be distinguished from other forms of internal representation? Evidence from studies of information retrieval times. *Memory and Cognition*, 4, 291–7.

Kosslyn, S. M. (1980) *Image and Mind*. Cambridge, MA: Harvard University Press.

Kosslyn, S. M. (1981) The medium and the message in mental imagery: A theory. *Psychological Review*, 88, 46–66.

Kosslyn, S. M. (1983) *Ghosts in the Mind's Machine: Creating and using images in the brain*. New York: W. W. Norton.

Kosslyn, S. M. (1984) Mental representation. In J. R. Anderson and S. M. Kosslyn (eds.), *Tutorials in Learning and Memory: Essays in honor of Gordon Bower*, San Francisco: W. H. Freeman, 91–117.

Kosslyn, S. M. (1987) Seeing and imagining in the cerebral hemispheres: A computational approach. *Psychological Review*, 94, 148–75.

Kosslyn, S. M. (1988) Aspects of a cognitive neuroscience of mental imagery. *Science*, 240, 1621–6.

Kosslyn, S. M. (1991) A cognitive neuroscience of visual cognition: Further developments. In R. H. Logie and M. Denis (eds.), *Mental Images in Human Cognition*, Amsterdam: North-Holland, 351–81.

Kosslyn, S. M., Ball, T. M. and Reiser, B. J. (1978) Visual images preserve metric spatial information: Evidence from studies of image scanning. *Journal of Experimental Psychology: Human Perception and Performance*, 4, 47–60.

Kosslyn, S. M. and Bower, G. H. (1974) The role of imagery in sentence memory: A developmental study. *Child Development*, 45, 30–8.

Kosslyn, S. M., Brunn, J., Cave, K. R. and Wallach, R. W. (1984) Individual differences in mental imagery: A computational analysis. *Cognition*, 18, 195–243.

Kosslyn, S. M., Cave, C. B., Provost, D. A. and von Gierke, S. M.

(1988) Sequential processes in image generation. *Cognitive Psychology*, 20, 319–43.

Kosslyn, S. M., Flynn, R. A., Amsterdam, J. B. and Wang, G. (1990a) Components of high-level vision: A cognitive neuroscience analysis and accounts of neurological syndromes. *Cognition*, 34, 203–77.

Kosslyn, S. M., Holtzman, J. D., Farah, M. J. and Gazzaniga, M. S. (1985) A computational analysis of mental image generation: Evidence from functional dissociations in split-brain patients. *Journal of Experimental Psychology: General*, 114, 311–41.

Kosslyn, S. M., Holyoak, K. J. and Huffman, C. S. (1976) A processing approach to the dual coding hypothesis. *Journal of Experimental Psychology: Human Learning and Memory*, 2, 223–33.

Kosslyn, S. M., Murphy, G. L., Bemesderfer, M. E. and Feinstein, K. J. (1977) Category and continuum in mental comparisons. *Journal of Experimental Psychology: General*, 106, 341–75.

Kosslyn, S. M., Pick, H. L., Jr and Fariello, G. R. (1974) Cognitive maps in children and men. *Child Development*, 45, 707–16.

Kosslyn, S. M., Pinker, S., Smith, G. E. and Shwartz, S. P. (1979) On the demystification of mental imagery. *The Behavioral and Brain Sciences*, 2, 535–81.

Kosslyn, S. M. and Pomerantz, J. R. (1977) Imagery, propositions, and the form of internal representations. *Cognitive Psychology*, 9, 52–76.

Kosslyn, S. M., Reiser, B. J., Farah, M. J. and Fliegel, S. L. (1983) Generating visual images: Units and relations. *Journal of Experimental Psychology: General*, 112, 278–303.

Kosslyn, S. M., Seger, C., Pani, J. R. and Hillger, L. A. (1990b) When is imagery used in everyday life? A diary study. *Journal of Mental Imagery*, 14 (3–4), 131–52.

Kosslyn, S. M. and Shwartz, S. P. (1977) A simulation of visual imagery. *Cognitive Science*, 1, 265–95.

Kosslyn, S. M., Van Kleeck, M. H. and Kirby, K. N. (1990) A neurologically plausible model of individual differences in visual mental imagery. In P. J. Hampson, D. F. Marks and J. T. E. Richardson (eds.), *Imagery: Current developments*, London: Routledge, 39–77.

Kuiper, N. A. and Paivio, A. (1977). Incidental recognition memory for concrete and abstract sentences equated for comprehensibility. *Bulletin of the Psychonomic Society*, 9, 247–9.

Lautrey, J. and Chartier, D. (1991) A developmental approach to mental imagery. In C. Cornoldi and M. A. McDaniel (eds.),

Imagery and Cognition, New York: Springer-Verlag, 247–82.

Le Ny, J.-F. (1979) *La Sémantique psychologique*. Paris: Presses Universitaires de France.

Le Ny, J.-F. (1985) Comment (se) représenter les représentations. *Psychologie Française*, 30, 231–8.

Le Ny, J.-F. (1989) *Science cognitive et compréhension du langage*. Paris: Presses Universitaires de France.

Levelt, W. J. M. (1982) Linearization in describing spatial networks. In S. Peters and E. Saarinen (eds.), *Processes, Beliefs, and Questions*, Dordrecht, The Netherlands: Reidel, 199–220.

Levelt, W. J. M. (1989) *Speaking: From intention to articulation*. Cambridge, MA: The MIT Press.

Levin, J. R. and Divine-Hawkins, P. (1974) Visual imagery as a prose-learning process. *Journal of Reading Behavior*, 6, 23–30.

Levine, M., Jankovic, I. N. and Palij, M. (1982) Principles of spatial problem solving. *Journal of Experimental Psychology: General*, 111, 157–75.

Light, L. L. and Berger, D. E. (1976) Are there long-term 'literal copies' of visually presented words? *Journal of Experimental Psychology: Human Learning and Memory*, 2, 654–62.

Logie, R. H. (1989) Characteristics of visual short-term memory. *European Journal of Cognitive Psychology*, 1, 275–84.

Logie, R. H. (1991) Visuo-spatial short-term memory: Visual working memory or visual buffer? In C. Cornoldi and M. A. McDaniel (eds.), *Imagery and Cognition*, New York: Springer-Verlag, 77–102.

Logie, R. H. and Baddeley, A. D. (1990) Imagery and working memory. In P. J. Hampson, D. F. Marks and J. T. E. Richardson (eds.), *Imagery: Current developments*, London: Routledge, 103–28.

Lynch, K. (1960) *The Image of the City*. Cambridge, MA: The MIT Press.

MacLeod, C. M., Hunt, E. B. and Mathews, N. N. (1978) Individual differences in the verification of sentence–picture relationships. *Journal of Verbal Learning and Verbal Behavior*, 17, 493–507.

Maher, J. H., Jr. and Sullivan, H. (1982) Effects of mental imagery and oral and print stimuli on prose learning of intermediate grade children. *Educational Communication and Technology*, 30, 175–83.

Mahoney, M. J. and Avener, M. (1977) Psychology of the elite athlete: An exploratory study. *Cognitive Therapy and Research*, 1, 135–41.

Mandler, J. M. (1983) Representation. In J. H. Flavell and E. M. Markman (eds.), *Cognitive Development*. Vol. 3 of P. Mussen (ed.), *Manual of Child Psychology*, New York: Wiley, 420–94.

Mandler, J. M. and Mandler, G. (1964) *Thinking: From association to Gestalt*, New York: Wiley.

Mani, K. and Johnson-Laird, P. N. (1982) The mental representation of spatial descriptions. *Memory and Cognition*, 10, 181–7.

Marks, D. F. (1973) Visual imagery differences in the recall of pictures. *British Journal of Psychology*, 64, 17–24.

Marks, D. F. (1977) Imagery and consciousness: A theoretical review from an individual differences perspective. *Journal of Mental Imagery*, 1, 275–90.

Marmor, G. S. (1977) Age of onset of blindness in visual imagery development. *Perceptual and Motor Skills*, 45, 1031–4.

Marschark, M. (1985) Imagery and organization in the recall of prose. *Journal of Memory and Language*, 24, 734–45.

Marschark, M. and Paivio, A. (1977) Integrative processing of concrete and abstract sentences. *Journal of Verbal Learning and Verbal Behavior*, 16, 217–31.

Marschark, M., Richman, C. L., Yuille, J. C. and Hunt, R. R. (1987) The role of imagery in memory: On shared and distinctive information. *Psychological Bulletin*, 102, 28–41.

Marschark, M., Warner, J., Thomson, R. and Huffman, C. (1991) Concreteness, imagery, and memory for prose. In R. H. Logie and M. Denis (eds.), *Mental Images in Human Cognition*, Amsterdam: North-Holland, 193–207.

Marteniuk, R. G. (1976) *Information Processing in Motor Skills*. New York: Holt, Rinehart & Winston.

Mathews, N. N., Hunt, E. B. and MacLeod, C. M. (1980) Strategy choice and strategy training in sentence–picture verification. *Journal of Verbal Learning and Verbal Behavior*, 19, 531–48.

McCollough, C. (1965) Color adaptation of edge-detectors in the human visual system. *Science*, 149, 1115–16.

McDaniel, M. A., Einstein, G. O., Dunay, P. K. and Cobb, R. E. (1986) Encoding difficulty and memory: Toward a unifying theory. *Journal of Memory and Language*, 25, 645–56.

McGlynn, F. D. and Gordon, B. C. (1973) Image latency and reported clarity as functions of image complexity. *Psychological Record*, 23, 223–7.

McGlynn, F. D., Hofius, D. and Watulak, G. (1974) Further evaluation of image latency and reported clarity as functions of image complexity. *Perceptual and Motor Skills*, 38, 559–65.

McKelvie, S. J. and Demers, E. G. (1979) Individual differences in reported visual imagery and memory performance. *British Journal of Psychology*, 70, 51–7.

McKelvie, S. J. and Rohrberg, M. M. (1978) Individual differences in reported visual imagery and cognitive performance. *Perceptual and Motor Skills*, 46, 451–8.

McNamara, T. P. (1986) Mental representations of spatial relations. *Cognitive Psychology*, 18, 87–121.

McNamara, T. P., Altarriba, J., Bendele, M., Johnson, S. C. and Clayton, K. N. (1989) Constraints on priming in spatial memory: Naturally learned versus experimentally learned environments. *Memory and Cognition*, 17, 444–53.

McNamara, T. P., Ratcliff, R. and McKoon, G. (1984) The mental representation of knowledge acquired from maps. *Journal of Experimental Psychology: Learning, Memory, and Cognition*, 10, 723–32.

McNamara, T. P. and Sternberg, R. J. (1983) Mental models of word meaning. *Journal of Verbal Learning and Verbal Behavior*, 22, 449–74.

Mehler, J., Walker, E. C. T. and Garrett, M. (1982) *Perspectives on Mental Representation: Experimental and theoretical studies of cognitive processes and capacities*. Hillsdale, NJ: Lawrence Erlbaum Associates.

Meyerson, I. (1932) Les images. In G. Dumas (ed.), *Nouveau traité de psychologie. Tome II: Les fondements de la vie mentale*, Paris: Alcan, 541–606.

Miller, A. I. (1984) *Imagery in Scientific Thought: Creating 20th-century physics*. Boston: Birkhäuser.

Miller, G. A. (1972) English verbs of motion: A case study in semantics and lexical memory. In A. W. Welton and E. Martin (eds.), *Coding Processes in Human Memory*, Washington, DC: Winston, 335–72.

Milner, B. (1974) Hemispheric specialization: Scope and limits. In F. O. Schmitt and F. G. Worden (eds.), *The Neurosciences: Third study program*. Cambridge, MA: The MIT Press, 75–89.

Mitchell, D. B. and Richman, C. L. (1980) Confirmed reservations: Mental travel. *Journal of Experimental Psychology: Human Perception and Performance*, 6, 58–66.

Moar, I. and Bower, G. H. (1983) Inconsistency in spatial knowledge. *Memory and Cognition*, 11, 107–13.

Moeser, S. D. (1974) Memory for meaning and wording in concrete and abstract sentences. *Journal of Verbal Learning and Verbal Behavior*, 13, 682–97.

Mohr, G. and Engelkamp, J. (1991) Size comparison with verbal and pictorial material. In R. H. Logie and M. Denis (eds.), *Mental Images in Human Cognition*, Amsterdam: North-Holland, 129–40.

Morra, S. (1989) Developmental differences in the use of verbatim versus spatial representations in the recall of spatial descriptions. *Journal of Memory and Language*, 28, 37–55.

Morris, P. E. and Reid, R. L. (1972) Imagery and the recall of adjectives and nouns from meaningful prose. *Psychonomic Science*, 27, 117–18.

Morris, P. E. and Reid, R. L. (1973) Recognition and recall: Latency and recurrence of images. *British Journal of Psychology*, 64, 161–7.

Mowrer, O. H. (1960) *Learning Theory and the Symbolic Processes*. New York: Wiley.

Moyer, R. S. (1973) Comparing objects in memory: Evidence suggesting an internal psychophysics. *Perception and Psychophysics*, 13, 180–4.

Murphy, G. L. and Smith, E. E. (1982) Basic-level superiority in picture categorization. *Journal of Verbal Learning and Verbal Behavior*, 21, 1–20.

Murray, F. S. and Szymczyk, J. M. (1978) Effects of distinctive features on recognition of incomplete pictures. *Developmental Psychology*, 14, 356–62.

Neisser, U. (1967) *Cognitive Psychology*. New York: Appleton-Century-Crofts.

Neisser, U. (1972) Changing conceptions of imagery. In P. W. Sheehan (ed.), *The Function and Nature of Imagery*, New York: Academic Press, 233–51.

Nelson, D. L., Reed, V. S. and McEvoy, C. L. (1977) Learning to order pictures and words: A model of sensory and semantic encoding. *Journal of Experimental Psychology: Human Learning and Memory*, 3, 485–97.

Newell, A. and Simon, H. A. (1972) *Human problem solving*. Englewood Cliffs, NJ: Prentice Hall.

Newstead, S. E., Manktelow, K. I. and Evans, J. St B. T. (1982) The role of imagery in the representation of linear orderings. *Current Psychological Research*, 2, 21–32.

Norman, D. A. and Rumelhart, D. E. (1975) *Explorations in Cognition*. San Francisco: W. H. Freeman.

Ochanine, D. (1978) Le rôle des images opératives dans la régulation des activités de travail. *Psychologie et Education*, 2 (2), 63–72.

Osgood, C. E. (1953) *Method and Theory in Experimental Psychology.* New York: Oxford.

Pailhous, J. (1970) *La Représentation de l'espace urbain.* Paris: Presses Universitaires de France.

Paivio, A. (1966) Latency of verbal associations and imagery to noun stimuli as a function of abstractness and generality. *Canadian Journal of Psychology,* 20, 378–87.

Paivio, A. (1971) *Imagery and Verbal Processes,* New York: Holt, Rinehart & Winston.

Paivio, A. (1974) Spacing of repetitions in the incidental and intentional free recall of pictures and words. *Journal of Verbal Learning and Verbal Behavior,* 13, 497–511.

Paivio, A. (1975a) Neomentalism. *Canadian Journal of Psychology,* 29, 263–91.

Paivio, A. (1975b) Imagery and synchronic thinking. *Canadian Psychological Review,* 16, 147–63.

Paivio, A. (1975c) Perceptual comparisons through the mind's eye. *Memory and Cognition,* 3, 635–47.

Paivio, A. (1977) Images, propositions, and knowledge. In J. M. Nicholas (ed.), *Images, Perception, and Knowledge.* Dordrecht: Reidel.

Paivio, A. (1978a) Comparison of mental clocks. *Journal of Experimental Psychology: Human Perception and Performance,* 4, 61–71.

Paivio, A. (1978b) Mental comparisons involving abstract attributes. *Memory and Cognition,* 6, 199–208.

Paivio, A. (1982) The empirical case for dual coding. In J. C. Yuille (ed.), *Imagery, Memory and Cognition: Essays in honor of Allan Paivio,* Hillsdale, NJ: Lawrence Erlbaum Associates, 307–32.

Paivio, A. (1986) *Mental Representations: A dual coding approach.* New York: Oxford University Press.

Paivio, A. (1991) *Images in Mind: The evolution of a theory.* Hemel Hempstead: Harvester Wheatsheaf.

Paivio, A. and Begg, I. (1971) Imagery and comprehension latencies as a function of sentence concreteness and structure. *Perception and Psychophysics,* 10, 408–12.

Paivio, A. and Begg, I. (1981) *Psychology of Language.* Englewood Cliffs, NJ: Prentice Hall.

Paivio, A., Clark, J. M., Digdon, N. and Bons, T. (1989) Referential processing: Reciprocity and correlates of naming and imaging. *Memory and Cognition,* 17, 163–74.

Paivio, A. and Csapo, K. (1973) Picture superiority in free recall: Imagery or dual coding? *Cognitive Psychology,* 5, 176–206.

Paivio, A. and Ernest, C. H. (1971) Imagery ability and visual perception of verbal and nonverbal stimuli. *Perception and Psychophysics*, 10, 429–32.

Paivio, A. and Harshman, R. (1983) Factor analysis of a questionnaire on imagery and verbal habits and skills. *Canadian Journal of Psychology*, 37, 461–83.

Paivio, A. and Okovita, H. W. (1971) Word imagery modalities and associative learning in blind and sighted subjects. *Journal of Verbal Learning and Verbal Behavior*, 10, 506–10.

Paivio, A., Rogers, T. B. and Smythe, P. C. (1968) Why are pictures easier to recall than words? *Psychonomic Science*, 11, 137–8.

Paivio, A. and te Linde, J. (1982) Imagery, memory, and the brain. *Canadian Journal of Psychology*, 36, 243–72.

Paivio, A., Yuille, J. C. and Madigan, S. A. (1968) Concreteness, imagery, and meaningfulness values for 925 nouns. *Journal of Experimental Psychology Monograph Supplement*, 76 (1, Pt 2).

Palmer, S. E. (1977) Hierarchical structure in perceptual representation. *Cognitive Psychology*, 9, 441–74.

Palmer, S. E. (1978) Fundamental aspects of cognitive representations. In E. Rosch and B. B. Lloyd (eds.), *Cognition and Categorization*, Hillsdale, NJ: Lawrence Erlbaum Associates, 259–303.

Patten, B. M. (1973) Visually mediated thinking: A report of the case of Albert Einstein. *Journal of Learning Disabilities*, 6, 415–20.

Perky, C. W. (1910) An experimental study of imagination. *American Journal of Psychology*, 21, 422–52.

Péronnet, F. and Farah, M. J. (1989) Mental rotation: An event-related potential study with a validated mental rotation task. *Brain and Cognition*, 9, 279–88.

Perrig, W. J. (1986) Imagery and the thematic storage of prose. In D. G. Russell, D. F. Marks and J. T. E. Richardson (eds.), *Imagery 2*, Dunedin, New Zealand: Human Performance Associates, 77–82.

Perrig, W. and Kintsch, W. (1985) Propositional and situational representations of text. *Journal of Memory and Language*, 24, 503–18.

Peterson, M. J. (1975) The retention of imagined and seen spatial matrices. *Cognitive Psychology*, 7, 181–93.

Peterson, M. J. and Graham, S. E. (1974) Visual detection and visual imagery. *Journal of Experimental Psychology*, 103, 509–14.

Pezdek, K. and Royer, J. M. (1974) The role of comprehension in learning concrete and abstract sentences. *Journal of Verbal Learning and Verbal Behavior*, 13, 551–8.

Philipchalk, R. P. (1972) Thematicity, abstractness, and the long-term recall of connected discourse. *Psychonomic Science*, 27, 361–2.

Piaget, J. and Inhelder, B. (1966) *L'Image mentale chez l'enfant*, Paris: Presses Universitaires de France.

Pinker, S. (1984) Visual cognition: An introduction. *Cognition*, 18, 1–63.

Pinker, S., Choate, P. A. and Finke, R. A. (1984) Mental extrapolation in patterns constructed from memory. *Memory and Cognition*, 12, 207–18.

Plant, D. C. and Farah, M. J. (1990) Visual object representation: Interpreting neurophysiological data within a computational framework. *Journal of Cognitive Neuroscience*, 2, 320–43.

Podgorny, P. and Shepard, R. N. (1978) Functional representations common to visual perception and imagination. *Journal of Experimental Psychology: Human Perception and Performance*, 4, 21–35.

Poltrock, S. E. and Brown, P. (1984) Individual differences in visual imagery and spatial ability. *Intelligence*, 8, 93–138.

Pomerantz, J. R., Sager, L. C. and Stoever, R. J. (1977) Perception of wholes and of their component parts: Some configural superiority effects. *Journal of Experimental Psychology: Human Perception and Performance*, 3, 422–35.

Potter, M. C. (1979) Mundane symbolism: The relations among objects, names, and ideas. In N. R. Smith and M. B. Franklin (eds.), *Symbolic Functioning in Childhood*, Hillsdale, NJ: Lawrence Erlbaum Associates, 41–65.

Potter, M. C., Valian, V. V. and Faulconer, B. A. (1977) Representation of a sentence and its pragmatic implications: Verbal, imagistic, or abstract? *Journal of Verbal Learning and Verbal Behavior*, 16, 1–12.

Presson, C. C., DeLange, N. and Hazelrigg, M. D. (1989) Orientation specificity in spatial memory: What makes a path different from a map of the path? *Journal of Experimental Psychology: Learning, Memory, and Cognition*, 15, 887–97.

Pylyshyn, Z. W. (1973) What the mind's eye tells the mind's brain: A critique of mental imagery. *Psychological Bulletin*, 80, 1–24.

Pylyshyn, Z. W. (1979) The rate of 'mental rotation' of images: A test of a holistic analogue hypothesis. *Memory and Cognition*, 7, 19–28.

Pylyshyn, Z. W. (1981) The imagery debate: Analogue media versus tacit knowledge. *Psychological Review*, 88, 16–45.

Quinton, G. and Fellows, B. J. (1975) 'Perceptual' strategies in the solving of three-term series problems. *British Journal of Psychology*, 66, 69–78.

Ramey, J.-C., Péruch, P. and Pailhous, J. (1982) Influence des relations entre les observables sur l'élaboration du référentiel spatial exocentré. *Cahiers de Psychologie Cognitive*, 2, 207–16.

Rasco, R. W., Tennyson, R. D. and Boutwell, R. C. (1975) Imagery instructions and drawings in learning prose. *Journal of Educational Psychology*, 67, 188–92.

Reeves, A. (1980) Visual imagery in backward masking. *Perception and Psychophysics*, 28, 118–24.

Rehm, L. P. (1973) Relationships among measures of visual imagery. *Behaviour Research and Therapy*, 11, 265–70.

Richard, J.-F. (1990) *Les Activités mentales: Comprendre, raisonner, trouver des solutions*. Paris: Armand Colin.

Richardson, A. (1969) *Mental Imagery*. New York: Springer-Verlag.

Richardson, J. T. E. (1979) Subjects' reports in mental comparisons. *Bulletin of the Psychonomic Society*, 14, 371–2.

Richardson, J. T. E. (1980) *Mental Imagery and Human Memory*. London: Macmillan.

Richardson, J. T. E. (1983) Mental imagery in thinking and problem solving. In J. St B. T. Evans (ed.), *Thinking and Reasoning: Psychological approaches*, London: Routledge & Kegan Paul, 197–226.

Richardson, J. T. E. (1987) The role of mental imagery in models of transitive inference. *British Journal of Psychology*, 78, 189–203.

Richardson, J. T. E. (1991) Imagery and the brain. In C. Cornoldi and M. A. McDaniel (eds.), *Imagery and Cognition*, New York: Springer-Verlag, 1–45.

Richman, C. L., Mitchell, D. B. and Reznick, J. S. (1979) Mental travel: Some reservations. *Journal of Experimental Psychology: Human Perception and Performance*, 5, 13–18.

Riding, R. J. and Calvey, I. (1981) The assessment of verbal-imagery learning styles and their effect on the recall of concrete and abstract prose passages by 11-year-old children. *British Journal of Psychology*, 72, 59–64.

Riding, R. J. and Taylor, E. M. (1976) Imagery performance and prose comprehension in seven-year-old children. *Educational Studies*, 2, 21–7.

Robin, F. and Denis, M. (1991) Description of perceived or imagined spatial networks. In R. H. Logie and M. Denis (eds.), *Mental Images in Human Cognition*, Amsterdam: North-Holland, 141–52.

Roland, P. E., Eriksson, L., Stone-Elander, S. and Widen, L. (1987) Does mental activity change the oxidative metabolism of the brain? *Journal of Neuroscience*, 7, 2373–89.

Roland, P. E. and Friberg, L. (1985) Localization of cortical areas activated by thinking. *Journal of Neurophysiology*, 53, 1219–43.

Rosch, E. (1975) Cognitive representations of semantic categories. *Journal of Experimental Psychology: General*, 104, 192–233.

Rosch, E., Mervis, C. B., Gray, W., Johnson, D. and Boyes-Braem, P. (1976) Basic objects in natural categories. *Cognitive Psychology*, 8, 382–439.

Rowe, E. J. and Rogers, T. B. (1975) Effects of concurrent auditory shadowing on free recall and recognition of pictures and words. *Journal of Experimental Psychology: Human Learning and Memory*, 1, 415–22.

Rumelhart, D. E. (1979) *Analogical Processes and Procedural Representations* (CHIP Report No. 81). La Jolla, CA: University of California, San Diego, Center for Human Information Processing.

Rumelhart, D. E., Lindsay, P. H. and Norman, D. A. (1972) A process model for long-term memory. In E. Tulving and W. Donaldson (eds.), *Organization of Memory*, New York: Academic Press, 197–246.

Rumelhart, D. E. and Norman, D. A. (1988) Representation in memory. In R. C. Atkinson, R. J. Herrnstein, G. Lindzey and R. D. Luce (eds.), *Stevens' Handbook of Experimental Psychology*: Vol. 2. *Learning and Cognition* (2nd edn.), New York: Wiley, 511–87.

Ryan, E. D. and Simons, J. (1982) Efficacy of mental imagery in enhancing mental rehearsal of motor skills. *Journal of Sport Psychology*, 4, 41–51.

Saariluoma, P. (1989) Chess players' recall of auditorily presented chess positions. *European Journal of Cognitive Psychology*, 1, 309–20.

Sachs, J. S. (1967) Recognition memory for syntactic and semantic aspects of connected discourse. *Perception and Psychophysics*, 2, 437–42.

Santa, J. L. (1977) Spatial transformations of words and pictures. *Journal of Experimental Psychology: Human Learning and Memory*, 3, 418–27.

Savoyant, A. (1988) Mental practice: Image and mental rehearsal of motor action. In M. Denis, J. Engelkamp and J. T. E. Richardson (eds.), *Cognitive and Neuropsychological Approaches to*

Mental Imagery, Dordrecht, The Netherlands: Martinus Nijhoff, 251–8.

Schmidt, R. A. (1982) *Motor Control and Learning*. Champaign, IL: Human Kinetics.

Schreuder, R., Flores d'Arcais, G. and Glazenborg, G. (1984) Effects of perceptual and conceptual similarity in semantic priming. *Psychological Research*, 45, 339–54.

Schwanenflugel, P. J., Harnishfeger, K. K. and Stowe, R. W. (1988) Context availability and lexical decisions for abstract and concrete words. *Journal of Memory and Language*, 27, 499–520.

Schwanenflugel, P. J. and Shoben, E. J. (1983) Differential context effects in the comprehension of abstract and concrete verbal materials. *Journal of Experimental Psychology: Learning, Memory, and Cognition*, 9, 82–102.

Seamon, J. G. and Gazzaniga, M. S. (1973) Coding strategies and cerebral laterality effects. *Cognitive Psychology*, 5, 249–56.

Segal, S. J. (1972) Assimilation of a stimulus in the construction of an image: The Perky effect revisited. In P. W. Sheehan (ed.), *The Function and Nature of Imagery*, New York: Academic Press, 203–30.

Segal, S. J. and Fusella, V. (1970) Influence of imaged pictures and sounds on detection of visual and auditory signals. *Journal of Experimental Psychology*, 83, 458–64.

Segui, J. and Fraisse, P. (1968) Le temps de réaction verbale: III. Réponses spécifiques et réponses catégorielles à des stimulus objets. *L'Année Psychologique*, 68, 69–82.

Sergent, J. (1990) The neuropsychology of visual image generation: Data, method, and theory. *Brain and Cognition*, 13, 98–129.

Seymour, P. H. K. (1975) Semantic equivalence of verbal and pictorial displays. In A. Kennedy and A. Wilkes (eds.), *Studies in Long-term Memory*, New York: Wiley, 253–87.

Shanon, B. (1984) Room descriptions. *Discourse Processes*, 7, 225–55.

Shaver, P., Pierson, L. and Lang, S. (1974–5) Converging evidence for the functional significance of imagery in problem solving. *Cognition*, 3, 359–75.

Shepard, R. N. (1975) Form, formation, and transformation of internal representations. In R. Solso (ed.), *Information Processing and Cognition: The Loyola Symposium*, Hillsdale, NJ: Lawrence Erlbaum Associates, 87–122.

Shepard, R. N. (1978) The mental image. *American Psychologist*, 33, 125–37.

Shepard, R. N. (1988) The imagination of the scientist. In K. Egan and D. Nadaner (eds.), *Imagination and Education*, New York: Teachers College Press, 153–85.

Shepard, R. N. and Chipman, S. (1970) Second-order isomorphism of internal representations: Shapes of states. *Cognitive Psychology*, 1, 1–17.

Shepard, R. N. and Cooper, L. A. (1982) *Mental Images and their Transformations*, Cambridge, MA: The MIT Press.

Shepard, R. N. and Metzler, J. (1971) Mental rotation of three-dimensional objects. *Science*, 171, 701–3.

Shepard, R. N. and Podgorny, P. (1978) Cognitive processes that resemble perceptual processes. In W. K. Estes (ed.), *Handbook of Learning and Cognitive Processes*, Hillsdale, NJ: Lawrence Erlbaum Associates, 189–237.

Sholl, M. J. (1987) Cognitive maps as orienting schemata. *Journal of Experimental Psychology: Learning, Memory, and Cognition*, 13, 615–28.

Simon, H. A. (1972) What is visual imagery? An information processing interpretation. In L. W. Gregg (ed.), *Cognition in Learning and Memory*, New York: Wiley, 183–204.

Singer, J. L. (1966) *Daydreaming: An introduction to the experimental study of inner experience*. New York: Random House.

Skinner, B. F. (1953) *Science and Human Behavior*. New York: Macmillan.

Skinner, B. F. (1975) The steep and thorny way to a science of behavior. *American Psychologist*, 30, 42–9.

Smith, E. E. and Medin, D. L. (1981) *Categories and Concepts*. Cambridge, MA: Harvard University Press.

Smith, E. E. and Nielsen, G. D. (1970) Representations and retrieval processes in short-term memory: Recognition and recall of faces. *Journal of Experimental Psychology*, 85, 397–405.

Snodgrass, J. G. (1984) Concepts and their surface representations. *Journal of Verbal Learning and Verbal Behavior*, 23, 3–22.

Staats, A. W. (1961) Verbal habit families, concepts, and the operant conditioning of word classes. *Psychological Review*, 68, 190–204.

Sternberg, R. J. (1980a) The development of linear syllogistic reasoning. *Journal of Experimental Child Psychology*, 29, 340–56.

Sternberg, R. J. (1980b) Representation and process in linear syllogistic reasoning. *Journal of Experimental Psychology: General*, 109, 119–59.

Sternberg, R. J. (1981) Reasoning with determinate and indeterminate linear syllogisms. *British Journal of Psychology*, 72, 407–20.

Sternberg, R. J. and Weil, E. M. (1980) An aptitude X strategy interaction in linear syllogistic reasoning. *Journal of Educational Psychology*, 72, 226–39.

Stevens, A. and Coupe, P. (1978) Distortions in judged spatial relations. *Cognitive Psychology*, 10, 422–37.

Tabossi, P. (1982) Sentential context and the interpretation of unambiguous words. *Quarterly Journal of Experimental Psychology*, 34A, 79–90.

Tabossi, P. (1988) Effects of context on the immediate interpretation of unambiguous nouns. *Journal of Experimental Psychology: Learning, Memory, and Cognition*, 14, 153–62.

Tabossi, P. and Johnson-Laird, P. N. (1980) Linguistic context and the priming of semantic information. *Quarterly Journal of Experimental Psychology*, 32, 595–603.

Thompson, A. L. and Klatzky, R. L. (1978) Studies of visual synthesis: Integration of fragments into forms. *Journal of Experimental Psychology: Human Perception and Performance*, 4, 244–63.

Thorndyke, P. W. (1981) Distance estimation from cognitive maps. *Cognitive Psychology*, 13, 526–50.

Thorndyke, P. W. and Hayes-Roth, B. (1982) Differences in spatial knowledge acquired from maps and navigation. *Cognitive Psychology*, 14, 560–89.

Thorndyke, P. W. and Stasz, C. (1980) Individual differences in procedures for knowledge acquisition from maps. *Cognitive Psychology*, 12, 137–75.

Thurstone, L. L. and Jeffrey, T. E. (1956) *Flags: A test of space thinking*. Chicago: Education Industry Service.

Titchener, E. B. (1898) *A Primer of Psychology*, New York: Macmillan.

Tolman, E. C. (1948) Cognitive maps in rats and men. *Psychological Review*, 55, 189–208.

Tversky, B. (1969) Pictorial and verbal encoding in a short-term memory task. *Perception and Psychophysics*, 6, 225–33.

Tversky, B. (1975) Pictorial encoding of sentences in sentence–picture comparison. *Quarterly Journal of Experimental Psychology*, 27, 405–10.

Tversky, B. (1981) Distortions in memory for maps. *Cognitive Psychology*, 13, 407–33.

Tversky, B. (1991) Spatial mental models. In G. H. Bower (ed.), *The Psychology of Learning and Motivation: Advances in research and theory* (Vol. 27), New York: Academic Press.

Tversky, B. and Hemenway, K. (1984) Objects, parts, and categories. *Journal of Experimental Psychology: General*, 113, 169–93.

Ullmer-Ehrich, V. (1982) The structure of living space descriptions. In R. J. Jarvella and W. Klein (eds.), *Speech, Place, and Action: Studies in deixis and related topics*, Chichester: Wiley, 219–49.

Valentine, T. and Bruce, V. (1988) Mental rotation of faces. *Memory and Cognition*, 16, 556–66.

Vandenberg, S. G. and Kuse, A. R. (1978) Mental Rotations, a group test of three-dimensional spatial visualization. *Perceptual and Motor Skills*, 47, 599–604.

Vinacke, W. E. (1952) *The Psychology of Thinking*. New York: McGraw-Hill.

Watson, J. B. (1913) Psychology as the behaviorist views it. *Psychological Review*, 20, 158–77.

Wattenmaker, W. D. and Shoben, E. J. (1987) Context and the recallability of concrete and abstract sentences. *Journal of Experimental Psychology: Learning, Memory, and Cognition*, 13, 140–50.

Wehner, T., Vogt, S. and Stadler, M. (1984) Task-specific EMG-characteristics during mental training. *Psychological Research*, 46, 389–401.

Wetherick, N. E. (1991) What goes on in the mind when we solve syllogisms? In R. H. Logie and M. Denis (eds.), *Mental Images in Human Cognition*, Amsterdam: North-Holland, 255–67.

Wilkins, A. and Moscovitch, M. (1978) Selective impairment of semantic memory after temporal lobectomy. *Neuropsychologia*, 16, 73–9.

Williams, R. L. (1979) Imagery and linguistic factors affecting the solution of linear syllogisms. *Journal of Psycholinguistic Research*, 8, 123–40.

Winograd, T. (1975) Frame representations and the declarative/procedural controversy. In D. G. Bobrow and A. M. Collins (eds.), *Representation and Understanding: Studies in cognitive science*, New York: Academic Press, 185–210.

Wunderlich, D. and Reinelt, R. (1982) How to get there from here. In R. J. Jarvella and W. Klein (eds.), *Speech, Place, and Action: Studies in deixis and related topics*. Chichester: Wiley, 183–201.

Yuille, J. C. and Catchpole, M. J. (1977) The role of imagery in models of cognition. *Journal of Mental Imagery*, 1, 171–80.

Yuille, J. C. and Paivio, A. (1969) Abstractness and recall of connected discourse. *Journal of Experimental Psychology*, 82, 467–71.

Author Index

Subject Index